Scoping the Amazon

Scoping the Amazon
Image, Icon, Ethnography

Stephen Nugent

Left Coast Press Inc.

Walnut Creek, CA

Left Coast Press, Inc.
1630 North Main Street, #400
Walnut Creek, California 94596
http://www.LCoastPress.com

Hardback ISBN 978-1-59874-176-6
Paperback ISBN 978-1-59874-177-3

Library of Congress Cataloging-in-Publication Data

Nugent, Stephen (Stephen L.)
Scoping the Amazon : image, icon, ethnography / Stephen Nugent.
   p. cm.
   Includes bibliographical references and index.
ISBN-13: 978-1-59874-176-6 (hardback : alk. paper)
ISBN-13: 978-1-59874-177-3 (pbk. : alk. paper)
1. Indians of South America–Amazon River Region–Public opinion.
2. Europeans–Attitudes. 3. Indigenous peoples in popular culture–Amazon River Region. 4. Indigenous peoples in motion pictures.
5. Stereotypes (Social psychology)–Amazon River Region. I. Title.
   F2519.1.A6N84 2007   981'.1–dc22   2007032740

07 08 09 5 4 3 2 1

Printed in the United States of America

⊗™ The paper used in this publication meets the minimum requirements of American National Standard for Information Sciences–Permanence of Paper for Printed Library Materials, ANSI/NISO Z39.48–1992.

Cover design by Andrew Brozyna

Left Coast Press Inc. is committed to preserving ancient forests and natural resources. We elected to print Scoping The Amazon on 30% post consumer recycled paper, processed chlorine free. As a result, for this printing, we have saved:

3 Trees (40' tall and 6-8" diameter)
1,329 Gallons of Wastewater
534 Kilowatt Hours of Electricity
147 Pounds of Solid Waste
288 Pounds of Greenhouse Gases

Left Coast Press Inc. made this paper choice because our printer, Thomson-Shore, Inc., is a member of Green Press Initiative, a nonprofit program dedicated to supporting authors, publishers, and suppliers in their efforts to reduce their use of fiber obtained from endangered forests.

For more information, visit www.greenpressinitiative.org

Contents

Illustrations

Note to readers:
Credits in the captions may refer to photographer or source of published photograph. Some photographs credited to Thomas Whiffen – a number of which appear under Sydney Paternoster – may actually have been taken by Eugene Robuchon, a French explorer who disappeared in the northwest Amazon ca. 1906.

Preface:
Talismanic Indians

Figure P.1 Huitoto captain. S. Paternoster 1913.

Declaration of Interests

I was brought up in a household in which the dictum '*Life* magazine is for people who can't read' (and its associate, '*Time* magazine is for people who can't think') was taken seriously, if not too earnestly. At least two family friends were photographers whose work often appeared in *Life*, and Steichen's (1955) *The Family of Man* was offered as a 'good' book to look at, so the judgement on documentary photography/photojournalism was certainly inconsistent – and its effects, persistent.

During fieldwork in Amazonia (initially 1975–76 and intermittently ever since) the idea that photographs might be a crucial part of research was not a strong one for me. My own photographs dating from the earliest – as well as more recent – forays are mainly nostalgia aids (or as they say in Brazil, *matar saudades*, to kill homesickness), many badly marked by the effects of temperature and humidity as well as poor craftsmanship.

There were two resistance-to-photography issues that were paramount. The first was the rather old-fashioned conviction that what was being researched was not really photographable – that is, something un-seeable about the logic of a social system. From this perspective, images were random ornamentation that might have a useful if modest illus-trative role (geophysical scene setting; crucial landmarks/monuments; the odd 'representative' person), but which were always threatening to reduce complexity (big crime, reductionism, in any form) to simple (which is to say simplistic and simple-minded) renditions. I am getting over some of those prejudices.

The second issue is one that, it seems, separates focused photographers from unfocused ones, and this concerns – in its brute form – sticking a lens unbidden into someone's face and in more subtle/artistic/artisanal/*et seq* form, establishing a relationship with the subject. What prevented my aspiring to this kind of photography while in the field was the double-edgedness of (and my ignorance and uncertainty about) Amazonian notions of racial stereotypes. It was evident from the outset of my first stay in Amazonia that racial encoding and photographic images were wrap-ped up in a way that I was ill prepared to deal with as part of my research. The racialized terrain was so vast and complex that the idea of attempting to contextualize it prior to getting down to the main dish was absurd. So I pretty much ignored it beyond skeletal remarks about the broad outlines of relations among Santarenos[1] who reference Indians, blacks, Africans, whites, Russians, French, pagans, Jews, Lebanese, Moroccans, English, Irish, Germans, Japanese, Europeans, *caboclos*, *nordestinos*, *sulistas*, *cearaenses*, *gauchos*, and others as part of their racial-identity-fixing discourse.

More recently, I embarked on a film project that was meant to elaborate aspects of 'Amazonianness' that are not widely recognized outside of Amazonia but indicate an historical depth and cultural diversity that have barely registered in the anthropological literature. This was a pilot film on Jewish communities in the lower Amazon (*Where's the Rabbi?* 2001), made with Renato Athias, subject matter that seems to most people so exotic and counter-intuitive as to be almost unprocessable.

I mention these matters of image and Amazonia not to establish any credentials in this area – for I really have very few – but in order to trace the path leading back to the photographic record of Amazonian Indians and my interest in looking at how a set of stereotyped images came to be established and the kinds of relationships it has with a late-arriving scholarly literature – ethnography – that could absorb, contest, coexist with, transcend, or otherwise cope with an image of Amazonians that is at once 'the real thing' and also an historical product of a protracted encounter that has contained elements of genocide/ethnocide, accommodation, religious conversion, patronage, duplicity, admiration/reverence, celebration, and cooperation.

This book is mainly concerned with photographs of Amazonian Indians and the ways in which these images have contributed to our understanding of them, past and present. In particular, the focus is on images that have been published as complements to ethnographic accounts rather than images available through less specialized publications – although, as it turns out, the overlap between the two set of images is greater (and more subtle) than might be expected.

The relationship between text and image in this Amazonian context is not a straightforward one, and one of the themes of this book is how that relationship has developed. When the earliest photographs of Amazonian Indians appeared in the third quarter of the 19th century, anthropology was in a state of transition with an explorer/naturalist mode gradually being replaced by a more explicitly scientifically oriented kind of investigation.[2] By the time an ethnographic reference literature had achieved dimensions that warranted encyclopaedic rendition – in Steward's (1948) *Handbook of South American Indians* – key elements of the image of the 'Amazonian Indian' already had wide recognition: headhunter, cannibal, primitive, naked, long haired, savage, nomad, bow hunter, and so on. Well established in pre-photographic media, in a crucial sense these conceits were consolidated by photography rather than displaced or significantly modified by it: the realism of the photographic image of the Indian became a new layer as much as a new kind of image.

In terms of the relationship between image and text, the image of the Amazonian Indian that eventually came to be grafted onto a complex ethnographic literature had two effects. First, the image had a documentary function in providing visual content that complements ethnographic analysis. Second, however, it had an iconic (and mythmaking/myth-sustaining) function in re-creating a primordial Indian whose current embodiment is thought to be an extension of the Indian of the past. There is a similarity here to what Faris (2003) has observed of Curtis's photographic portrayals of North American Indians – namely the attempt to invoke a timeless 'ethnographic present' through removing from the frame material (or other: facial expressions?) evidence that historicizes portraits, with the result that the Indian of the present is seamlessly folded into the Indian of the past. While this effort to idealize may be understandable as motivated by a desire to encapsulate some kind of authenticity, it also cultivates stereotype and cliché, and over time the relationship between ethnographic text and image may become stressed – texts becoming more complex, nuanced, and ambitious, images becoming rigid and hackneyed.

The focal set of images reviewed in *Scoping the Amazon* comes from an ethnographic literature comprised of 140 single-authored volumes running to almost 40,000 pages of text. Together, these books include 2,500 photographic images. In terms of pages published, the photographic images account for a small percentage (less than 6 per cent).[3] Such a gross relative measure need not indicate anything of significance, but the comparison serves to underline a key feature of the text/image relationship noted above: a small population of images conveys unitary, powerful impressions that in many respects challenge the subtleties of the explanatory texts to which such photographs are supposed to be sub-servient or ancillary. The forcefulness with which the stereotyped image of the Amazonian Indian dominates the cultural landscape of Amazonia is indicated not only in public perceptions of what is 'typically' Amazonian, but also in the narrowness of an anthropological gaze that has tended to disregard non-Indian (or *mestiço*) Amazonians. This material and symbolic over-representation of the Indian does not just reflect tendencies within English-speaking anthropology and its associated popular cultures, but also finds expression in Brazil where the symbolic power of the Indian – the original Brazilian and one of the three strands of Brazil's syncretic uniqueness – far outweighs the political power of Indians (fragile-to-nonexistent) or their numerical strength (far less than 1 per cent of the national population), a phenomenon aptly described by Ramos (1992) as the 'hyperreal Indian'.

A vivid image of *the* Amazonian Indian has been in place for about five hundred years. The continued cultivation of this image has taken place against a backdrop of systematic eradication of actual Amazonian Indians, one of whose contemporary defenses – paradoxically and contradictorily – lies in both recovering and rejecting that image, but this is a backdrop that has itself been repainted a number of times. The first backdrop is commonly referred to as the Conquest, but also identified as globalization. The second backdrop – globalization Mk II – is provided by the mercantile apparatus epitomized by the British Empire during the 19th century and in local terms is represented by the rubber industry, a phenomenon of pan-Amazonian impact. The third backdrop, what is also currently referred to – memory loss not withstanding – as globalization is represented in local terms by the developmentalist integration of Amazonia and the Brazilian

As principais províncias indígenas do Médio Amazonas, em 1550-1650

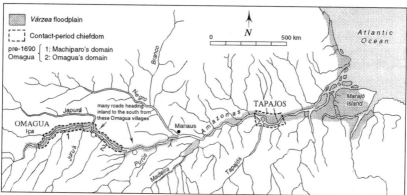

Figures P.2 & P.3 Two maps showing riverine chiefdoms/proto-states based on accounts and drawings from earliest voyages descending the river. Amazonia's first globalization experience. A. Porro 1996; R. Wilson 1999.

state through programmes such as PIN (centerpiece: the Transamazon Highway) and the Greater Carajás Project.

In all three cases, the mode by which Amazonia has been part of the globalization process has mainly been characterized by extractive production that has become successively more territorially expansionist. During the first phase (commencing mid-16th century), the riverbank societies of Amazonia were effaced in the course of Portuguese efforts to exploit what was then thought to be a gold-poor area.[4]

During phase two (latter part of the 19th century), the paramount commodity was rubber and Indian groups hitherto insulated from immediate post-Conquest society were further reduced in the face of extractivist expansion closely tied to rising industrial output in Europe and North America.

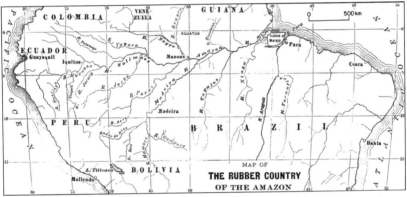

Figure P.4 Map of Brazilian rubber country ca. 1900, Amazonia's second experience of globalization.

During phase three, the state itself was primarily responsible for administering the region's integration into the global economy mainly through making the region available to highly unregulated investment of national and international capital. This version of Amazonia is a landscape of roads and mineral deposits.

The Indian societies that survived these great transformations have a prehistoric and historical significance that sometimes sits uneasily with the talismanic significance of the image of the iconic forest Indian who so often stands for them all, past and present, uneasily because he seems to embody the anti-history of the ancient tribal isolate yet also exemplify the survivor of a crushing set of historical transformations. The societies themselves – the collective subjects of anthropological inquiry – harbour elements of a relatively unrecoverable past – an incomplete record of material culture, ethnographic documentation, and testimony, but most crucially cohering in the modern image of the forest Indian.

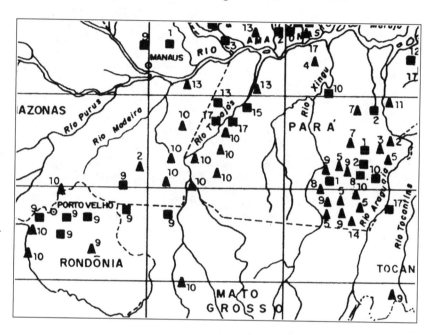

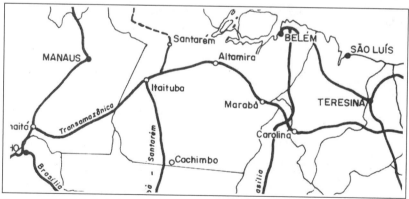

Figures P.5 & P.6 Typical cartographic representations of Amazonia – resource frontier – facing its third globalization experience.

Figure P.7 Wakonti-re. © Christine Burrill.

Acknowledgements

I am grateful to the Arts and Humanities Research Council (AHRC) for support while writing this book. I would also like to acknowledge the assistance of the staff of the British Museum's Centre for Anthropology.

A number of friends have helped enormously over the past few years – Mike and Sue Rowlands, Humphrey Ocean, Mitch Sedgwick, Marc and Wendover Brown. And special thanks to June, Zoe, and Zac.

Notes

1 A reference to residents of the city and municipality of Santarém, a city of the lower Amazon, Brazil.
2 Koch-Grunberg (2004) and Im Thurn (1934) characterize this phase. Nimendajú (1939) is arguably the first modern ethnographer of the region.
3. There is methodological discussion in later chapters, but for the present note that only photographs depicting actual subjects caught being anthropological subjects have been counted. Landscapes, material artefacts, and aerial photographs (classically, of village clearings) have been excluded.
4 Gold was extracted during early colonial phases, but it was not until the 1980s that anything approaching the long-awaited boom occurred.

1

Introduction:
Anthropology with
Pictures

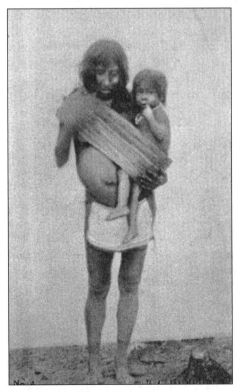

Figure 1.1 Postcard

Since its emergence in modern form, anthropology has sought to distance itself from the original application of photography in the field – the first instantiation of visual anthropology – namely anthropometry and derivatives such as criminal anthropology. Soon after, in the early twentieth century, and with a positivist bravado still evident in the enthusiasm for an unadorned observational style or approach, ethnographic film – the new visual anthropology – was heavily promoted as a 'research tool', a means of gathering and recording data that exceeded the potential of the pencil and notebook. In general, the prevailing notion is that the core purpose of image taking in an ethnographic context is for the gathering of observational data.

Despite its status as a core notion, however, there is wide acknowledgement – even among those stridently committed to an ideal of pure information flowing through lens onto recording medium – that ethnographic data are mediated, that their uncooked status is (minimally) questionable. Lombroso's criminal archetypes, for instance, were selected with purpose and didn't just pop up as data; cine-cameras have to be pointed, focused, turned on; what qualifies as an informative image (a portrait of a tribesman gazing over a distant horizon; a woman washing manioc tubers) reflects non-trivial editorial decisions. In short, a set of fieldwork images is a motivated assemblage of visual facts requiring critical judgement as to its relevance or importance, as is the case with other kinds of data; yet there persists the belief that there is in visual anthropology some kind of medium-specific, revelatory possibility with respect to a kind of knowledge unhelpfully, but almost provocatively, qualified as *visual* – often without much clarification or precise characterization of its qualitative difference.[1]

While the promise of great explanatory and theoretical possibilities is widely voiced, even one of the most vocal champions (Ruby 2000:38) of these possibilities for the use – in this case – of film in communicating anthropological knowledge concedes that the strongest claim for 'communicating anthropological knowledge' really lies in the use of films for undergraduate teaching. This pedagogic function is hardly unimportant, but one suspects that 'visual, anthropological knowledge' is meant to imply more than screening *Nanook* or *Dead Birds* in introductory anthropology courses. Ruby (2000:26) goes on to cite MacDougall in his comments about the continuing quest for an adequate theory.

> As should be clear by now, no one has articulated a theory or practice of ethnographic film adequate to the task. More than twenty years ago, MacDougall pointed out that ethnographic film needs 'a new paradigm, another way of seeing, not necessarily incompatible with written anthropology but at least governed by a distinct set of criteria' (MacDougall 1978:405). It has not been an easy task. In fact the search continues.

Moving images provide only one of the main contexts for debates about the elaboration of visual anthropology theory. Elsewhere, part of the problem associated with the conflict between just-the-facts documentary and facts-plus documentary[2] has been side stepped in recent work involving still photography, accomplished in part through shifting attention away from images made in the name of anthropological information gathering toward images that depict or address the colonial (or analogous[3]) situation (see, for example, Edwards 1994; Pinney and Peterson 2003).

While this shift partially resolves the dilemma by making the artefact-image itself the focus of attention rather than the narrowly defined ethnoscape, it might otherwise be intended to illustrate, it still leaves open the question of what constitutes distinctively anthropological knowledge, for one of the claims of a more prosaic ethnographic-documentary approach is that there is something different about an image (or series of images) taken with anthropological purpose (see Ruby 2000:6). In the case of both tendencies – the image as document, the image as aperture to an interpretive space – much rides on the artifactual status of the image, the first being ethnographically authoritative, the second being carefully situated in space and time (e.g., the 'colonial situation').

In the introduction to *Photography's Other Histories*, Pinney (2003a:3), for example, writes:

> That the formal qualities of images themselves may be in large part irrelevant is suggested by their historical trajectories and the radical re-evaluations that they undergo. If an image that appears to do a particular kind of work in one episteme is able to perform radically different work in another, it appears inappropriate to propose inflexible links between formal qualities and effect. Instead, we need a more nuanced reading of the affinities between particular discursive formations and the image worlds that parallel them, as well as sophisticated analyses of their transformational potentialities.

If the formal qualities of images were, as imagined above, irrelevant, then the image is no longer the object of analysis; the context is, but what precisely is this context? A specified sociohistorical context appears to be precluded, for this would be epistemically presumptuous. A context that allows nuanced reading is the proposed alternative, but this is one – curiously – that articulates 'image worlds', the essentialness of which (formal qualities) has already been disallowed.

Regardless of the very real and substantial differences between an ethnographic approach in which the image enhances a superordinate, traditional anthropological analysis and the 'reading' approach sketched above, there is a common claim to be able to exploit the visual in a way that satisfies explanatory goals as well as being open to interpretation and nuance inaccessible to Popper-style framing as testable notions. Intrinsic to what now seems to be the mainstream position is the idea that somehow 'the visual' in itself provides a translation medium. The 'givenness' of this notion of the visual is widespread in current visual studies and visual anthropology.[4]

The main aim of this book does not include a discussion conducted along the lines of *what is the theoretical adequacy or viability of either visual anthropology or visual studies*, for it is not clear that either of those labels identifies a clear objective or object of analysis. Now, it might be objected that phrased that way, such vast covering terms could hardly be expected to have achieved a rigour and cohesion to make the notions meaningfully subject to critique – but that is precisely the problem. Within visual anthropology, for instance, is there actually a unified approach (a theory?) that can deal with still images, moving images, observationalism, auteurism, the image as fact, the image as ideological projection, the image as colonial-historical material artefact, and so on? It hasn't appeared yet and shows no sign of doing so imminently, and those dilemmas are (in any case) grist for the mill as far as the fragmentation-with-stability state of anthropological theory goes. What could a special visual theory provide at this stage beyond the rather ineffable 'greater communicative possibilities'?

With respect to visual studies, a similar set of conditions applies: the identity trauma of visual studies as the all-embracing synthetic is still so closely bound up with its attempts to distance itself from art history (to name but one foundation) and forge alliances with other fields (some, such as cultural studies, themselves still unsure about how to configure their institutional maturity) that the specificity of these dilemmas to *visual studies* per se is hard to distinguish from the normal routine of disciplinary turf wars and scholarly disagreement (however considerate or ill tempered). What does the arena of visual studies provide or allow that isn't already on the table?[5]

These brief comments about the relationship between core issues in visual anthropology and the emergence of kinds of academic disciplinary authority that aspire to levels of generality that erode the boundaries among various humanities and social science fields are meant only to indicate some of the broader contexts into which ethnographic photography and filmmaking extend. These aspirations are driven by important and interesting evaluations of various relationships between modernity and *the visual*, not least being the disputed claims about the dominance of scopic regimes in the twentieth century (of which Jay 2003 is the commanding text).

In relation to this broad perspective, however, the aims of *Scoping the Amazon* are quite prosaic. Instead of framing issues of the visual, anthropology, and Amazonia in terms of a collection of debates and discussions about the epistemological status of visual knowledge, *Scoping the Amazon* draws a distinction between the dominant images historically associated with Amazonia (through scholarly and general publications as well as other media such as films), and the *actual* images that form the substratum or base repertoire of authoritative accounts – by anthropologists, for example – of Amazonia and Amazonian peoples. Thus, instead of assuming that there is an obvious relationship between the visual record and perceptions of what is visual culture, I take it as a problematic relationship.

In a sense, the argument that there is not a straightforward relationship between the visual record and the perception of the visual record may amount to little more than a restatement of scepticism about the reliability of a purely observational record, but more than that is intended here. Through examining the growth of the visual record – a chronological sequence of photographic images – and correlating that sequence with other kinds of knowledge about Amazonians (traveller/explorer accounts, anthropological accounts, narrative accounts based on documentary sources, e.g., films 'based on true stories') the visual culture of Amazonia will be presented not as an autonomous semiosphere of images, but as a contingent representation of Amazonia, a representation that has elements of accuracy as well as those of cliché, stereotype, and distortion.

The interplay or contingency of photographic images of Amazonia and the meanings ascribed to them is revealed in several ways. In comparing the most attention-grabbing images of the region's peoples – the stereotypes/clichés – with what is written about these peoples, there

Figure 1.2 Simply titled 'Indians of the Peruvian Amazon'. W. E. Hardenburg 1912.

are important contrasts. The images tend to be highly routinized, the text intensely nuanced. Images of among the best known exemplars of 'Amazonian forest Indian' – the Yanam, Yanomam, Sanema, Xilixana, Ajarani, Catrimani, Malaxi, Sanuma, Surucucu, Auaris, Palimi, Yanomami (terms designating different fractions or segments of people known as 'the Yanomami') – require textual elaboration if they are to be faithful to what is actually known about relevant/non-trivial distinctions within the effective generic: Yanomami.

Another manifestation of contingency lies in specialists' criticism of the accuracy of many features about Amazonian Indians that appear to be salient to the general public. This is hardly unusual in relations between anthropology and public culture but should not be ignored on grounds of its normality. It is analogous to the popular claim that chimpanzees share 98 per cent of their DNA with humans. While this statement is not untrue, many complications are masked behind 'share'.

Given the prominent role that Amazonia plays in discussions about climate change/human impact on the environment (and its global implications), the relationship between research and popular myth is a compelling – if disturbing – phenomenon. Poor public understanding of the relentless persecution of Amazonian Indians (the same ones whose images in shop windows have been used to connote respectful ethnic affiliation and alliance à la Body Shop International), the hollow certification of tropical forest products, and the crass promotion of eco-trek salvation are indicators of some of the inadequacies of representational strategies in which 'images talk'. The authentication function of the forest Indian image is wildly disproportionate to the actual sharing of material resources implied by the trade-not-aid ethos, not dissimilar to the 'certification of sustainable Amazonian forests'.

The images that represent the visual contents of key anthropological contributions to the study of Amazonian Indians require textual elaboration, but paradoxically that elaboration tends to be quite restricted; a few words of caption, for example, typically suffice. Thus, an image isn't often able to speak for itself, but the text offered to bring it fully to life is almost nothing. In fact, if the images were acknowledged as playing a major role, they would be granted the critical interpretation typical of the 'colonial photography' approach; yet as argued above, such interpretive bringing to life of the image renders the image per se contingent, its meaning revealed in different combinations of features that are idiomatically coherent, but requiring explication.

Perceptions of Amazonia tend to be distorted by the predominance of a set of clichéd images, icons of the neo-tropics. To say distorted is not simply to offer a negative evaluation, only to note some kind of transience in the movement of information. Over the period of time during which

Amazonia has been recognized and to some degree well understood (or its distinctiveness appreciated) by a public in the West, the images and icons of Amazonia that have tended to prevail have been remarkably durable even though the world and Amazonia have changed in many ways since these clichéd views of Amazonia became part of a received view. Some of the earliest images of Amazonia (so-called 'Amazon women' themselves; cannibals presiding over cooking pots)[6] have faded over time, but others persist even in the face of serious challenge to their representational adequacy. While there may be significant differences in the meanings carried by anthropological and non-anthropological images of the region and its peoples, the images themselves don't necessarily reveal such differences in affiliation. The image of the forest Indian retains an iconic quality even when subject to such different contextual renderings as those offered by, for example, Jacques Cousteau and Mose Richards's (1984) *Jacques Cousteau's Amazon Journey*, Sebastiao Salgado's *Genesis* project (Hattenstone 2006), Elizabeth Bishop's (1962) *Brazil*, or Kaj Arhem's (1998) *Makuna* – explorer, photographer, poet, and anthropologist, respectively.

Figure 1.3 'Indians of the Amazon'. Albert Frisch ca. 1860.

The easy convergence, the cliché, is partly due to the historical remoteness of Amazonian Indians – hence the limited number of inter-locuters, partly due to their actual situation as forest refugees whose life chances are positively correlated with distance from national society, and partly due to global process of familiarization through tourism, the mod-ernization/development industry, and mass media.

In this new global context the familiar images – the cliché renditions of cultural difference - function quite well.[7] There is a sense that the kind of world that is re-represented and reproduced in the course of new forms of tourism and travel and trekking and so on – sought for exotic qualities, but simultaneously familiarized as new frontiers are domesticated – is one meant always to be experientially rich for the visitor; yet that assumption of experiential richness – let's call it internationalist narcissism – puts a relatively sober and uncelebratory anthropology on its back foot. Whereas anthropology once had a recognized, semi-official responsibility for representing anthropological subjects, there are other interests that now perform parallel tasks and whose mediation between the metropolitan West and the non-specific exotic undermines, challenges, complements, or perhaps simply complicates anthropological authority.

Culture Industry, Amazonia, Anthropology

Whether the modern anthropological project (and accompanying pre-scriptions) is intact or not,[8] there is a significant continuity between the founding of the field and its current state, and this is represented by the notion of anthropology as a culture industry – that is, a branch of scientific inquiry that is expected to produce a particular kind of know-ledge. While the conceptual distinctiveness of that branch of knowledge continues to be a matter of dispute, there are several clear markers.

One of these is represented by celebrity anthropologists whose professional work has found significant resonance in public spheres. Mead's work on Samoan adolescent sexuality, Lévi-Strauss's structur-alist codifications, Geertz, Sahlins, Harris, and Wolf represent significant public acknowledgment of the so-called 'anthropological gaze'. Another is represented by what are regarded as exotic or esoteric aspects of anthropological research: cannibalism, hominid predecessors, ancient cityscapes, witchcraft, and the like. A third is represented by the promise of genealogical lifelines reaching from the present to the remote past.[9]

These culture industry products are problematic. Mitigation of the polarized positions of Harris and Sahlins (Harris and Sahlins 1979) with respect to Aztec cannibalism, for example, requires detailed (and to out-siders, pedantic) contextualization that typically holds little appeal for the casual inquirer. Does Freeman's (1983) methodological critique of Mead efface the broad, culturally relativistic implications to which a broad public responded? Notions of kin relatedness invariably contain elements of risible folk science.

As with other culture industries, anthropological producers cannot really stipulate the meanings to be attached to them. The concept of race, for example, falls well within the anthropological orbit, but has folkloric salience on one hand and vacuity as an anthropological or scientific notion on the other. The term 'culture' itself is so all embracing as to be capable of descent to the irretrievably trivial (e.g., 'blame culture').

This book is primarily concerned with one product line in the anthropological culture industry – Amazonia – and its portrayal in three different, though linked, guises: the 'green hell' of Victorian naturalism; the hunter-gatherer landscape of modern ethnography; the Amazonia of Hollywood.

These versions of Amazonia clearly represent different interests (discovery, inventory, explanation, commercial exploitation), but are linked by a set of durable images that prevail despite their dubious accuracy. The 'green hell/Lost World' images dating from the earliest Western penetration of the region connote flagrant disregard for order, an uncontrolled fertility and luxuriance; yet the biosystem is highly ordered and, far from representing an emergent landscape, is actually a senile one (or, more charitably, oligarchic). The typical Amazonian indigenous society recorded in the ethnographic literature (small, mobile, egalitarian, hunting/gathering/horticultural) may be less typical than the contemporary record indicates, as much an artefact of conquest as indicative of the possible social forms that might emerge in the humid neo-tropics. Feature film portrayals of Amazonia unhesitatingly privilege megafauna, malign agents, or devious toxin bearers – animal, vegetable, mineral, and human.

This general set of affairs is hardly unique to the Amazonian anthropological terrain but there are distinctive features. One of these is the role of Amazonian studies in the emergence of evolutionary theory (mainly through Wallace 1889). A second is the biodiversity represented in the high species number/low species density of the neo-humid tropics. A third is the long-term (but now undoubtedly revoked) marginality of Amazonian societies from the mainstream of Brazilian modernization and – earlier – national identity.

The prevalence of naturalist imagery in Amazonian studies reinforces the tendency (in anthropology and elsewhere) to associate particular geographical locations and particular kinds of social formation. There are many versions of the virtuous association (Sun People in the tropics, snow people in the North; noble savages and tropical forests; entrepreneurs and frontiers; etc.), but one of the consequences in Amazonia of an overbearing naturalism has been the oversimplification of the notion 'Amazonian society'.

Early accounts by European travellers, explorers, conquistadors, and scientists of Amazonian peoples were filtered through a variety of self-interested perceptions and considerably refined by the codifications provided by professional (mainly post-World War II) anthropology. A stereotype emerged that was almost indistinguishable from the archetype, an exaggeration based on a residual focal example: the interfluve hunter/gatherer/horticulturalist whose complexities of social organization and symbolic life often stood in stark contrast to a rudimentary technology and nomadism. Under the strong influence of idioms of human and cultural ecology, this typical Amazonian sociality was seen to be heavily constrained by the biosystem. Curtailed by unambiguous material constraints, so the argument went, the social in Amazonia was seen to be contingent on the natural, tolerated to a rather low threshold.

The anthropological 'typical Indian' coexists comfortably with its derived public version in contemporary portrayals of Amazonia – in cinema, for example. There are fiction/faction portrayals of Amazonia that draw with considerable accuracy on the ethnographic record, such as Boorman's (1985b) *Emerald Forest* and Babenco's (1991) *At Play in the Fields of the Lord* (based on the Peter Matthiessen novel of the same name). There are also selective and opportunistic appropriations of Amazonian symbols of dubious provenance – *The Creature from the Black Lagoon* (Arnold 1954), *Anaconda* (Llosa 1997), or *The Rundown* (Berg 2003).

There is not always a stable relationship between anthropology and public culture, the former typically receiving a public airing over matters of food and sex,[10] primates, lost worlds, and preserved bodies/missing links. Cannibalism, as well, continues to be a compelling topic – not, however, because anthropology has ever had a lot to say about it, but because the public assumes there is something anthropology can contribute to polite discussion of the topic.

The time frame for this book is mid-19th century to the present, roughly from the period during which the British naturalists Bates, Spruce, and Wallace provided – on the basis of extended field studies – the first widely disseminated, systematic accounts of *o inferno verde* (green hell) until the segment 1970 to the present, a period during which Amazonia came to be treated as a coherent category of public culture, an eco-political entity still passed off as green hell.

There are strong similarities between these two periods. While both are characterized by an intensity of scientific activity unmatched outside those boundaries, they also mark significant epochs of imperial hegemony and global restructuring; yet Amazonia is represented as a domain beyond the scope of such structural shifts, a domain that resists incorporation by virtue of its green hellness.

Amazonian anthropological discourse (traditionally focused on Amerindian societies) and public culture both conceive of the Amazonian landscape (cultural and natural) as one that disavows the legitimacy (and, at times, even the existence) of kinds of Amazonians who are neither Indian (and, in this context, *natural*) nor modern (frontier colonists, entrepreneurs, eminently *social* however pathologically characterized). The 'other Amazonians', in fact, are a vital link between the Victorian-science Amazonia of Bates, Spruce, and Wallace and the modern science Amazonia of fire-ant-kin selection, biodiversity, and *Relic* (Hyams 1996). They are the Amazonians with names such as Nelson, Wilson, and Lady Di (Fleming n.d.) and whose world is lost only to others.

Prehistoric Amazonians do not register as forcefully as do their few descendants, in part because lacking representation in other than pre-photographic, expressive realist drawings and etchings, they are lost to that area of social memory that claims the heightened reality fix of the observational image. The contemporary, invisible Amazonian – the *mestiço* in many guises[11] – also fails to register imagistically except, by and large, as a victim. That unfortunate condition (which is its own stereotype – exaggerated, yet not without real content) is perhaps too much for photographic representation, for it seems to demand more information and explication than is available to the eye, as in Salgado's (1993) images of miners and the landscapes they occupy at Serra de Pelada in Eastern

Figure 1.4 G. Huebner 1888.

Amazonia. Without elaboration the images appear almost fantastical, an evisceration of the myth of a green hell that is far from green, but patently hellish.[12]

Chronologically, at either limit of the record of photographic images of the Amazonian forest Indian who embodies the venerated archetype-stereotype lie two Amazonias that do not lend themselves so easily to photographic representation – the one prehistoric because there are not enough traces, no living examples, no 'pyramids'; the other because there are too many traces, and mainly profoundly unpleasant and daunting ones, of the intense interaction between Amazonians and the world system over the last five hundred years.

Caution: Objects in Mirror Are Closer Than They Appear

Why Anthropology, Visual Anthropology, and Visual Studies Might Be Further Apart Than They Appear

The emphasis in this book is on the relationship between photography and ethnographic writing in Amazonia, more specifically with the way images serve the text rather than as codifications of anthropological knowledge in their own right. Books in which that relationship is reversed – typically disparaged as 'coffee-table' books – stand outside the core literature considered here, but they are key to a wider understanding of the relationship between images of anthropological subjects and public culture in as much as their consumption demands no commitment to an anthropological gaze, only the exotic icons associated with that gaze. These include, for example, Ricciardi's (1991) *Vanishing Amazon* as well as Lévi-Strauss's (1994) *Saudades do Brasil* (and many lesser offerings). There are a handful of anthropological monographs that fall outside the core literature, in which the arrays of photographic images take precedence over textual explanation and bear the narrative weight, as in Arhem's (1998) *Makuna: Portrait of an Amazonian People* and Verswijver's (1996) *Mekranoti: Living among the Painted People of the Amazon*.

The historical relationship between ethnographic text and ethnographic images of Amazonians has been an uneven one with images invariably relegated to a subservient position and often not present at all – or included with such casualness and lack of interest in production values as to be distracting or detracting features.[13]

Ethnographic filmmaking, widely regarded as having commenced with Flaherty (1922) and *Nanook*, has until recently borne most of the responsibility for anthropology-and-image. The more recent emergence of the category visual anthropology, perhaps drawing strength from both the literary turn in anthropology and material culture over the last two decades,[14] has drawn new attention to general issues of representation that embrace both still and moving images in anthropology; but despite this renewal, there is little sense in which the image has come to prevail over the text as the main medium for anthropological expression.[15]

Part of the reason for this marginalization of the image in anthropology may lie in the way modern anthropology promoted the notion of society/ culture/system as scientific object of analysis rather than the received folk conceptions along the lines of savagery/primitivism/cannibalism – the former a more abstract object than could be effectively displayed in a photograph, the latter too closely linked to the raciological reductionism evident in the mug-shot approach of tendencies such as criminal anthropology.

Another part of the reason may lie in what Prosser (2005) has described as 'photography's hidden truth': that what a photograph does is represent something – a real moment – that no longer exists. In other words, a photographic image is about loss,[16] yet the thrust of the new fieldwork-based enterprise was not *only* about such loss[17] (societies that represented the past) but societies that were tangible coevals, still within the anthropological gaze. Photographs are *memento mori* and as such may send out the wrong message.

Curiously, what does provide plausibility to the notion of a (relatively) unified visual anthropology discourse is precisely the notion of traditional anthropological holism that is ostensibly challenged by visual anthropology. An added twist lies in the fact that holism was to a considerable extent a marker of the scientific ambitions of the discipline, ambitions not particularly welcomed (or obviously) welcomed by those championing a visually oriented anthropology.

Visual Anthropology as a Departure from Anthropology

There is a core contradiction in anthropology that provides much of its dynamism and this is simultaneous commitment to universalism and particularism. Visual anthropology plays with the core contradiction by substituting one of the terms with an appealing, but ultimately nonrevealing, metaphor: instead of using scientific knowledge as the universalizing pole, it grants vision that authority on the assumption that there is something like a 'language of vision' that permits images to be 'read'.[18] These readings, cross-culturally, may not achieve full translation, but even the aspiration is based on the idea that vision in principle affords that possibility.[19]

A visual approach displaces the text and its apparently forbidding tendency toward logocentric command and control. It also preys upon a key concept that appeared in company with a mainstream rejection of normal science: reflexivity. The associated preoccupation with subject positions seems to provide a conceptual clarity appropriate to the visual, and it re-situates knowledge away from the binding rules of 'text' and 'language' and offers it up as a gift of the senses. Hume and Locke live on in unlikely garb, as post-structuralist visionaries, and it is no small irony that a trend-setting multidisciplinary synthesis such as visual studies – of which visual anthropology is a subset – should be so beholden to such unambiguously empiricist foundations.

What this reformulation of anthropology's core contradiction – replacing the universalism of science with the universalism of visualism – does is offer a new(ish) medium, photography[20] as a way of retaining the possibility of cross-cultural discourse while disavowing scientific pretensions or association.

The coordinated attention[21] to the image in anthropology[22] is certainly a provocative challenge to the earnest natural history approach caricature of an expeditionary and data-collection-obsessed version of scientific anthropology. In addition to the medium-specific dimensions that image-focused work offers (a very material kind of reflexivity, finite historical slices or frame-grabs, a different kind of social memory, and so on) it also forces aesthetic considerations into the frame as well as putting some overlooked names to some faces.[23] In terms of anthropological knowledge, however, the image-focused change doesn't really shift the core problematic/contradiction. It enhances it, certainly, not least by the persistent materiality on display, but visual anthropology rather overplays its adjectival status.

An example of overplaying the hand of visual anthropology is the use/misuse of the linguistic metaphor (that is, the notion that there is a language of vision – or film for that matter[24]). Further, the notion that, as Gell (1998) succinctly claims, 'objects have agency',[25] is a closely related though more sophisticated proposal.

There is a firm tradition of use of the linguistic metaphor, but little evidence that it has content in a rigorous sense. If what is meant, in an anthropological or other context, by a language of imagery/vision is simply that representations carry meaning, then there is little to get excited about; but it seems clear that something stronger is intended, minimally that representations communicate in a rule-like (grammatical) fashion. This connotation, however, doesn't go far enough to justify the talk of a language/grammar of vision. While perception and representation are clearly constrained by certain kinds of rules (optical illusions provide a classic example of some of these: one perceives but cannot settle on a stable representation of an image), what is the evidence that the structure of the putative 'language' of vision is anything like the structure (grammar) of language? Language-like it may be in some respects, but that doesn't necessarily help much.

As noted earlier, it is unlikely that proponents of a 'visual language' notion would be happy to see vision reduced to 'just language' (i.e., derivative) or 'just communication', but nor does the coherence of a 'visual language' grammar seem within reach at this stage. Recourse to a general theory of semiotics has long seemed to provide a safe redoubt within which the linguistic metaphor can be cultivated by language-of-vision proponents, but it is precisely the generality of such a theory that restricts its applicability in much the same way that theories of culture are so vague and ubiquitous[26] as to preclude useful refinement. Sperber (1980) despatches this linguistic metaphor in a brief article on the semiotic function. He notes that a key difference between the kinds of codes implicated in semiotic communication and linguistic communication is that the former is non-enumerated while the latter is strictly enumerated, which is to say that the latter entails syntactic *and* semantic coherence (*that is the ugliest jumper I have ever seen*) while the former does not (*blue flip-flops in pink frogs climb El Capitan*). In what sense is semiotic communication 'linguistic' if it defies the syntactic principles that distinguish linguistic structure? In what useful sense does the 'linguistic' qualifier apply at all? Hence in what sense can images be read without resort to the extra-visual means at our disposal?

That the theoretical status of visual anthropology is problematic is not a new idea, and although there is a general notion that visual anthropology is an innovative departure and a number of well-established positions have been marked out, the generic visual anthropology actually embraces quite incompatible tendencies – narrow observationalism and auteurism. MacDougall (1999:276) – whose comments are echoed in others' work – notes that '[a]nthropology has had no lack of interest in the visual; its problem has always been what to do with it'.

Answers to that question are highly varied. These include Bloch's withering comment that too much interest in film indicates a loss of 'confidence in their own ideas' (Houtman 1988:20); Ruby's (2000) and MacDougall's (1999) quite different, but similarly optimistic views about a shift toward a plausible notion of visual explanation in anthropology; Ginsburg's (1995) and Turner's (1992) espousal of indigenous media; Thomas's (1999) conjoining of the anthropology of art and visual anthropology; and Hastrup's (1992) calibration of ethnographic density in film and text.

In the South American context, Poole (1997) and Taussig (1987, 1993) offer two quite different examples of how photographic images have been incorporated into the analysis of a colonial context in which images of the past are recycled as part of a process of denouncing and reclaiming the past, and reflecting some of the particularities of indigenous identity building/culture formation in the post-colonial state. Taussig's (1987)

Shamanism, Colonialism, and the Wildman makes extensive use of historical images (mainly from the early 20th century Putumayo scandal) in order to explore the violent setting within which a usually benignly depicted *syncretic culture* actually transmogrified as a *culture of terror*, subsequently depicted (1993) as 'intercultural space of magical power'. Poole's (1997) work on Peruvians' use of images emphasizes not the notion of *visual culture*, but *visual economy*, importantly drawing attention to the fact that the apparently unifying effect of images and their seeming representation of collectivities[27] are crosscutting: there are issues of production, consumption, and distribution that defy some of the effects of limited dimensionality represented in photographic images.

Figure 1.5 Macuxi. © Stephen Baines.

Figure 1.6 Shipibo. G. Huebner 1888.

In the material that follows, the visual space considered is very limited. It concerns the allocation of photographic images within a professional literature – that is, what images have actually been included in ethnographic monographs and what function they appear to serve. The narrowness of this particular visual space is meant to provide a realistic reference against which to contrast a more diffuse and extensive set of images, what has been referred to as the stereotype/cliché of the Amazonian forest Indian. To the degree that the anthropological literature provides a culturally authorized/approved body of knowledge, the ways in which images are used in this context should inform the manner in which both accurate and mystified notions of Indianness, green hell, the lost world, tropical nastiness/despair, and connections between past and present are taken up in other, public cultural spheres.

Notes

1 An obvious strategy, but not one taken up as far as I know, would be to follow a modular approach à la Fodor, but this is anathema in a field committed to representational holism.

2 Frequently, this conflict is simply portrayed as one between 'positivism' and 'reflexivity', a rather sad comment on the state of theoretical debate.

3 The chapter on Hawaiian travel literature in Hight and Sampson's (2002a) *Colonialist Photography*, for instance, is quite differently 'colonial' from the other contributions there.

4 See Elkins (2003) for a sceptical overview of a core concept of 'visual culture'.

5 This point is pressed by Elkins (2003).

6 See Mason (1990) for examples.

7 White (2004) offers a clinical assessment of what might be characterized as the 'authoritative cliché mentality'.

8 See Segal and Yanagisako (2005) for various discussions, mainly concerned with professional boundary disputes.

9 Although this also represents a case in which there is almost complete untranslatability between anthropological notions of what is interesting about kinship and popular notions, the former focusing on systems in which Ego is virtually a cipher, the latter concerned with links literally embodied in John or Jane Ego.

10 The idioms of this fascination have changed, though, from imaginary-visual (savage free sex) to imaginary-invisible (sociobiology, genetics).

11 That is to say, *mestiço* in more than a racial sense. See Schwartz and Salomon (1999) for a discussion of ethnogenesis in South America not restricted to indigenous discourse (cf. Hill n.d., 1996).

12 In the same way that the so-called 'rubber boom' label is perversely preferred over the 'rubber industry' label (it did, after all, dominate the Amazonian economy for about a century), so is the 'gold rush' from the 1980s onward typically depicted in a manner that enhances the episodic aspects and ignores the broader systemic and structural effects. The gold industry in Amazonia – which has a long history at modest scale – attracted about one million miners to the region. See Cleary (1990) and MacMillan (1995). Closely related in terms of the region's international financial integration are money laundering and drug industries. See Machado (n.d.) for a fascinating look at the role of local bank branches in the region.

13 The advent of digital reproduction has not necessarily enhanced the role of photographs in ethnographic monographs. Many published in recent years are little better than smudges.

14 See MacDougall's (1999) historical overview in this regard.

15 See Edwards's (1994) wide-ranging discussion. The notion that a photograph is somehow too easy to consume and comprehend seems widely believed.

16 He cites Sontag (1977), Benjamin (1992 [1968]), and Barthes (1993) in this regard and Lévi-Strauss's (1994) *Saudades* is the subject of a chapter.

17 Although the 'salvage' aspect of modern anthropology clearly provides such a connotation.

18 The credibility widely granted 'visual language' often appears greater than that granted the much more convincing and systematically explored universal model provided by theoretical linguistics.

19 A close relation of the notion that 'seeing is believing'.

20 And soon after, cinema.

21 Which is to say the encoding of a subdiscipline.

22 Although photography has a key place both in the early anthropometric chapter of modern anthropology (as in the Torres Straits investigations) and in the methods of ethnographic documentation that became the hallmark of the field in the 20th century, visual anthropology as a recognized subfield is quite recent.

23 Putting names to faces is a highly charged ethnographic act. First, it personalizes relationships between researchers and subjects in a context often presented as clinical (subjects = informants) and in which anonymity may be desirable (to protect the innocent and the guilty). Second, it may expose subjects to various unforeseen, subsequent dangers (e.g., attention from police). Third, it may impose an unwanted or unwarranted iconic status (look at the image careers of the Kayapó Raoni and Payakan). Fourth, it often connotes a mug-shot/usual suspect portrayal as well as harking back to explicitly anthropometric photography; of the 177 Yanomami portraits in Chagnon (1974), most are for purposes of identifying genetically related individuals, not simply documenting the many faces of the Yanomami. Fifth, identifying individual subjects in this way may be seen to obscure or distract from the real object of analysis, the system/society/culture.

24 A recent, interesting, and damning, commentary on the 'language of film' notion that comes from a practitioner rather than a theoretician is provided by celebrated film editor Walter Murch (Ondaatje 2002).

25 Which is to say that the intentions of artefact creators are embodied in objects such that these artefacts themselves address viewers. An art object, in short, may function as a medium for social action (for a discussion, see Thomas and Pinney 2001).

26 Such that the theory includes cultures of shame, blame, dogs, snorkeling, the office, the car, dub, etc.

27 See also Thomas (1999:273) in this regard.

2

The Head Hunter
Cliché

Figure 2.1 L. Cotlow 1954

Although Amazonia[1] is widely perceived as a region dominated by nature, not by culture, it has been part of the modern world system for five hundred years. It exemplifies 'wilderness region' yet has been massively altered in many ways since first invaded by Europeans.[2] The main images used to represent Amazonia, however, tend not to reveal this complexity or contradiction. Instead, they invoke a unified, dehistoricized domain of dolphin, Indian, jaguar and piranha, and forest canopy and orchid. These images are artefacts of early exploration and natural history such as the influential texts of the Victorian naturalists Bates (1892), Wallace (1889), and Spruce (1908) – among numerous others – reinforced by reportage and systematic modern ethnographic investigation and consolidated by the culture industry (e.g., coffee table book, Hollywood). The pictorial record of Amazonia is a cliché with deep and interesting historical roots.[3]

The term 'scoping' now usually connotes a particular technical procedure, something along the lines of an endoscopy that involves viewing an object normally inaccessible to scrutiny. Previously, scoping implied a different kind of invasive view, something akin to rubber necking – an overtly intrusive gaze. These two notions of scoping share the idea of going beyond what is normally available for view by physically overcoming obstacles, in the case of an endoscopy or x-ray, or by defying cultural norms in the case of predatory staring.

The title of this book draws on both connotations: it is intrusive, without question, but it also has an investigative purpose. The object of analysis is a group of images that appears to provide focal referents for primary notions about Amazonia and its peoples. A characteristic image is exemplified in the book jacket reproduced above.

Cotlow's (1954) *Amazon Head Hunters* is described by its publisher as a 'travel-adventure book' and while it looks like a typical pulp product (mildly sensationalist, exotic, perhaps lurid), it also has claims to respectability – a cover blurb from the *Sunday Times*, for example, and a list of acknowledgements to generals, politicians, priests, and fellow explorers.

The opening line of the book is 'Why does a man cut off another man's head, shrink it to the size of his fist, and then dance around it?' (1954:7); and although the subsequent text doesn't provide an answer as startling as the question, lacks useful specialist focus, and is without much in the way of formal ethnographic dimensions, the conclusions reached are not anthropologically contentious. Jivaro, as the author refers to the Shuar people, prize *tsantsas* (shrunken heads) for reasons that seem sensible within their own cultural logic: 'Utitiaja . . . was still ranging the forest, dispensing justice and living the good life of a competent and dedicated human being' (1954:255). The message of the text, then, is somewhat at odds with the cover image, which reduces Jivaroness to a single major activity: head hunting.

Cotlow (1954) is further illustrated with a handful of similarly reductionist, authenticating plates, the first showing the author standing with a pair of head hunters, the other three showing shrunken heads (one in preparation and two as finished artefacts, one showing the use of a head as a teaching device: hands-on, head-off pedagogy). The selection of head hunting as the outstanding characteristic of the Jivaro is not unusual[4], cannibalism and savagery comprising one of the dominant themes employed by Europeans to typify New World peoples since contact, and the scene setting in *Amazon Head Hunters* brings forward other familiar and recurring tropical suspects: 'the half-breed'; 'damp rotting vegetation'; streaming sweat; swarming insects; and so on.

The cover of Michael Harner's (1973) *The Jivaro: People of the Sacred Waterfalls* is superficially similar to that of *Amazon Head Hunters*, though based on a photograph rather than illustration. This book, however, is a respectable anthropological monograph with chapters on historical background, material culture, social relations, and law/feuding/war as well as Jivaro cosmology. The book has 22 photographs and various figures, only one of which includes *tsantsas* (and these are not artefacts of Harner's fieldwork, but specimens held by the American Museum of Natural History in New York). The other photographs are landscapes and portraits, or show Jivaro engaged in various daily tasks. Text and photographs convey, in conventional ethnographic manner, the contextualization of this Jivaro culture feature, yet the focal image is still the dramatic, decorative *tsantsa*.[5]

One reason to contrast these two takes on head hunters – the populist and the specialist – is to point toward anthropological self-consciousness about the way in which the meanings of certain concepts are in danger of escaping control. Anthropologists typically try to avoid usages, for example, that conjure up unreconstructed versions of their subject matter – 'savage' and 'primitive' and so on[6] – and are careful to qualify usages that are subject to highjacking.[7] The acceptability of 'head hunter' (or Jivaro, for that matter) is questionable,[8] yet the focal image – the full-haired *tsantsa* – retains the same expressive power. In fact, the dominant imagery of the region as a whole (Amazonian green hell) has been remarkably stable across both public and specialist cultural domains – those addressed, for example, by Cotlow and Harner.[9]

That relative stability characterizes the separate genealogies of both popular and scholarly traditions, but is recurrently challenged by interpretations of the images used to illustrate the points so forcefully established in the written accounts. There are paradoxical aspects to this challenge:

Figure 2.2 © Michael Harner.

in a field in which detailed written documentation and argument have long prevailed over the use of images to represent anthropological knowledge, the power of 'mere' images to provoke disputes about interpretation is undeniable.

An example of disputed interpretations of Amazonian anthropology is provided by Gow and Harris's (1985) commentary on *Hidden Peoples of the Amazon,* an exhibition on Amazonian Indians mounted at the British Museum in 1985. The reviewers take issue with the inclusion of a photograph of a native man astride a motorbike. Their objection is not that the juxtaposition of the modern and the traditional is transgressive[10] in that it trivializes or in some other way diminishes an unfettered anthropological subject, but that the image is incapable of expressing the historical depth of contact between Amazonians and Europeans – in other words, that the motorcycle is tokenistic (which is also to say, in this context, misrepresentative).

While it is true that the exhibition did not provide much material of historical depth[11] – and this was not its goal – it is the motorcycle image that offends (misrepresents), not the overall exhibition. There are two issues here. The first is the power of an image itself to bear such interpretive weight. The second is specialist anthropological intervention in order to correct a public misrepresentation. One of the recurring features in comparing specialist and popular portrayals of Amazonia, however, is convergence rather than divergence.

A Transformed Amazonia

The misrepresentative powers of ethnographic photography are not new. Levine (1989:92–3) writes with respect to Im Thurn's (1893) early essay on anthropological photography that:

> [s]ome anthropologists spoke out against such degrading portrayals, but to little avail. Everard E. im Thurn,[12] who used photography as part of his field research in Guiana, addressed the Anthropological Institute after returning to London, complaining that poses of native people taken by outsiders were 'merely pictures of lifeless bodies,' and stating that the 'ordinary photographs of uncharacteristically miserable natives . . . seem comparable to the photographs which one occasionally sees of badly stuffed and distorted birds and animals.

Levine (1989:31) also notes, however, that the preference for unimaginatively posed photographs did not merely reflect a crude ideological bias – not that that was inconsequential by any means – but also reflected technical limitations such as long exposure times and the practical burden of heavy cameras. Success in the emergent, international *carte-de-visite* industry did not seem to be impaired by stylistic crudity in representations of strange peoples from strange lands.

In the particular case of Amazonia, however (albeit hardly uniquely), it is sometimes difficult to ascertain a baseline against which one might measure the accuracy of representations, whether images or not. In order to appreciate the reasons underlying the apparent stability of the clichéd Amazonian image set, it is worth looking at standard and revised accounts of Amazonia as a more or less uniform culture area.

Figure 2.3 Miranha Indians. Albert Frisch ca. 1860.

The Elements of Cliché: Who Are Amazonians?

Migration

There is no serious alternative to the view that Amazonia was occupied, like the rest of the New World, by peoples from Asia who crossed a land bridge (at the Bering Straits) during the previous ice age. Assertions of trans-Pacific migration or more outlandish origin myths (Nazca) have little serious support. Earlier dates for humans in Brazil (i.e., prior to ca. 10,000 BP) associated with the research of Guidon (Bahn 1991), and which complicate the standard account, remain in confirmation/refutation limbo.

Despite the strength of the Bering Straits migration theory and the substantial body of supporting empirical material (linguistic, archaeological, mitochondrial, ecological) and absence of any plausible alternative account, there is still a persistent sense of mystery surrounding the origins of Amazonians, one reinforced by the recurrent of the notion of 'lost tribe'.[13] In contemporary Brazil, the mystery of the 'lost tribe' is now mainly represented in the journalistic coverage of the activities of the former director of the National Indian Foundation, Sidney Posuello (see Bellos 2000 for a recent example) with the collaboration of *National Geographic*.[14]

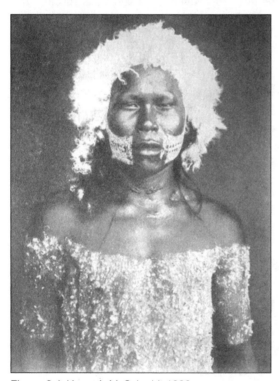

Figure 2.4 Kayapó. M. Schmidt 1926.

Other Amazonians

While Indian Amazonians – First Nations Amazonians – have an unrivalled iconic status as 'real' Amazonians, the history of their contact with

European interlopers dramatically illustrates the general disdain in which they have been held and the systematic persecution, neglect, and violence to which they have been and continue to be subjected.[15] The disparity between Indians' high symbolic capital and their impoverished circumstances is part of the construction of Ramos's (1992, 1998) afore-mentioned 'hyperreal Indian'.

This contradictory representation – that is, the simultaneous over- and under-valuation of Indians – is mirrored in the representation of non-Indian Amazonians who, despite five hundred years of occupation/residence, are typically described as settlers, frontier folk, peoples of the forest, or haphazard interlopers. While it is true that the commencement of development projects associated with the Transamazon Highway (ca. 1970) prompted an unprecedented wave of immigration,[16] from the time of Cabral's laying of Portuguese claims on Brazil in 1500 and the 1542 descent by Orellana of the Amazon River, the region has supported a cosmopolitan population – Dutch, English, French, Japanese, Moroccan (Sephardic), Lebanese, Africans, and Caribbeans (among many others).

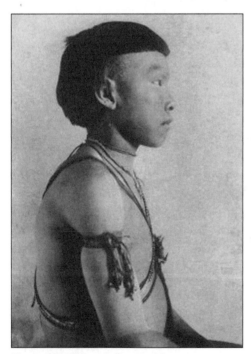

Figure 2.5 Postcard, Bororo girl.

The actual diversity of Amazonians, however, does not often disrupt the characterization of the region as a social as well as natural frontier.

Lorimer's (1989) detailed account of various English and Irish colonial enterprises in the 16th century gives a flavour of the early international-ization of the region,[17] but while Brazil's nation-building project based on eclectic sources continues to command much attention,[18] Amazonia is pre-sumed to stand outside the mainstream of neo-tropical syncretism.

Demography and Environment

An underlying reason for the widely held belief in Amazonia's being endurably 'Indian territory' is the belief that in the profoundly non-/anti-social space of the hideous tropics (see further discussion below), no one else would tolerate it – or, in a modern recapitulation of the Rousseauean savage-in-harmony-with-nature equation, the belief in a primordial and exclusive Indian integration with nature.

Early accounts of the densely populated banks of the Solimoes/Amazon[19] did not inspire much investigation until very recently and the notion of 'lost cities of the Amazon' lay in the world of fiction rather than fact. With the rejection of the implications of early travellers' accounts, estimates of pre-colonial Amerindian populations presented in authoritative work well into the last quarter of the 20th century are significantly lower than contemporary estimates (500,000 versus 15 million cf. Hecht and Cockburn 1989). Denevan's (1976) influential collection (revised in 1992) established a new, much higher baseline estimate, and in recent years there has been convergence around the figure 5–10 million.

These revisions have had provocative and in many respects still not fully realized implications for long-established views of pre- and post-colonial Amerindians[20]. Centrally, they challenge the almost sacred as-sociation between rigid environmental constraint and the possibility for the emergence of social complexity that has been a keystone of much Amazonianist research and, crucially, they give pause to the notion that the predominant form of contemporary Amerindian societies is typical of pre-Conquest societies (i.e., small scale, upland forest, etc.).

In the face of growing scepticism about the established ideal typifi-cation of 'Amazonian' and 'Amazonia', there has been little transform-ation of the basic image set. The significant modifications take the form of novel, allochthonous pathologies – marginals with chainsaws, desperate goldminers, multinationals, bulldozers, soya farmers – a familiar set of journalistic tokens. These pathologies are unquestionably real, yet they are generally not presented as *integral* to Amazonia but as disruptive factors that may individually be mollified ('stop the loggers'; 'retain biodiversity'), thereby maintaining the conventional separation of biological systems and social systems as well as denying the long history of human modification of the terrain.[21] The tropical forest so represented is not dissimilar from

Ramos's 'hyperreal Indian'. Both Indians and the idealized, pristine forest-river system hark back to some authentic, pre-modern original condition, but that representation is incomplete and bears few of the traces of history even in the face of substantial documentation and recognition of those shortcomings.

Figure 2.6 Postcard, Salesian nun and Indians.

Tropical Nastiness

In his analysis of what he calls 'the doctrine of tropical nastiness', Blaut (1993) illustrates how certain conceits regarding geographical determinism persist in the face of compelling empirical refutation – an argument that has considerable bearing on Amazonia.[22] The claim that this kind of naturalistic tropicalism represents an intrinsic and rigid obstacle to sociocultural complexity is a long established notion although contradicted by the archaeological and historical records, as well as the current phase of agribusiness (soya production[23]).

The burden of pathological tropicalism falls mainly on two groups in Amazonia – Indians whose allegedly stunted sociocultural development is claimed to be causally linked to features of the natural landscape (e.g., protein shortage; cf. Gross 1975 and Beckerman 1979 for critiques); and small-scale colonists/peasants whose predatory swidden agriculture is so often incorrectly highlighted as the ultimate, rather than proximate, cause of deforestation.

While these causal, geographically deterministic claims are not as well supported by evidence as proponents claim, they are key elements of folk wisdom and from the perspective of the focal set of images of Amazonia and Amazonians, what is crucial is that clichéd Indians and peasants/ farmers represent 'before' (state of nature/society grace) and 'after' (state of rupture), respectively.

Phases of Amazonian Development

Michael Heckenberger (2005), who employs the notion 'deep temporality' to describe the synthetic project earlier outlined by Roosevelt (1994) to combine history, archaeology, and ethnography, draws attention to the discontinuities in Amazonian history that have given rise to a selective portrayal of Amerindian response to colonialism (2005:xiii–xi) such that there·is unwarranted 'durability of the false notion that the present is a version of the past in Amazonia'.

Of particular importance in terms of the establishment of received views about and images of Amazonian Indian societies are two facts. First is the long gap between early European penetration of the region and the onset of serious scientific inquiry (from the early 16th century to the late 18th century).[24] Second is the belated recognition of the extent of demographic collapse of Amerindian societies. Even if one takes a conservative estimate of the indigenous population at the time of conquest – five million, say – the contrast with the estimated indigenous population provided by the Aborigine Protection Society in 1973 (Brooks et al. 1973) of ca. 50,000 is dramatic.[25]

To put this into context with respect to the representativeness of the images of Indians (and Amazonia) that form the focal set, the majority of them had certainly disappeared before the 'Victorian age' of natural history in the region (which was responsible for establishing some of the key images). By the time professional anthropology arrived in strength in Amazonia (and anthropology is one of the major sources of knowledge about Amazonians for the general public), the representativeness of extant Amazonian Indians was highly questionable.

Regionalism

The way in which Amazonian history articulates with Brazilian colonial and national history contributes to the mystifying aspects of the set of focal images. Until the mid-19th century, Amazonia was – and in many respects still is – 'the interior' and offered little in the way of remuneration within a colonial export economy. With the rising demand for rubber,[26] a large-scale extractive industry emerged and was to prevail as a virtual global monopoly until the second decade of the 20th century. This industry, which grew and remained profitable for almost 100 years, tends to be viewed as one of a series of boom-and-bust economies that character-ized the economic history of the colony and early Republic. The fact that its transformative powers within the region (in terms of the wide-spread promotion of a range of petty commodity production, urbanization, and links with North America and Europe) were considerable is subsumed under a national boom-and-bust idiom of economic growth that is not really accurate. Despite the intensity and duration of rubber exploitation, Amazonia was not actually meaningfully integrated. The rubber economy remained overwhelmingly regional, and national (and international) conceits about the region (miserable source of mere *drogas do sertão*[27] – exotics from the interior) prevailed, only to be partially dislodged much later in the 20th century when exotic extractivist products were redefined as key elements in the 'green harvest' and other scripts of sustainable development.[28]

Figure 2.7 Parakuta family. R. C. Humphrey.

It is no novelty to argue that Amazonia (and its history) occupies a marginal position within Brazil and Brazilian studies, but that marginality is qualified: quite a lot is known about Amazonia and its peoples, yet that knowledge tends to be sequestered. Complementing that seclusion, however, is the high visibility and plausibility of certain longstanding and convenient images, what have been referred to thus far as belonging to a focal set/clichés. These images are inaccurate in an absolute sense, but they are indicative rather than representative. The predominance of these indicative images impedes an adequate appreciation of the state of Brazilian Indians past and present. The images, in other words, may be worth thousands of words, but some of them are the wrong words.

Notes

1   The Brazilian Amazon is the focal – but not exclusive – area considered here. Amazonia refers to a social landscape that includes indigenous and non-indigenous peoples and a natural landscape of river/forest (and savannah) typically referred to as humid neo-tropics.

2   In recent years, there has also been increasing attention to the extent of prehistoric human modification to the landscape. See Balée (1994) and Heckenberger (2005) for overviews.

3   Redfern observes that "[t]he study of clichés is inescapably a study of knowledge (and of ignorance), of how we transmit or acquire it, and of what difference it makes to us" (1989: 5).

4   It is probably the *shrunken* aspect of Jivaro head hunting that makes it an outstanding example (lots of peoples hunt heads – the Mundurucú, for instance) – that is, its artefactual, transformed character (Jivaro shrunken heads tend to be polished and the facial features intentionally distorted). Stirling (1938:76) notes that most heads in private collections are counterfeits – attesting to non-Jivaro fascination with the artefacts – a tendency dating from at least the mid-19th century. Jivaro also shrunk the heads of the sloth, jaguar, and condor (1938:73–4). Conklin's (2001) *Consuming Grief* presents a strong example of a measured anthropological approach to the issue of anthropophagy.

5   Noteworthy recent contributions to Jivaro/Shuar studies – by Descola (1994, 1997) and Taylor (2003), for instance – signally do not exploit the head-hunting issue.

6   Note, for example, the disappearance of the subtitle *The Fierce People* from Chagnon's celebrated *Yanomamo*. For some reason, the expression *The Other* escapes wide condemnation and indeed appears for many to be a preferred usage despite its dehumanizing connotations.

7   Whitehead and Wright's recent (2004) *In Darkness and Secrecy: The Anthropology of Assault Sorcery and Witchcraft in Amazonia* provides an interesting example:

while the 'sorcery' and 'witchcraft' usages are relatively unproblematic in a South American context, many Africanists would think twice before employing them. In the introductory pages, however, the editors go to some lengths to specify/qualify what they mean by 'shamanism' in light of the widespread misappropriation of the term by New Age therapists.

8 As is the display of such artefacts.

9 Harner, being the core figure in The Foundation for Shamanic Studies, has forsaken the latter for the former.

10 That is to say not ethno-appropriate. There is widespread overvaluation – not least by many anthropologists – of the polluting/transgressive effects of culture contact. While for some culture contactees the wearing of a U2 tee-shirt may well indicate cultural pathology, for others it may only represent a piece of clothing.

11 Quite different from a successor exhibition at the same museum (when the Museum of Mankind had been incorporated into the main site of the British Museum). See McEwan, Barreto, and Neves (2001).

12 In some publications, the surname is Thurn; in others, Im Thurn. The knowledgeable Rosalind Poignant, among other things a former photographic archivist at the the Royal Anthropological Institute, insists on Im Thurn – the convention followed here.

13 The answer to 'Lost in relation to what?' remains ambiguous. There is the connotation of 'without known origin' as well as the connotation 'not yet encountered by European/white man'.

14 This is hardly a uniquely Amazonian phenomenon. The Mormon church, for example, represents a powerful interest group committed to completely unsubstantiated 'lost tribes' claims. A two-tiered model has developed in the Philippines: the 'Tasady' represent the classic 'lost tribe' (Nance 1975), while Japanese soldiers ignorant of the end of World War II represent an updated version. Wauchope (1962) is a classic discussion of speculation surrounding Amerindian origins.

15 Hemming (1978, 1987a, 1987b, 2003) provides an authoritative overview of the decline of Amerindian societies. See Crosby (1972, 1986) for an analysis of macro-ecological dimensions. The Comissao Pro-Yanomami (http://www.proyanomami.org.br) and Instituto Socio-Ambiental (http://www.socioambiental.org/) provide ongoing coverage.

16 Although it should be noted that such was the demographic collapse following conquest that it was only in the post-Transamazon decades that the Amazonian population (Indian and non-Indian) achieved its pre-conquest levels.

17 See Bethell (2003) for a discussion of British and Irish sources for the period.

18 For an interesting anthropological analysis of the early racialized politics of this ongoing debate, see Schwarcz (1999).

19 Above Manaus the river has historically been referred to as the Solimoes. For a discussion of the first accounts of the peoples of the Amazon, see Porro (1994, 1996).

20 See Roosevelt (1994) and Heckenberger (2005) for overviews and Roosevelt (1989) on the specific question of representativeness.

21 To bear down on an obvious – if insufficiently – explored point, Amazonia-the-natural-system clearly tolerated large societies of some complexity for some millennia; Amazonia (post-16th century) has significantly regressed since its incorporation into the modern world system. One familiar index is deforestation, taken by experts and non-experts as an important indicator of system health. Under pre-capitalism, deforestation leading (as far as we know, and megafauna, probably, excepted) to significant subversion of the overall viability of the forest-river biome was negligible; deforestation since 1970 approaches 20 per cent of the area of Legal Amazonia.

22 In particular, Blaut (1993) challenges the notions that humans are physiologically ill adapted to tropical existence (hence, in part, the 'lazy native' thesis); that 'poor soils' are an absolute rather than relative limitation on agricultural output; and that the 'diseases of the tropics' are intrinsic to the tropics and not more usefully perceived as correlates of poverty and poor public health provision.

23 See Brown (2005), especially Chapter 9 'The Brazilian Dilemma'. It remains to be seen whether soya production will escape the fate of its predecessor mono-cultures in Amazonia.

24 See also Nugent (2004).

25 Ribeiro (1967) provides a widely cited and now, it appears, overly pessimistic prediction of the complete demise of the Brazilian Indian. Current estimates (300,000–400,000) represent something of a turnaround, but it is not clear how much of the increase is due to natural growth and how much is due to the (qualified) advantages of Indian identity under revised demarcation statutes (and there is by no means a consensus that demarcation is a panacea). Indians represent less than 0.25 per cent of the Brazilian population of ca. 180 million.

26 The major commercial species was *hevea brasiliensis*. See Dean (1987) and Weinstein (1983) for standard accounts of the period.

27 A label for extractive produce.

28 For a pointed discussion, see Turner (1995).

3

Visualizing Social Memory: Race, Class, and Ethnicity in Amazonia

Figure 3.1 Barqueiros Bolivianos. Albert Frisch, 1860–65.

The focal anthropological material considered here is in some respects very easy to summarize: it consists mainly of a set of photographic images taken in the course of fieldwork[1] by diverse anthropologists and used to illustrate monograph publications that have served as standard ethnographic references for students, teachers, and field researchers.

Images from other sources that constitute – very unevenly – a photographic record of Amazonia, and Amazonians as they have come to be known by European and North American explorers, travellers, naturalists, and writers and their audiences, are also part of the anthropological record. These two sets of images' respective status as professional record and public record have been shaped by diverse institutional, technical, and historical factors, but they merge around a set of stereotypes congealed as cliché: the Amazonian Indian of green hell.

Figure 3.2 *Açaizal*, Rio Guama. © Stephen Nugent.

This cliché is not just an amalgamation of fragments of portrayals culled from the diverse sources documenting the region and its peoples since the 16th century, but is also actively – if often indirectly or inadvertently – promoted by Amazonianists themselves seeking to highlight the distinctiveness of their objects of anthropological analysis. If one looks, for example, at overviews of the ethnographic literature from the 1970s,

1980s, and 1990s (Jackson 1975; Overing 1981; Viveiros de Castro 1996; see also Hill n.d.), a recurrent theme is the search for a pan-Amazonian Indian model of sociality – that is, a concept that refutes the crude labels of the past ('noble savages', 'simple, tribal peoples', and so on) and provides an adequate generic category. All the authors concede that such a model remains out of reach, but the quest provides a common focus. Hill (n.d.) ingeniously if unconvincingly identifies the missing unity in Lowland sociality as lying in the promise of *ethnogenesis*, although

> [the] emergence of ethnogenesis as a core concept in Lowland South American ethnology is not reflected in any single book or edited volume but can be inferred from the number of conferences, symposia, and short pub-lications that deal with indigenous cultures as practical ways of historically constructing social identities.

In the absence of a satisfactory, revised cover term, the historically grounded cliché retains its force; while we may reject the base and de-meaning portrayals of Amazonian Indians as – crudely – tropical victims, there is still the binding image of a hunter-gatherer sociality so heavily constrained by the environmental features of the humid neo-tropics that culture is super-naturalized. Consequently, the anthropological record both challenges the 'primitive peoples' stereotype (especially through the detailed examination of the complexities of myth, rhetoric, and ritual) and confirms crucial broad features of the stereotype (naked people who live directly from forest and river). Outside professional anthropo-logical circles, the subtleties of specialist debate are largely irrelevant and the predominant image of the Indian is basically the befeathered spear thrower or manioc processor. Ultimately, the professional, specialist image and the popular, public image feed off and reinforce each other such that the ethnogenesis identified by Hill (n.d.) as a 'practical way of historically constructing social identities' is not just confined to the social worlds of anthropological subjects, but is part of what anthropologists themselves do. It is part of the anthropological (and, to a degree, the public) record.

Although anthropological attention to Amazonian identity (and repre-sentation of Amazonian identity through images) now has an undoubted authority, one wrested away from the adventurer-traveller, this authority emerged rather late – almost 400 years after the first European exploration of the region – and the professional anthropological record sits atop many layers of description, commencing with the accounts of Carvajal (1934[1555]) and his contemporaries.[2] That long time lag, as well as the very different agendas of subsequent explorers and others (religious conversion, basic inventories of flora and fauna, plunder), contribute to an unsettled background for the emergence of a highly focused anthro-pological discourse. Further complicating matters have been the dramatic demographic collapse in the early years of contact followed by steady, piecemeal decline of surviving Indian groups; state Indian policy positioned somewhere between genocide and assimilation; and the marginality of the Amazon region from the main currents of national development (such that in many respects, Amazonian Indians are as exotic to Brazilian nationals[3] as they are to Europeans).

The tendency to promote the stereotype, the cliché, is not – as I hope the above comments make clear – a matter of misrepresentation in the sense of corruption, but misrepresentation in the sense of accommodating an incomplete and fragmented body of knowledge. It is also the case that from the Indian perspective, the attempt to mobilize around indigenous goals has required (and at times achieved) the construction of a generic Indian as well. The history of UNI – the Union of Indian Nations – reveals this well. Formed in the aftermath of initiatives by CIMI (Indigenist Missionary Council, a militant tendency within the National Council of Bishops) to mobilize so-called 'indigenous assemblies', UNI was in part an attempt to provide a pan-Indian (which is in many respects also pan-Amazonian) image to stand for the 'proliferation of small societies living relatively independent lives with few common concerns apart from the underlying predicament of being Indian in a country that strongly favors cultural homogeneity' (Ramos 1998:176). Ramos also underscores the role that anthropologists themselves played in advancing an image of the Indians, which once seized upon had the effect of 'surprising and even shocking many a friend of the Indians' (1998:176–7), revealing in yet another way the close and complex intermingling of the elements used to construct the cliché.

There is another anthropological realm (archaeology) in which the received image of the Amazonian Indian plays an important role and also contributes significantly[4] to public understandings (or misunderstandings) about the origins and general features of indigenous Amazonian peoples and societies. The highly influential work of Meggers and Evans (1957; Meggers 1971, 1996) encapsulates long-standing views about neo-tropical pathology, particularly with regard to the notion that the biogeography of Amazonia cannot support societies of great social complexity or size. High temperatures and humidity (encouraging the too-rapid decomposition of organic material) and the poverty of the heavily leached soils are among the factors cited in defense of the notion that Amazonia is anathema to humans. The fact that the demographic collapse following conquest so rapidly rendered a landscape notably lacking in human presence no doubt contributed to the idea that environmental constraints in Amazonia were highly rigid and highly effective.[5]

While there has long been criticism of the particular 'rigid environmental constraints' view of Meggers's counterfeit paradise notion,[6] and despite the fact that recent excavations in Amazonia further undermine the confident claims of Meggers and her allies,[7] the forest-dwelling-Indian stereotype prevails.

To express scepticism about the typicality of the green hell-savage cliché is neither to challenge the legitimacy of contemporary Indians' claims to be representative of Indian interests (and their links with the past are mainly expressed through song, myth, and other such codes) nor deny the overwhelming importance of environmental constraint, but the evidence to date very clearly challenges in non-trivial ways some crucial underlying assumptions about Amazonia that have prevailed in specialist circles as well as within public/popular culture, and it is these assumptions' resilience in the face of empirical challenge that is partially revealed in the photographic record of Amazonian research.

While there are important disagreements about the prehistory of Amazonian peoples and large gaps in our understanding of the early and late colonial periods, there is little disagreement about what kinds of societies Amazonian Indians live in today and have lived in during the 20th century, and it is almost certainly the case that the tendency by anthropologists and other allies of Indians to highlight essentialist features of Amazonian Indianness has contributed in vital ways to the defense of the modern Indian and some improvement in life chances.[8] That is to say the idealization of what might be called the 'derived Indian' is accurate, but also somewhat incomplete. Two major factors contributing to this incompleteness have already been noted: demographic collapse and the resulting lacunae in the historical record, and recent archaeological supposition that questions some basic terms of reference (e.g., to what degree contemporary 'typical' Amazonian societies are representative of societies of the past).

While historical portrayals of Indians have usually carried references to practices that attract easy attention and comment (savagery, cannibalism, infanticide, spirit-possession, shamanism, use of psychotropics, and so on – exotic, real, imagined), public perception in Europe and North America of Indians as inveterate perpetrators of violence was put into perspective in the early 20th century during the investigation of allegations of torture and persecution of Indians on the rubber estates of the Putumayo region of northwest Amazonia.[9]

Sir Roger Casement, a British civil servant who had already overseen an investigation into enslavement and brutalization of Congolese on Belgian King Leopold's rubber estates in 1904, was appointed to investigate first hand the Putumayo estates following charges brought to international attention by William Hardenberg, an American engineer. The investigation revealed extraordinary crimes against Indians and in the face of government indifference was aggressively supported by the

Anti-Slavery Society and the periodical *The Truth*. Both Paternoster's (1913) *The Lords of the Devil's Paradise* – compiled from *The Truth* – and Hardenburg's (1912) *The Putumayo: The Devil's Paradise* appealed to broad audiences and the latter featured photographic documentation.

Figure 3.3 Smoking rubber. H. C. Pearson 1911.

The extensive introduction to *The Putumayo: The Devil's Paradise* was provided by C. R. Enock, author of *The Andes and the Amazon* (1907) and a member of the Royal Geographical Society. His comments reveal a number of telling undercurrents to the defense of the Indian. These include the mobilization of the Indian as a token of anti-modernism and anti-commercialism, an affiliation with biogeographical determinism, and a racial categorizing typical of the period.

While 'commercialism' lay behind the evil perpetrated against the Indians (Hardenburg 1912: 22–4), according to Enock, he also asserts that Indians had a natural affinity for work in the tropics that was not possessed by others.

> No foreign or imported race can perform the work of the Peruvian miner or rubber-gatherer. Due to the peculiar conditions of climate – the great altitude in the one case and the humidity in the other – no European or Asiatic people could take the place of these people, whose work can only be accomplished by those who have paid Nature the homage of being born upon the soil and inured to its conditions throughout many generations. (Hardenburg 1912: 27)

This frankly culturalist and adaptationist argument (cultivation over generations), overlaid on an essentialist claim ('born upon the soil') and combined with a quasi-religious reverence toward nature, is consistent with many contemporary claims about stewardship and the maintenance of a pre-modern relationship between the land and those who directly occupy it.[10] Thus, one reading of Enock concerns the fitness of the Indian to Amazonian circumstances. What is disruptive is the violent intervention (literally, as through persecution and physical torture, and more abstractly as through the introduction of commercialism and its mentality), a dystopia in place of an original state-of-grace utopia.

Another of Enock's themes, and one that also has contemporary resonances, concerns issues of racial purity and national culture. The alleged shortcomings of racial mixing are illustrated for Enock by a 'sinister' and 'callous' Spanish and Portuguese character resulting from the influence of 'Moor, Goth, Semite, Vandal and other peoples' (Hardenburg 1912: 37). This character is, according to Enock, complemented by the innate savagery of Barbadian slave drivers imported by estate owners: 'But probably the savage depth of the negro is easily stirred, as all know who had dealings therewith (Hardenburg 1912: 39–40).[11]

The contrast between the 'pure' Indian and the *mestiço* continues to feature prominently in anthropological discourse in Amazonia despite the fact that most serious researchers acknowledge the variability and uncertainty of criteria and contexts invoked in making authoritative Indian/non-Indian distinctions in Amazonia, but the ideal typification of the Amazonian Indian – the cliché – commands an authority that other Amazonians do not.[12]

The idealization of the Amazonian Indian – what has been referred to as the focal cliché – draws upon a number of sources and kinds of material of which the anthropological is a relatively recent one. Having established authority (in most respects) as the official authoritative mediator between Amazonian Indians and other constituencies, anthropology still carries others' histories with it, including images that convey an ideological baggage that fits uncomfortably – in most cases – in modern accounts.

Faces, Races, and the Anthropological Record

The unavoidable associations with highly racialized discourse that early anthropologically minded photography maintained is largely forgotten in the face of the serious critical attention accorded historical anthropology and photography in much recent work (see Banks and Morphy 1999; Edwards 1994; Pinney and Peterson 2003), and within visual anthropology there is a conceptual vocabulary that is at one time generic enough to accommodate moving images, still photographs, and mixed media, while also being attentive to historicist demands. In addition, new frameworks offered by the material culture subfield, for example, as well as technological advances[13] and art world/museum world overlaps, cultivate new audiences and new kinds of practice. Considerable cohesion is provided by a common concern with photography as a colonial practice, specifically with regard to its codifying subjects according to racial criteria (see Stoler 1995), but also with the way in which photography and its traditions are taken up, modified, and used by subjects to advance their own accounts of the colonial and post-colonial situation (see Pinney 1999; Poole 1997).

Much of the emphasis on photography's specific significance within the colonial situation seems to rest on the way racial stereotyping functioned in service of colonialism, although as Thomas (1994) has argued, there is also a broader cultural brief implicated in the documentation record that the racial emphasis may over-represent presentist concerns. In either case, however, the normative colonial references/dimensions seem to be those largely characteristic of the British Empire.[14]

In some circumstances – in Brazil, for example, and in Mexico, not to mention the United States – quite different features of internal colonialism stand out. One implication of this contrast between kinds of colonial experience is that the first photographic documentation of imperial/colonial subjects captures the unevenness of imperial/colonial reach, but also submits to the influence of what was arguably the dominant mode of the moment. The similarities between colonial photograpy in Africa for example (see Landau 1999) and the *cartes de visite* industry in South America may be weak or strong depending on sensitivity to local/regional factors. This is not to suggest that it is a straightforward matter to disengage the various racial rhetorics of the late 19th century, but the peculiarities of their fit and lack of fit have some relevance. The British imperial voices of Enoch (1907) and Im Thurn (1934), for example, share in crucial respects Euclides da Cunha's (1944 [1902]) preoccupations with the consequences of miscegenation in colonial South America; their respective imperial and nation-building gazes are hardly reducible to each other.

The unevenness of these racialized discourses – and inevitably expressed in the photographic record (and subsequent commentaries on) – is discernible, but not necessarily accessible to any great degree. In Brazilian Amazonia, the foundational images seem to represent the work of commercial photographers about whom little is known (e.g., Frisch), but whose presence in the region is undoubtedly linked to the rubber industry and the direct transport and mercantile links made with Northern Europe. In some cases – unusually, and unlike that of Frisch – there is quite a lot known about the circumstances surrounding early images. Huebner's Manaus studio and expeditionary photographs (Schoepf 2000) reveal the overlaps between scientific and commercial activities in the region over a period of decades, but the kind of administrative colonial context within which this documentation took place is very far removed from that of other imperial/bureaucratic regimes. The syncretic character of Amazonian colonial society, the early severing of Lusitanian control (1822) and the rise of the Republic (1889), and the geographical isolation of the region all shape the colonial depiction. Again, this is not to deny the enormous impact of other European/imperial racial doctrines on how Brazilian subjects were portrayed (Schwarcz 1999), but only to note that there are distinctive local features of the colonial situation in Brazil and Amazonia whose relegation may contribute to the shaping of a stereotype/cliché (of the 'Amazonian Indian') – some of whose cardinal qualities reflect others' histories and preoccupations.

Similar caution with respect to the level at which a transhistorical[15] notion of colonial photography is germane may also apply to assessments of Curtis's (2003) work with North American Indians. While criticized for an excess of aestheticism from one quarter because of his portraiture and the artifice of the 'ethnographic present', his position with respect to anthropometry and 'the personality study' – as well as his harsh comments on the U.S. government attitude toward treaties with Indian groups – displays a sensibility close to that of many current indigenist militants: 'The conditions are still so acute that, after spending many months among these scattered groups of Indians, the author finds it difficult even to mention the subject with calmness' (quoted in Adam 2003:23).

In the following discussion of the Amazonian material, the colonial idiom has a background status. This is hardly to discount or ignore the importance of colonial regimes, but the main focus of attention is on anthropological idiom itself – that is, the portrayal by text and image of Indians as subjects of modern anthropological inquiry, itself a legatee of 'the colonial situation', a successor in the lineage of conquest, exploration, and development.

Figure 3.4 Paressi headball. M. Schmidt 1926.

The kinds of knowledge about Amazonia widely available to and/or promulgated to non-specialist audiences – images purported to represent various 'Amazonian realities' and drawn from a variety of sources – may be mythical/fantastical or documentary/realist. These images, and the knowledge embodied, are in a crucial sense contingent, but that contingency is itself accessible to examination and critique.

Notes

1 There is also a limited use of historical images in these monographs (see Table 6.1).

2 Nimuendajú (1939, 1942, 1946, 1952) is the key figure in early Amazonian anthropology. Born Curt Unckel, he adopted a Tupi name.

3 The question of Indians being Brazilian nationals themselves is examined by Ramos (1998), yielding such paradoxes as the fact that it is in some ways easier (practically and conceptually) for a foreigner to become Brazilian (i.e., natural-ized) than it is for an Indian to achieve that status (without, of course, revoking Indianness).

4 As measured by the volume of coverage in newspapers and journals.

5 It may seem paradoxical that the field research upon which these generaliz-ations were based took place in Marajoara, the one area of Amazonia at that time (late 1940s/early 1950s) acknowledged as having supported a large, com-plex, and 'atypical' Amazonian society, but the explanation offered is that Marajoarans were Caribbean incomers.

6 Lathrap (1968, 1970) having been the most aggressive and persistent critic.

7 See, in particular, Roosevelt (1991), McEwan, Barreto, and Neves (2001), Heckenberger (2005), and Heckenberger, Peterson, and Neves (2001).

8 In particular, access to an international platform/audience has allowed some mitigation of ruthless state policies toward Indians in Brazil.

9 Taussig's (1987) celebrated examination of the culture of terror in the Putumayo region addresses events there from a variety of perspectives representing diverse interests present at the time (e.g., travellers, missionaries, scientists, etc.) and draws attention to the way in which the culture of terror was not only imposed upon Indians of the region but also internalized by them in the form, for example, of co-opted Indian youths (muchachos) who became agents of rubber estate owners against their own people. The Huitoto are one of the main groups involved. See Gray (1996a, 1996b) for a detailed ethnography of contemporary Huitoto.

10 He writes, 'Tribal people like the Aborigines, Amerindians and Bushmen are the heirs to all the richness and diversity of the natural world. They have a special understanding of nature through their long and intimate relationship with it and they are prepared to lay down their lives to defend it. The least we should do is listen to their arguments before we allow the juggernaut of 'progress' to sweep away what we no longer understand. What is the point of trying to save the world if you destroy its diversity, both natural and human, in the process?'

Enock's speculations about the purity of those most closely in touch with nature are oddly echoed in Survival International, of which Robin Hanbury-Tenison – who is also a key figure in the Countryside Alliance – is founder and president.

11 This kind of racialized, confused, and contradictory discourse is typical of other writers of the time. Paternoster (1913:323), for example, quotes from Colonel H. Fawcett in the *Manchester Guardian*: 'What is the matter with this country [Peru]? Part of it, particularly the governing class, suffers from the inevitable moral atrophy of a white and hybrid race born and bred at sea level near the Equator'. Woodroffe (1914) quotes extensively and admiringly from Enock's introduction to Hardenburg (1912), and in his enthusiasm for racist posturing and pronouncement becomes totally lost amidst all the racial markers. Arguing, for example, that '[i]f it ever comes to a question of extermination, those whom I would like to see removed are the low-class half-breeds', and adding to Enock's list of Moor, Goth, Semite, and Vandal the 'Negro and Indian', he rushes on to define 'native races' including both 'pure' Indian and Negro, but also 'Cholo (half Negro, half Indian), Mestizo (white and Indian), Mulatto (white and Negro)' as among those who 'must, in all cases, form the basis of society' (1914:11).

12 And, of course, it is largely a symbolic authority. For an analysis of the paradoxes of such symbolic authority, see especially Ramos (1998, Chap. 3 'The Indian Against the State').

13 Although there is much talk of a digital revolution, much of the technological impact in anthropology is actually pre-revolutionary: digitizing material from outdated formats and stirring up dust in the archives.

14 This is by no means a hard and fast claim. In an indicative volume (Pinney and Peterson 2003), for example, there is material from outside the British Empire (Japan, the United States, Peru), but the basic – and still emergent framework – bears heavily on UK imperial constructions.

15 In Hight and Sampson (2002a), for instance, the colonial examples in twelve chapters include Australian aborigines, Nubians, Indians (South Asian X2), Turks under the Ottoman Empire, Japanese, Algerians, Fijians, Hawaiians, diverse prisoners of war (Germany), West Africans, and Puerto Ricans (*jíbaros*). Despite lip service to the idea of colonial complexity, the overall impression is of a discourse of 'the other', 'alterity', and other typical markers of a voracious and leveling 'post-colonial theory'. See Jacoby (1995) for a hyper-sceptical critique of the ambitions of post-colonial theory.

4

The Tropic of Amazon: Missing Peoples and Lingering Metaphors

'A cliché is not a half-dead metaphor, it is one that refuses to die.'
[Lerner 1956:250, quoted in Redfern 1989:102]

It is itself a cliché to say that images of Amazonia are stereotypical and in some respects the origins of key relationships between cliché and stereotype are far from obscure. They are revealed in a literature, beginning in the mid-19th century, when long-term field research by the Victorian naturalists Bates, Spruce, and Wallace (and others less celebrated) first provided detailed – if hardly complete – descriptions of significant portions of the basin, flora, and fauna (and, to a much lesser degree, its human occupants). The essence of their depictions, reinforced by Conan Doyle's (1912) widely disseminated *Lost World*, have held sway until the present, several decades after the science- and modernization-led 'conquest of the tropics,'[1] the implementation of the Transamazon Highway, and associated development projects in ca. 1970. Throughout that period, there has been a significant immutability of representations of both the natural and social spheres, the persistent imagery of green hell, natural exuberance, and cultural parsimony such that the centrality of the image of the forest-dwelling hunter-gatherer is coherent in terms of an authoritative, detailed ethnographic literature, but is also compatible with a crudely stereotypical 'noble savage'/'stone-age people' characterization that prevails in public culture.

This coexistence of more and less accurate notions of 'Amazonian Indian' or 'Amazonian society' is hardly controversial – the same could be said of most ethnographic areas – and what is also shared in these

Figure 4.1 Andoke couple. T. Whiffen ca. 1904: Copyright of the Royal Anthropological Institute of Great Britain and Ireland.

two views of Amazonia is a curiously ahistorical place, a place in which the idioms of naturalism still serve to provide the basic references for the social, as they still do for many hunting and gathering societies.

In a crucial respect, however, the ahistoricism and persistent naturalism are surprising. Amazonia may yet appear as one of the last frontiers, but since the earliest phases of New World colonization, Amazonia has been part of the modern world.

Even as a narrowly defined anthropological object, Amazonia is fragmented, but there is a general notion – especially among Indianists who tend to provide the focus for sociocultural anthropological research – of a division of labour among symbolists, structuralists, and cultural ecologists.[2] Such a classification is not exhaustive of the sociocultural anthropology of the region as it little acknowledges the anthropology of non-Indian Amazonians or the appeals to multidisciplinary syntheses (see Balée 1994; Heckenberger 2005; Roosevelt 1994), but the core ethnographic literature is unquestionably centred on a highly recognizable 'Amazonian Indian subject'.

Alongside this fairly unambiguous anthropological object is a tradition of Amazonian studies that converges, however awkwardly at times, with

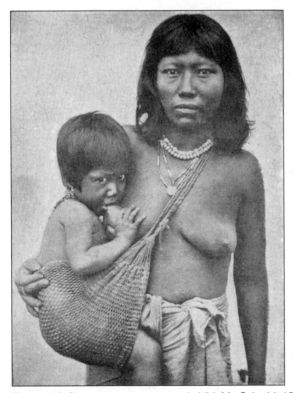

Figure 4.2 Chamacocco woman and child. M. Schmidt 1926.

Figure 4.3 Bates versus the toucans. H. Bates 1892.

the official anthropological literature.[3] There are key elements of this tradition regularly invoked to provide a general background that highlights both natural (*inferno verde*) and cultural (Manuas opera house) features. Against this background are actors generally designated with no great subtlety as Indians, *caboclos*, or whites (from an indigenist's perspective) or Indians, *mestiços*, and nationals (from a national perspective).[4] There is a relative and significant absence of autochthonous historical figures, no analogues of Sitting Bull, Geronimo, or Black Elk.[5] Instead, outside actors such as Colonel Fawcett, Henry Ford, and Euclides da Cunha provide iconic reference.[6]

For the purposes of this book, there are roughly five phases of documentation of Amazonia (both natural and social landscapes) in which there is an intermixing of anthropological and non-anthropological stereotypes. Obviously, an official anthropological idiom only emerges in the 20th century, but that idiom inevitably draws heavily – if selectively – on earlier sources.

The first phase is associated with accounts provided by religious chroniclers who accompanied, respectively, the first descent and first ascent of the river: Carvajal who documented the voyage of Orellana (1542), and Acuna who documented Teixeira's expedition a century later (1637). La Condamine (1737), von Humboldt (1799), von Spix and von Martius (1817) – and, subsequently, Agassiz – represent the explorer/scientist phase.[7] Phase three is closely associated with Wallace (1889), Bates (1892), and Spruce (1908), independent scientists[8] whose work was mainly funded through the sale of collections. Phase four is the official ethnographic record, effectively commencing with Curt Nimuendajú (1939, 1942, 1946, 1949, 1952). And the fifth phase commences with the so-called 'opening' of Amazonia via the projects associated with – and superseding – the construction of the Transamazon Highway.

There is a sixth phase, though perhaps not so much a stage of the sequence as it is an accumulation and aggregation of images that represent a stereotypical Amazonia, one whose mythic elements – challenged by new research – are not so much displaced as enhanced. An early example of this is the myth of Amazon warriors, an image of dubious reliability, yet still a centerpiece of folkloric accounts, kept alive as much through its repeatedly being cited as inaccurate as through its being ascribed any credibility. Henry Hoyt's (2001 [1925]) *Lost World* (based on Conan Doyle's 1912 novel) is undoubtedly one of the most influential in terms of popular perceptions of Amazonia, reinforced by updates such as Crichton's novel and film *Jurassic Park* (1990 and Spielberg 1993) and feature films such as *Anaconda* (Llosa 1997) and *Relic* (Hyams 1996) (see Chapter 7). A more time-bound, but still significantly influential, literature also dates from the declining years of the rubber industry (early 20th century; see, for example, Woodroffe and Smith 1915).[9]

As this sketch of phases indicates, Amazonia has long been the subject of serious scrutiny from diverse quarters, but the guiding images – the melange of tropical associations (see Stepan 2001) – tend to repeat themselves. The net effect is of an Amazonia repeatedly re-invented under the terms of the current prevailing research programme (anthropology, economic botany, mineral extraction, non-timber forest products, etc.), but with continued deference to the fundamental immutability of the so-called *hyleia*,[10] a nature yet to be brought to bear under the force of civil society, a frontier laboratory setting out limitless research and social engineering possibilities. Granted that between the 16th century discovery of 'Amazon warriors' and the 20th century discovery of 'wise forest-managers,'[11] there have been significant changes in the public perception of the region and its peoples (witness the centrality of the rain forest in contemporary eco-discourse), but there is still a strong sense of time suspension in Amazonian studies.

Founding Stereotypes

Amazonia was first explored by Europeans in the early 16th century (1541–2). That voyage was documented by Friar Gaspar de Carvajal, published in Spanish in 1855 (complete version, 1895) and revised and published in English (Heaton 1934). A closely following descent of the river (replete with hostile encounters with Amerindians) found cinematic representation in the form of *Aguirre: Wrath of God* (Herzog 1972), an impressive, low-budget, didactic costume drama. Although in many respects textually accurate, it fails to convey a controversial feature of the Amazonian landscape of the 16th century that has come to prominence in recent debates (see Meggers 1996) about the character of prehistorical Amazonian social formations: the Amerindian adversaries were not bow-wielding hunter-gatherers diverted from their normal task of procuring food for dinner, but were armed representatives of complex and large societies.

The Societies

What Carvajal documented has been slighted for two quite separate reasons. The first is that Orellana's voyage failed to consolidate the gold-driven aims of Spanish conquerors. Passage down the river did not reveal monumental societies that could provide the material wealth sought by the Spanish. Second, Carvajal documented kinds of societies that so rapidly disappeared under the impact of conquest that by the time one could speak of colonial society in Amazonia, indigenous peoples were largely represented by mere fragments of their antecedents; and by the time serious anthropological investigation was undertaken, indigenous Amazonian societies were representative of pre-Conquest societies in a manner so slight as to allow only piecemeal speculation (Lathrap 1968; Porro 1994; Roosevelt 1994).

The first ascent of the river did not take place until the early 17th century. Led by Pedro Teixeira, the expedition documented a social landscape comparable in scale to that encountered by Orellana (i.e., high density, riverine chieftainships, proto-states), but the benchmarks of pillageable wealth established by the conquest of Andean societies were still not approachable.[12]

Subsequent exploration and colonization of the region (see Hemming 1978, 1987a, 1987b) conducted by private, crown, and religious groups did result in unsteady commercial exploitation of the region (see Anderson 1999) and the decimation and further fragmentation of indigenous societies. Scientific exploration by Condamine, von Humboldt, Agassiz, von Martius, and Spix – 18th until early 19th centuries – and by Spruce, Wallace, and Bates in the mid-to-late 19th century was conducted in a highly truncated social landscape. The Amazonia that presented itself to these Victorian naturalists was a wilderness previously occupied by many humans. The relative absence of a social Amazonia was not an original condition but the outcome of hundreds of years of contact.

There are many reasons for highlighting the contributions of the trio of Victorian naturalists and for setting them apart from their predecessors. They were neither gentleman-scholars of private means nor direct employees of church or crown, but freelance/independent scholars hired as consultants, and they had much greater exposure to the lives of diverse, ordinary Amazonians. The images of Amazonia in the 19th century that emerge from the work of Bates, Spruce, and Wallace are based on extended periods in the field (their tenures perhaps only exceeded by Schultes in the mid-20th century; see Davis 1996), models for the kind of ethnographic fieldwork subsequently employed by anthropologists.

While Spruce's account of his time in Amazonia is mainly limited to an edited edition of his notebooks compiled by Wallace (1908), both Bates (1892) and Wallace (1889) are illustrated accounts that attracted large popular audiences (Stepan 2001:34) and were reviewed in periodicals for the educated public (e.g., *Dial, Academy*). These accounts carried the authority of a new scientific culture represented not only in such figures as Darwin (who with Wallace shares credit for introducing the notion of natural selection), but also institutions such as the Royal Geographic Society and the Royal Anthropological Institute of England and Wales. Unlike earlier woodcuts and engravings of more sensationalist (scenes of cannibalism feature prominently; see Mason 1990) and religious themes, those of Bates's and Wallace's illustrations that included depictions of humans – relatively few – showed a savage nature (aggressive crocodiles, vengeful toucans, towering forest) and anticipated the structure of the dioramas popularized by the American Museum of Natural History.

Bates's (1892) *The Naturalist on the River Amazons* – 470 pages in length – includes four maps (the Amazon basin, the upper Amazon River and Solimoes River, the lower Amazon River, and the Amazon estuary).

There are nine landscapes (including the widely reproduced 'Adventures with Toucans'; see above) and prints of twenty-two animal species and six plant species. Wallace's (1889) *A Narrative of Travels on the Amazon and Rio Negro* includes three maps (Rio Negro, Vaupes River, the Amazon basin), six landscapes, ten charts (e.g., annual rainfall), and illustrations of domestic articles (e.g., manioc grater) and geological formations.

Photography was then only an emerging technology and not, in any case, suited to the regime of solo collector,[13] and Bates and Wallace were not members of large teams, but more like freelance operators. Although the scientific goal of providing basic inventories was paramount, all three naturalists were dependent on the sales of their collections for their livelihoods and this was the priority.

Despite the natural history focus, Bates's and Wallace's texts include accounts of encounters with many different kinds of Amazonians; although not systematic, the ethnographic content is substantial. It is important to recognize that in this period, there is no ethnographic tradition with which to compare these accounts of field stays that are unprecedented in terms of the depth and length. The antecedents of these accounts are of very different character, either official reports to imperial sponsors and religious authorities or quasi-heroic explorer accounts (a genre that persists today and still constitutes a significant portion of the Amazonianist literature). Bates's and Wallace's accounts (not to overlook entirely Spruce's notebooks) were not the only contributions to this kind of narrative literature, but even though they comment extensively if unsystematically about the new Amazonian social landscape,[14] the main focus of their attention was on flora and fauna. An explicitly ethnographic and photographic counterpoint to the illustrative aims of the naturalists is provided by their contemporary E. Im Thurn who, although initially trained as a botanist, pursued an explicitly anthropological project.

Im Thurn on Anthropological Uses of the Camera

Im Thurn, probably best known for *Among the Indians of Guiana* (1883), provides two crucial links between the explorer/natural history Amazonianist literature (which is to say accounts of the period between the mid-16th century and the mid-to-late 19th century) and two modern bodies of Amazonian literature and images, those of academic anthropology and those of the culture industry (and, centrally, Hollywood feature films). In the first case, he brings to bear the documentary/classificatory impulse of modern ethnography (embodied in the Torres Straits Expedition, for example). In the second case, his account of his ascent of Mount Roraima (near the Guyanese/Venezuelan/Brazilian borders) is the source of Conan Doyle's 'lost world' representation of Amazonia (Conan Doyle 1912) – a

Figure 4.4 Riverbank. E. Im Thurn 1883.

Figure 4.5 Macusi dancing outfit. E. Im Thurn 1893.

version that not only continues to encapsulate received notions of tropical Amazonia and Amazonians, but is also the basis for other continental models (cf. Bond 1992a, 1992b) as well as modern mutations such as *Jurassic Park III* (Johnston 2001).

Figure 4.6 Warrau *cafuzo*. E. Im Thurn 1893.

Figure 4.7 Macusi boy. E. Im Thurn 1893.

Im Thurn's 1893 article on anthropology and photography is based on his considerable field experience in Guyana,[15] his familiarity with emerging trends within an anthropology represented by a newly formed professional association (the Royal Anthropological Institute of England and Wales) and on the verge of becoming a university discipline, and a concern to document 'primitive phases of life [that] are fast fading from the world in this age of restless travel and exploration' (1893:184). Despite his criticism of the restricted use of photography only for the accurate measuring of 'mere bodies of primitive folk' (1893:184) and his claim that the photographing of living beings should be a priority – another swipe at anthropometry – the position he espouses is still heavily flavoured by raciological preoccupations and archaic notions about the relationship between genotype and phenotype. Although more than mere physiology is to be captured by the camera, according to Im Thurn more accurate than even the detailed draftsmanship of a Catlin can achieve, he argues (more importantly) that the camera can record under natural conditions (1893:196), a claim somewhat undermined by the images (see above) he uses to illustrate his case.

It takes considerable faith to recognize in the *carte postale/carte de visite* format of these images the lifefulness claimed. Im Thurn writes:

> Just as the purely physiological photographs of the anthropometrists are merely pictures of lifeless bodies, so the ordinary photographs of uncharac- teristically miserable natives, such as that which I have just described, seem comparable to the photographs which one occasionally sees of badly stuffed and distorted birds and animals. (1893:187)

His commentary on each photograph makes clear that the step from 'stuffed animal' to 'living being' is less than it first appears, for each photo- graph – according to his commentary – is of interest because of the way it provides a context for the material culture displayed by each of the models. Hence, the first photograph (Partomona man in palm leaf dress) is of interest because the dress itself is brought to life by being worn: '[W]hen seen off the body of the wearer it would look like nothing in the world but a small bundle of withered palm leaves, and would to the uninitiated seem supremely uninteresting' (1893:195). Similarly, the photograph of the Macusi 'lad in full dancing dress' has merit because 'these articles seen, as in this photograph, *in situ*, acquire new interest' (1893:195). The caption to the photograph of Gabriel reverts to a raciological idiom, being an illus- tration of the offspring of a 'red-skinned mother' and 'black father'.

The initial claims for accuracy and lifefulness[16] are fully relegated in Im Thurn's own summary of what the photographs show: 'In short, a good series of photographs showing each of the possessions of a primitive folk, and its use, would be far more instructive and far more interesting that any collection of the articles themselves' (1893:197).

These are rather modest claims for the advantages brought to anthro- pology by the use of photography, and far from making a case for the superior accuracy of photography over textual or figurative accounts, Im Thurn's essay is basically an encomium to the forensic superiority of photography in deconstructing the racial elements to be found among various Guianese peoples. Ordinary illustrations make difficult 'discern- ing . . . the real bodily appearance of uncivilised folk' (1893:189).

With reference to images screened during the presentation of this paper to the Royal Anthropological Institute of England and Wales, but not reproduced in the published version, Im Thurn comments on what is crucially revealed in photographs: 'though not tall, are a fine people in the point of physical and muscular development'; 'the ordinary conception of these people as dull and expressionless should give place to the truer idea that . . . there is a great deal of life and even in some cases of beauty in their appearance' (1893:190); 'from the first instant that the stronger European influence meets and touches the weaker native American race, it is absolutely unavoidable that a change should begin in the latter' (1893:191).

Once launched on this line of speculation – and virtually abandoning the idea that photography can lift anthropology beyond the crude goals of anthropometry and allied conceits – Im Thurn is submerged in racio-logical dross (see, in particular, pp. 192–3), concluding with the damp re-commendation that 'the Institute should make it its business to collect and arrange in some suitable manner all photographs of the kind here alluded to, which the travelling anthropologist may secure' (1893:203).

Im Thurn's contribution to early analysis of the role of photography in modern anthropology is undeniable, but equivocal in key respects. One aspect has already been noted: the predominance of a forensic approach – ridiculed by Im Thurn as akin to taxidermy – makes any alternative approach appear a more radical departure than it may actually be. What Im Thurn takes to be naturalistic representations of Indians look contrived – stiff studio fare. Second, despite his enthusiastic, programmatic espousal of photography, Im Thurn himself seemed to lose interest in pursuing his craft. His prominence as a public figure (and promoter of anthropology) and association with the long-term study of the peoples of British Guyana resulted only in a very small number of prints held by the Royal Geo-graphical Society, the Royal Anthropological Institute, and the Pitt Rivers Museum (Ayler 1994).[17] Third, images of native peoples provided by serious scholars and explorers (often merged categories in this period)[18] represented an extremely small portion of image production of that epoch. The success of international trade fairs and theatrical exhibitions that included humans in native dress (see Poignant 2004 for a compelling his-torical case study of Australian travelling exhibits/subjects); the jumbling of categories of the exotic, as in the exhibition of pygmies, polar bears, and Scottish dancers cited by Street (1994:122); and the fashion for *cartes postale* – of which 866 million were posted in the United Kingdom in 1909–10 (Street 1994:122) – all overshadowed ethnographically inspired images as core representations of exotic natives.

The emergence of a substantial body of ethnographic images of Ama-zonians was delayed for several decades and the popularization of the clichéd image set was consolidated not only by the *cartes de visite*/travel image industry, but also through expression via other genres and media, a major example being *The Lost World* novel (Conan Doyle 1912) and feature film (Hoyt 2001 [1925]).[19] Im Thurn appears to have tried to minimize the association between the account of his ascent of Mount Roraima and Conan Doyle's fictional re-rendering, but despite his attempts to emphasize 'the scientific and practical aspects of his ascent [and the fact that it was a first ascent], possibly to counteract Conan Doyle's sensation-alising transformation of his achievement . . . his efforts were in vain' (Dalziell 2002:151). Only two years after his death, even his friend the anthropologist R. R. Marett and his widow Hannah would refer to the 'lost world' in their introduction to a commemorative set of essays (Dalziell 2002:151).

In her comparison of the parallel careers of Im Thurn's Mount Roraima and Conan Doyle's 'lost world',[20] Dalziell shows how Conan Doyle's rendition is not only obviously fashioned after Im Thurn's account, but also how it blatantly distorts key points. While the contents of the Mount Roraima plateau are mainly of botanical interest, and quietly odd, the contents of the 'lost world' plateau are rather more exotic.

> Im Thurn's peaceful summit, with dwarf, alpine-like vegetation and strange rock formations, is not the stuff of an imperial adventure story. . . . Before nightfall the dinosaur spotting has begun, and as the plot unfolds, the heroes are pursued by primeval carnivores, disturb a pterodactyl flock, are captured by hostile ape-men, trigger a war and rescue a grateful Indian tribe. (Dalziell 2002:148)

The scientific impulse of Im Thurn (e.g., collecting specimens for Kew Gardens) is overwhelmed by the appeal of dinosaurs on Tower Bridge, a tendency reflected as well in the contemporary discrepancy in symbolic weight between befeathered-Indian-with-blowpipe and genetically modified soya – the former a focal cliché, the latter a pedestrian, if potentially cataclysmic, footnote.

A similar example of the easy coexistence of contradictory empirical and mythical content in Amazonianist literature and imagery of that time is provided by Colonel Fawcett, an English explorer who disappeared in May 1925 – presumed killed by Indians – during a search for an ancient Amazonian city. His disappearance has continued to prompt speculation (intensity level: that of the Loch Ness monster or *yeti* rather than UFO) a lot of which has appeared in print,[21] and despite the absence of conclusive evidence, there is a folk attribution of responsibility to the Kalapalo Indians of the upper Xingu region. Basso (1973:4), the most assiduous student of the Kalapalo, recounts their denial of responsibility, yet

> during the period of my own research [mid-1960s], I met several persons visiting the Upper Xingu who were willing to pay for information about Colonel Fawcett. This was particularly true of Englishmen seeking to solve the mystery which apparently is still alive (at least in some circles) in Great Britain.

Im Thurn's work and reaction to it provide an example of folk knowledge prevailing over an emerging scientific literature, but it is important to note the very different dynamics characteristic of the scientific and folkloric bodies of the knowledge. The latter tends to be cumulative or iterative, the contemporary 'wise forest manager' being a clear transformation of the 'noble savage', and gives the impression of stability. The former, however, has an illusory stability despite the rigour provided by an increasingly sophisticated anthropology. The main reason for this is the fact that in terms of demographic collapse, by 1750 the 'worst was already over in most areas' (Heckenberger 2005:10) and that the move toward ethnography – by the Victorians, for example – took place against an impoverished backdrop of fragmented knowledge, and the photographic record of this period consists mainly of posed studio products.

Figure 4.8 Postcard, Macuchi Indian. G. Huebner 1903–04.

There were sound reasons for studio dependence, such as cumbersome equipment and the need for long exposure times, but it's also true that a documentary/observational approach toward ordinary life scenes had yet to challenge the idealized photographic object (Levine 1989:32).

The simple contrast between the idealized and the ordinary, however, does not seem to capture the actual variety represented in collections such as that of Kroehle and Huebner (Schoepf 2000). The photograph of the Macuxi youth above, and that of the couple below, are unambiguously posed studio images.

Figure 4.9 Amerindian couple. G. Huebner 1900–05.

As an alternative to the clinical/forensic style derided by Im Thurn, there is a female Xipibo couple posed against a drop cloth.

Figure 4.10 Xipibo women on the Ucayali. G. Huebner 1888.

Figure 4.11 Okaina girls. T. Whiffen ca. 1904: Copyright of the Royal Anthropological Institute of Great Britain and Ireland.

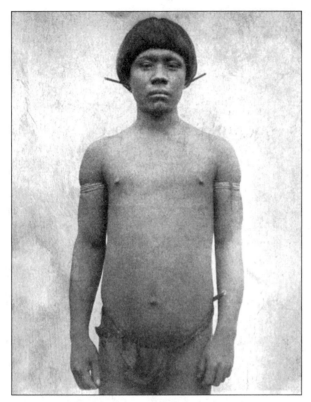

Figure 4.12 Yekuana man. M. Schmidt 1926.

Figure 4.13 Kobeua potter. M. Schmidt 1926.

Figure 4.14 Kobeua woman and children using *tipití* to squeeze juice from manioc pulp. M. Schmidt 1926.

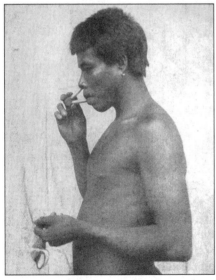

Figure 4.15 Tukuya snuff taker. M. Schmidt 1926.

Figure 4.16 Postcard, Carajá basketmaker.

Figure 4.17 Serra do Araraquara, Rio Branco. G. Huebner 1904.

In terms of the photographic conventions that came to prevail once a professional ethnographic literature could be recognized, taking the work of Nimuendajú (1939, 1942, 1946, 1949, 1952) as foundational, the range of subject matter represented in Huebner's work[22] is transgressive. Not only does it include Amazonians who are not indigenes, but it also shows a socially more complex Amazonia than is typical of 'green/vegetation hell'.

Im Thurn's dual role as a contributor to a maturing anthropology and, however inadvertently, contributor to a competing repertoire of Amazonian cliché might seem curious, but it accurately reflects key changes then occurring in the region. First, the rubber industry that had held sway over the regional economy of the Brazilian Amazon (and significant parts of other Amazonian countries) rapidly declined in the first decades of the 20th century, and in the absence of a substitute industry, the region was undergoing an involution later characterized as 'economic stagnation'.

Second, this relegation of the region from its previous position in the world economy coincided with the emergence of a new kind of anthropology that emphasized – in departing from the dominance of diffusionism, evolutionism, or raciology – a Boasian cultural relativism and the integrity of different kinds of pre-capitalist social systems as well as the structure functionalist notion of a self-contained system. Im Thurn flags these shifts in his references to the shortcomings of anthropometric materials in representing native peoples and in being caught up in the new projections of imperial culture. The *Lost World* phenomenon was not only literary, but also reflected a new kind of scientific culture within cosmopolitan circles (and in which the Darwinian revolution and the roles of learned societies featured prominently). Additionally, there were important political dimensions especially with regard to the high visibility of certain colonial and imperial practices.

The South American hinterland depicted by Im Thurn and the enterprising Conan Doyle was explicitly colonial Guiana (then British Guyana) for government employee and scientist Im Thurn, but a generic 'tropics' for Conan Doyle. This generic depiction and the ascendancy of a natural domain over a more political one is not unrealistic. Brazilian Amazonia had, after all, been initially claimed by Spain and de facto absorbed by a motley set of interests in the corner of the Portuguese colony. Effectively administered by the Jesuit order until Pombal's interventions in the mid-18th century, it was, (until the rubber boom) a not particularly desirable colonial territory. Borders between and among Brazil, Peru, Bolivia, Venezuela, Colombia, and the Guianas were uncertainly drawn and certainly permeable, a situation maintained in some subregions today; significant boundary re-drawing had taken place (e.g., Acre's shift from Bolivian to Brazilian control; the resolution of the Venezuela/British Guyana border dispute); and Colombia and Peru had tried to use the Putumayo scandal as the basis for pursuing a new set of territorial claims. The fact that travel in the region was mainly restricted to river routes certainly reinforced the perception of the interior as uncharted space.

This generic tropical forest – the lost world – was also laid before the public eye in other ways. Casement's report on Belgian labour practices on Congo Free State rubber estates in 1904 had drawn international attention to a shocking level of barbarism (indeed, an African 'heart of darkness' cognate of 'green hell'). In Amazonia, shortly afterward, allegations of the enslavement and torture of rubber estate workers in the Northwest Amazon (Putumayo region) were investigated by Casement[23] and the case was publicized by the Anti-Slavery and Aborigines Protection Society and intensely covered by the London periodical *The Truth*, whose editor Sydney Paternoster published a book-length account (*The Lords of the Devil's Paradise*) in 1913.[24]

The turn-of-the-century Amazonia depicted in literary, journalistic, and – to a limited degree – photographic accounts was not in any simple sense an 'occidentalist' construction of green hell, and while it is clear what elements were employed in the cliché assembly of 'the lost world/green hell' complex achieved by Conan Doyle (and many other lesser writers who also provided – and continue to provide – a deep jungle fix), many of the elements engaged were based, as the cinematic qualification has it, on 'real events/a true story'.[25]

The caricature of Amazonia as a lost, interior space populated by semi-mythic features and peoples was hardly confined to non-Brazilians, although in the case of Brazilian commentators (such as da Cunha 1944 [1902]), much more emphasis was placed on the national issue of the ethnic melting pot (and fears of the mongrelization of Brazil; Schwarcz 1999) than it was on Indians per se.

In looking at some of the photographic images available from late 19th century Amazonia, Im Thurn's criticism of what he clearly regards as a dominant mode (or genre) of representation is difficult to interpret.

First, the swipes at taxidermic photography seem directed at a general anthropological practice, not specifically an Amazonian one; yet as an overtly anthropological practice (as pursued, for example, by Rivers and his associates on the Torres Straits Expedition), photographic anthropometry was only really emerging at the time Im Thurn was writing. The reference may well be to the criminal identification system of Bertillon (1882–83) or to Lombroso (1876), but that is not clear. It is more likely a reference to the way photography had overtaken painting – e.g., the 'Company School' (Landau 1999:1) – in providing a record of human types disappearing under various colonial regimes.

Second, it is difficult to recognize the distinctive advance of an anthropologically informed photography over what was being achieved by, say, Frisch. Early photographs of Amazonians adhere quite well to Im Thurn's prescriptions, rendering his critique a bit lifeless.

It is known that an American photographer based in Belém in 1844, Charles Deforest Frederick, spent almost a decade photographing in the region and along the Brazilian coast, but no works seem to survive (Ferrez and Naef 1976:24). Among the earliest photographs available are those of Albert Frisch.[26] (Aside from Frisch's photographs, the only other 'Amazonian' image in Ferrez and Naef's [1976] *Pioneer Photographers of Brazil* – by Fidanza – shows Dom Pedro II arriving in Belém in 1867.) These show Indians in poses hardly dissimilar from those of contemporary postcards, and, as noted above, not at all dissimilar from what Im Thurn was later to achieve.

Figure 4.18 Albert Frisch ca. 1860.

Figure 4.19 Albert Frisch ca. 1860.

Figure 4.20 Albert Frisch ca. 1860.

Figure 4.21 Albert Frisch ca. 1860.

Figure 4.22 Indians on Solimoes. Albert Frisch ca. 1865.

Figure 4.23 Indian on Solimoes. Albert Frisch ca. 1865.

Although these are all of the *cartes de visite* style, they are neither pure 'portrait' nor 'view' – as the two prevalent types of the late 19th century were designated. Although clearly posed, prints 1–3 (Figures 4.18–4.20) in particular show what was to become an ethnographic photographic convention in subsequent decades: a scene of daily life that showed human actors and material culture (and/or spatial setting).

There are important similarities and differences between Amazonian anthropology of this period and photographic developments in other colonial settings. Landau (1999) observes that among the roles assumed by photography were reportorial and documentary (including anthropometric) functions, providing tokens for raciologists (1999:2) and assisting colonial administration (as in Watson and Kaye's [1868–75] *The People of India*).

The documentary importance of the Indian phenotype in Brazil was modest, perhaps overshadowed in the context of late-19th/20th century national debates about race and identity in which a discourse about white and black dominated (see Ramos 1998; Schwarcz 1999; Skidmore 1993). In terms of administration,[27] however, documentary photography rather than ethnography featured in the state's promotion of a national Indian bureaucracy – initially the SPI (Society for the Protection of Indians), later FUNAI (National Indian Foundation).[28]

The three volumes published under Rondon's name and entitled *The Indians of Brazil* (1946, 1953a, 1953b) include 1,515 images, the vast majority being of human subjects rather than material culture objects or landscapes.[29] Volume I – *Indians of the Centre, of the Northeast, and of the South of Mato Grosso* – is comprised of reports on 36 Indian groups and includes 573 images, a number of which are frame grabs from the films of Colonel Thomaz Reis who accompanied the expeditions as the official army cinematographer. Volume II, on Indians of the Xingu, Araguaia, and Oipoque rivers, includes four hundred images of sixteen groups. Volume III – *Indians North of the Amazon River* – includes accounts of fifteen groups and 540 images.

This is a formidable set of official images, and as Landau (1999:6) observes of a different setting (colonial Africa):

> The forces that marshalled and distributed images, were also those that propagated the dominant interpretations of what the images were taken to mean. From the 1890s through the 1930s, the Zulu 'warrior', the Maasai murran, the 'hunter' in Duggan-Cronin's beautiful photographs, all metonymically identified their 'tribes' in various books, lantern slides and postcards.

Much the same might be claimed for Amazonia with the important difference that a generic Indian (later to become Ramos's 'hyperreal Indian') took precedence over named tribes. In two senses, this generic tendency is not surprising. On one hand, the extermination of Amazonian Indians during the first two hundred years of contact was so extensive that it is now convincingly established – if not necessarily widely conceded – that in general terms contemporary Indian groups are very poorly representative of the situation just prior to and at the time of contact. On the other hand, by the time that photographic documentation emerges in the late-19th century, there is not a single example of the kind of large, possibly proto-state society that dominated the banks of the Amazon (Porro 1996). What the photographic image of an Amazonian subject has come to represent is (likely) at odds with what it is widely thought to represent.

This tension between the adequacy of what is represented by the image of the Indian, however, has its own history, and one that is sharply informed by the fact that the existence of any Indians – by whatever criteria of typicality – is precarious. When the development of a professional anthropology of Amazonian Indians did emerge, the considered view (if perhaps the dominant one) was that the collectivity of Indian groups was in such a fragile state that the process of modernization would rapidly complete the process of assimilation and cultural decline (Ribeiro 1967); thus, much emphasis in the field of Indian studies – indigenism – was placed on what little was still represented at all by Indians rather than representativeness in the longer term. The consolidation of indigenism as a clear position within the anthropology of Brazil and the Amazon bore with it the effect of creating a necessary Indian, a conception that might advance the cause of Indian rights even at the expense of precision. The designation 'Xingu Indian', for example, which has a high recognition factor, doesn't actually refer to an ethnos, or even meaningfully to the various ethnic groups (or fragments of) that live in or near the Xingu River and Reserve.[30]

One of the reality trade-offs is that classificatory simplifications are politically strategic in helping to identify a constituency that is recognizable within national and international political discourse; of course, however, that strategy is also enhanced by the cliché heritage. Again, a comparison with Africa (Landau 1999:8) is instructive: whereas in Africa photography relied on a number of stereotypes (albeit a small number), which is to say so-called 'tribes', colonial[31] photography in Amazonia was not so directly a reflection of administrative prerogatives. Although Rondon's heavily photographed expeditions were clearly part of a state project to extend and consolidate its influence in the more remote regions of interior Brazil, it was hardly either systematic or closely tied to a comprehensive administrative apparatus. The 67 tribes identified and photographed in the course of the Rondon expeditions provides a partial yet compelling collective portrait, an inventory[32] that includes and reinforces the key elements of the long-lasting aggregated icons – naked, befeathered, spear wielding, forest dwellers, etc.

Of the 437 peoples/tribes currently identified and documented by the Brazilian Social-Environmental Institute (*Instituto Socioambiental*), 37 also appear on the list of 67 provided in Rondon (1946, 1953a, 1953b), and of these sixteen were initially (i.e., by Rondon) cited with different names (e.g., Rondon *Massacá* appears on the ISA list as a subgroup of *Tuberão*). Given the greater size of the ISA list, it is not surprising that some of the Rondon names are duplicated – as in the case of the Nambiquara, for example, with a single entry in Rondon but 35 entries on the ISA list (e.g., Anunsu, Halotesu, Kithaulu, Wakalitesu, Sawentesu, Negarotê, Mamaindê, Latundê, Sabanê e Manduka, Tawandê, Hahaintesu, Alantesu, Waikisu, Alaketesu, Wasusu, Sararé).

There are a number of ways to read the comparison between the Rondon and ISA lists. The proportion of Rondon entries that recurs almost one hundred years later is only about 55 per cent, a decline not out of line with the well-known pessimistic predictions of authorities such as Ribeiro (1967). While the ISA survey is obviously more comprehensive in terms of both Amazonian and non-Amazonian Brazilian Indians, and the Rondon list reflects a far narrower explorer's brief, in both cases the images of Indians are different from those highlighted by Landau in his analysis of images of Africans, and different in ways that reflect fundamental differences between the colonial regimes. Just as the labelling and depiction of African natives were in part functions of the ways they were administered, so in Amazonia does the consolidation of a generic Indian reflect a particular political regime.[33]

Figure 4.24 Patamona group. J. F. Woodroffe 1914.

Notes

1 Heroic metaphors have been characteristic of colonial discourse in Amazonia since the first entry by Europeans, and in the 21st century the region is still being 'conquered'. The idea of a systematic relationship between the region and the nation-and-world-system is obscured by repeated recourse to an episodic notion of history.

2 See the overview by Viveiros de Castro (1996).

3 Many of these, especially of the 'traveller/adventurer' genre, make only fleeting reappearances, but others have well-established roles – e.g., the above widely reproduced engraving of Bates being attacked by toucans.

4 The classification of Amazonians is not straightforward. Among Indianists a short-hand evolutionary model tends to prevail: Indians – assimilated Indian (*caboclo*) – white man. For a detailed and interesting discussion of aspects of the modern politics of Indian identity, see Oakdale (2005).

5 Post-Transamazonia, this situation has changed; cf. Raoni, Davi Yanomami, Chico Mendes.

6 In the very recent past, however, named Amazonian representatives have emerged (e.g., Mario Juruan, Davi Yanomami, Raoni, Paulo Payakan).

7 See Smith (1990).

8 Although they maintained some kind of affiliation with such bodies as the Royal Botanical Gardens at Kew.

9 Excluded from this discussion is the 'coffee-table' and reference literature. This would include, for example, Cousteau and Richards's (1984) *Jacques Cousteau's Amazon Journey*; Ricciardi's (1991) *Vanishing Amazon*; H. and F. Schreider's (1970) National Geographic Society *Exploring the Amazon*; Bates et al.'s (1964) TIME-LIFE International *The Land and Wildlife of South America*; Bishop's (1962) Sunday Times World Library *Brazil*; and Willis's (1971) *Jungle Rivers and Mountain Peaks*.

10 A term first used by von Humboldt – 'forest' in Greek (Kricher 1989:16, citing Richards 1952).

11 A reference to an upward re-evaluation of native scientific capacity that followed the political mobilization of Amazonian peoples in response to the development assault on the region post-1970. There is serious dispute about the degree to which this re-evaluation of native science reflects anything more than a front for new forms of commercial exploitation, trading on the branding value Indian authenticity. See Turner (1995) and Corry (1993).

12 Smith (1990) provides a concise account of exploration from the early 16th until the early 20th centuries.

13 The Amazonian photographic record of this period is very slim. For an unusual and recently revealed archive, see Schoepf (2000) on George Huebner who worked with Koch-Grunberg and maintained a studio in Manaus.

14 The rubber industry of the late 19th century represented the apex of Amazonian integration in the world economy to date.

15 Im Thurn was curator of the British Guyana Museum (1877–82), government agent in Guyana (1891–99), and later governor of Fiji (1904). He was the first president of the Royal Anthropological Institute (1919–20).

16 Views on the degree to which Im Thurn departed from the forensic anthropological approach differ. Ayler (1994), for example, claims that the photographs of the subjects posing on palm thatch (above) 'involve no unnatural poses or contortions of the body, or anthropometric devices' (1994:188). The last clause is correct (if we exclude the camera itself from consideration), but the basis of Ayler's core claim is not wholly convincing, namely that the natives aren't actually posing because such manners of presentation of self come naturally to them: 'Most tropical-forest Indians are, in my experience, extraordinarily graceful while still in the prime of life'.

17 *Among the Indians of Guiana* (1883), his most durable contribution, includes 53 illustrations – ten plates and 43 woodcuts – but no photographs.

18 And photographers such as Huebner (Schoepf 2000) who maintained a commercial studio output as well as providing documentary facilities for explorers.

19 Anthropological documentary – or ethnographic film – emerged later (regardless of whether one classifies *Nanook* as a feature or documentary film). Extensive early observational footage of Amazonian Indians was taken by Colonel Thomaz Reis who established the Photographic and Cinema Department of the Rondon Commission in 1912. Another relatively neglected Amazonian image pioneer is Hercules Florence, credited with developing a photographic process before Daguerre and Fox Talbot (see Carelli 1995).

20 Bleiler (1996) notes that Conan Doyle's novel was one of many of that period that exploited the 'lost world' theme.

21 See Orcutt (2000) who cites Fawcett (1953), Dyott (1930), Fleming (1933), and Churchward (1936).

22 Huebner, that is, and his various Manaus collaborators.

23 Casement, who subsequently came to support the Irish Republican movement – and was hanged for treason – was an acquaintance of Conan Doyle, who offered some support in Casement's defense.

24 Taussig (1987) provides a celebrated discussion of the culture of violence in the Putumayo region.

25 Boorman's (1985a) memoir about the making of *The Emerald Forest* describes how the attention to accurate ethnographic detail provided by consultant anthropologists on the production finally became unsupportable. Such fidelity exceeded what was required in order to establish, for a cinema audience, ethnographic authenticity.

26 According to the catalogue entry for 'Nineteenth-Century Brazilian Views' of the University of New Mexico's Center for Southwest Research Pictorial Collections, Frisch's are the first known photographs of Amazonian Indians.

27 The 'colonial administration' in Africa and India referred to by Landau departs in many respects from what was encountered in Brazil. Initially, the administration of Brazilian Indians was split among (fought over by) private, crown, and religious interests, a system formalized under the Directorate in 1757. Although SPI was not ostensibly within the military sector of the government, Rondon's headship forged a durable link between Amazonia and the military, an association graphically revealed throughout the modernization process commencing with the construction of the Transamazon Highway (1970).

28 Hemming's (2003) *Die If You Must* traces the development of Brazil's Indian bureaucracy.

29 Compare this with Steward (1948a, 1948b), which has a high proportion of object images.

30 There are more than a dozen ethno-linguistic groups on the Reserve.

31 This is a very imprecise designation. 'Late colonial' in Brazil, for example, is reckoned to refer to the second half of the 18th century (cf. Alden 1987). What the adjective means in the current context is pre-Republican (roughly late 19th/early 20th century).

32 Of course, this is not an Amazonian inventory much less a national one, yet it provides an indicative baseline.

33 Although the Jesuit administration of Indians until 1750 bears striking similarities to the situation outlined by Landau for 'Africa'.

5

The Professional Literature: *'What I Saw in the Tropics'*

Figure 5.1 H. C. Pearson 1904.

In earlier chapters, the image of the Amazonian Indian that dominated at the beginning of the 20th century was attributed to various motivated and unmotivated sources. In the case of the former, for example, the Rousseauean idealization of a utopian state of balanced nature/culture grace was in part a critique of modernity of which the Indian was a vivid paragon.[1] In addition, religious orders enthusiastically confronted potential conscripts who might be retrieved from their sad state.[2] Similarly, a tropical frontier sparsely occupied by atomized social units of simple foragers was well suited as a background against which the civilizing forces of European societies could pursue progress, in part (self-)justified by their willingness to 'conquer the tropics'.

In the case of the less motivated sources, a public perception of the stereotyped or clichéd Indian emerged from journalistic accounts, international exhibitions, and various exploration-in-remote-parts motifs. Key images from the late 19th and early 20th centuries include woodland scenes familiar from antecedent watercolours and engravings[3] such as this from Bates (1892) in which the Indians are almost invisible, nearly absorbed into the landscape.

Figure 5.2 H. Bates 1892.

Transferred to studios, Indians were depicted still in hunting mode and in various kinds of domestic groups. Huebner's Canela group and a family (Wapixana) group photographed in the field are typical.

These kinds of images of normal folks at work or play, whether staged or observational, are strikingly different from those that emerged very early in the 20th century during the investigation of slavery on the Putumayo rubber estates – among the first Amazonian photographs with a topical documentary profile.[4]

Photographic documentation of Putumayo events concentrates on the persecution of Indian victims, and while the moral and ethical dimensions are at the fore, the larger commercial context (the rubber industry) is also shown[5] – not from the deck of an ocean liner, but from the riverbank.

Figure 5.3 Canela group. G. Huebner 1906–10.

Figure 5.4 Postcard, Macuchi group. G. Huebner 1903–04.

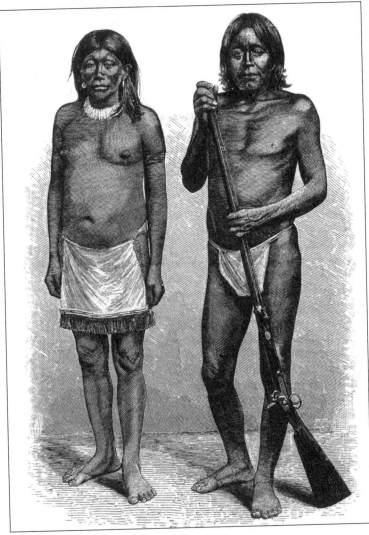

Figure 5.5 Ackawoi couple. E. Im Thurn 1883.

Photographs from the Putumayo region available through Hardenburg (1912) and Paternoster (1913) document a social landscape just prior to its being recalibrated by professional anthropology. As the rubber industry rapidly wound down in the face of competition from Southeast Asian plantation rubber between 1914 and 1920[6], modern anthropology (initially through the activities of Nimuendajú) inserted itself into Amazonia – not the Amazonia of a regional economy dominated by an export-oriented extractivism, but an 'economically stagnant' Amazonia

Figure 5.6 Booth Line ship.

Figure 5.7 Embarking rubber. S. Paternoster 1913.

that included Indian societies which, despite the vigorous efforts of the government and private interests, had managed to survive into the 20th century. These were Indian societies for whom the region was to become, for a few decades at least, something of a refuge[7] as national society and international trade retreated.

The 'Putumayo images' include those of the standard pseudo-observational style; those depicting violence; and those emphasizing the rubber industry context. Examples of the first are provided by Paternoster and Hardenburg.

Figure 5.8 House interior. J. F. Woodroffe 1914.

Figure 5.9 Rubber warehouse. H. C. Pearson 1911.

Figure 5.10 Amazon 'belles'. S. Paternoster 1913.

Figure 5.11 Huitoto. S. Paternoster 1913.

In the second (violent) category, there are fewer images.

Figure 5.12 Starved to death. W. E. Hardenburg 1912.

Figure 5.13 Indians and Indian overseer. H. C. Pearson 1911.

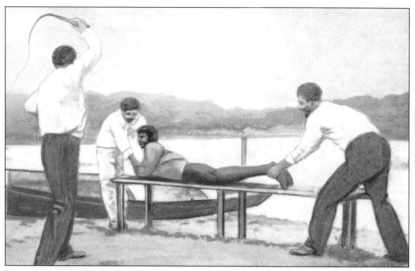

Figure 5.14[8] Flogging. S. Paternoster 1913.

Paternoster, unusually, includes some more narrowly observational/ethnographic images attributed to Whiffen (1915).

Figure 5.15 Huitoto dance I. S. Paternoster 1913.

The rubber industry setting is most fully represented in Pearson (1911), as might be expected of the editor of *The India Rubber World* and author of *Crude Rubber and Compounding Ingredients* and *Rubber Tires and All About Them*, subtitled for clarification *(A Book for Everybody Who Has to Do with Rubber Tires for Business or Pleasure)*.

Figure 5.16 Itaituba. H. C. Pearson 1911.

Figure 5.17 Rubber entrepreneurs, estuary near Belém. H. C. Pearson 1911.

Figure 5.18 *Seringueiros*. H. C. Pearson 1911.

Figure 5.19 Mosquito-phobic rubber engineers. H. C. Pearson 1911.

Figure 5.20 Rubber cloth. H. C. Pearson 1911.

In addition to the photographic documentation of a declining rubber industry, the other significant precursor to professional anthropology's refining and redefining of stereotypical views of Amazonian Indians was the large collection amassed by Rondon (1946, 1953a, 1953b) in the course of his various expeditions.

Rondon, a devotée of Benjamin Constant's brand of positivism, was faithful to the then-and-present Brazilian government line on the future of the Indian – that is to say, an assimilationist prescription. While Indians were literally consumed by the rubber industry, under the regime that Rondon personified, they were to be effaced in a different way, through being seduced into a role as well-behaved children who could grow up to be fully formed Brazilians.

Figure 5.21 Before: Indians of the upper Xingu. C. M. Rondon 1953a (Museo do Índio/FUNAI – Brasil collection).

Figure 5.22 After: Indians of the upper Xingu. C. M. Rondon 1953a (Museo do Índio/ FUNAI – Brasil collection).

As a collection, the photographs from the Rondon expeditions are far more numerous and stylistically diverse than those of other collections of the period. There are some passing similarities with Curtis's approach in North America (that is, portraits and iconic renditions), and although the artless approach frequently projects an appealing naiveté, there is little of Curtis's careful composition and artful, big statement.

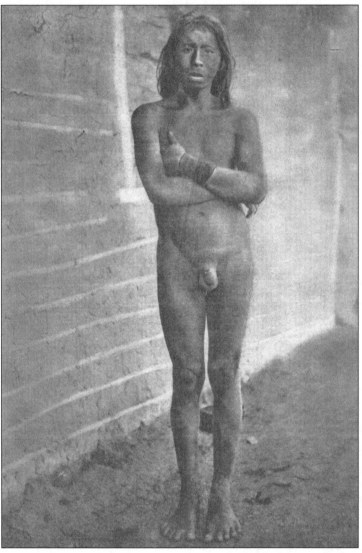

Figure 5.23 Cajabi man. C. M. Rondon 1953a (Museo do Índio/FUNAI – Brasil collection).

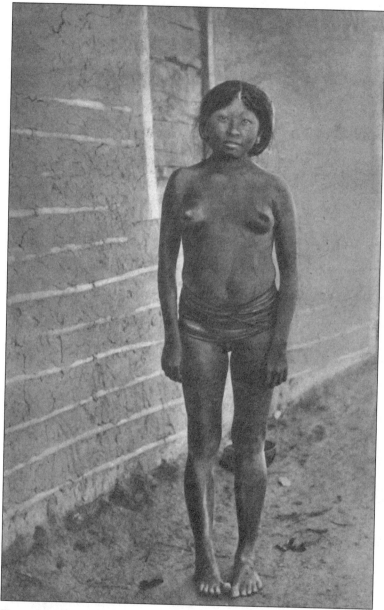

Figure 5.24 Cajabi woman. C. M. Rondon 1953a (Museo do Índio/FUNAI – Brasil collection).

Figure 5.25 Carajá man and boy. C. M. Rondon 1953a (Museo do Índio/FUNAI – Brasil collection).

Figure 5.26 Camairua man. C. M. Rondon 1953a (Museo do Índio/FUNAI – Brasil collection).

Figure 5.27 Bacairi family. C. M. Rondon 1953a.

Figure 5.28 Young Carajá pipe smoker. C. M. Rondon 1953a (Museo do Índio/ FUNAI – Brasil collection).

Figure 5.29 Carajá. C. M. Rondon 1953a.

Figure 5.30 Bacairi man and C. M. Rondon Commission marker. C. M. Rondon 1953a (Museo do Índio/FUNAI – Brasil collection).

These images were the immediate precursors of those that would emerge as part of the systematic ethnographic documentation provided by anthropologists, but there is not so obvious a shift in the photographic record as there is in the literature that has emerged. The images soon to emerge in service to ethnography entered a well-cultivated terrain of cliché.

Narrowing the Field

The focal literature discussed in the following chapter consists of ethnographic monographs on Amazonians published in English. This set does not include important work in cognate areas (e.g., history, ecology, rural sociology), nor does it include work that – largely for language reasons – is primarily situated in other, non-Anglo-American traditions of sociocultural anthropology.

The reason for these exclusions is, with respect to the former, to concentrate as much as possible on specifically anthropological knowledge as a source of popular conceptions about Amazonia and Amazonians; and with respect to the latter, to restrict the anthropological/public culture reckoning to the idiom with which I am most familiar. Linked to what might seem a provincial retreat, in particular setting aside the Brazilian literature not also published in English, is the argument that the trajectories of different anthropological traditions are not necessarily well served by being elided with the Anglo-American traditions.[9] The naturalist-explorer-scientist figure depicted in *The Lost World*, for example, may find parallels within the Brazilian cultural field (e.g., the Villas Boas brothers, Rondon, Possuelo)[10] but is embedded in a quite different imperial and cultural context, and as such is afflicted by its own kinds of national tradition and parochialism. Certainly, there are other texts – translations (mainly from Portuguese) and images that register as fully paid-up elements of the secondary literature – but any claims for the representativeness of the set are based on relevance primarily within an Anglo-American teaching and research milieu.

There is a further reason for restricting the literature mainly to that published in English: regardless of the many important connections between South American anthropology and anthropology as practised in the United States and United Kingdom (as well as France), the Amazonian Indian –'hyperreal' or just real – has a different political subjectivity from a Brazilian (or Colombian, Bolivian, Venezuelan, Guyanese, Peruvian) point of view than it does from an Anglo-American one. There are, as Ramos (1990) has noted, dimensions in the relationship between Brazilian anthropologists and Brazilian Indians that are not well served by generic accounts. In a broader context, the centrality of the symbol of the Indian in the long-standing nation-building project in Brazil (see Schwarcz 1999) entails a conception of the Amazonian Indian that has no neat analogy in North America, much less the United Kingdom, and their respective anthropological traditions.[11]

Criteria for Inclusion and Exclusion

While the core literature is single-author monographs – generally tribal case studies – other kinds of publications are included if, by virtue of significant citation or frequency of reference, they seem to have been important in shaping general conceptions of Amazonianness à la the stereotype/cliché. In detailing all the exceptions to the 'monographs about Indians' rule, there is the danger of erasing any important boundaries between a professional anthropological literature – mainly represented in monographs and articles – and what might be termed a 'literature of relevance' with respect to anthropological investigation; but it is import- ant to acknowledge the overlaps of these different subsets of literatures, as well as the fact that the anthropological literature, however much it might depart from its antecedents, emerges rather late in the post-contact story. Meggers's (1971) *Amazonia: Man and Culture in a Counterfeit Paradise*, for example, is not an ethnographic monograph, yet is included in the core literature on the grounds that the position it promotes (significantly sustained with ethnographic material) represents a long-standing received view about intrinsic features of Amazonian peoples and societies as culturally fragile and dominated by an unforgiving and intractable set of environmental constraints.

Nimuendajú (1939, 1942, 1946, 1952) is another contributor who does not neatly fit the single-author ethnographic monograph brief, but there would appear to be little disputing the lasting influence that his pioneering work has had both in shaping a very Boasian-inflected 'salvage' approach to ethnography and ethnology in Amazonia[12] as well as prefiguring the serious investigation of proto-state, '*terra prêta*' societies (see McEwan, Barreto, and Neves 2001).

Collections such as Lyons (1979) and Gross (1973) have been included on the grounds that they contain key articles/arguments/materials that do not otherwise appear in monograph form, but which have had an undeniable effect on the development of Amazonianist research trad- itions. Carneiro's (1973 [1961]) 'Slash-and-Burn Cultivation Among the Kuikuru and Its Implications for Cultural Development in the Amazon Basin' is one such example.

The historian Hemming (1978, 1987a, 1987b, 2003) has provided an invaluable and extensive account of Amazonian tribes for which there is no equivalent from an explicitly anthropological perspective (although see Gomes 1992 [1988] and Carneiro da Cunha 1992), and has been included on the grounds of providing a link between anthropological research (and photographic documentation) and a general audience more prepared to read history than anthropology.

A number of monographs that deal with non-indigenous themes, but which represent an extension of the traditional anthropological brief, might also have been included on the grounds that they build upon problematics developed within an indigenist framework (e.g., Cleary 1990; Harris 2000; Macmillan 1995; S. L. Nugent 1990, 1993; Raffles 2002). Cowell's (1960, 1973, 1990) documentary work (in text and film) does not position itself anthropologically but certainly falls within an explorer/traveller tradition (with antecedents in work such as Cotlow 1954) that has become increasingly relevant anthropologically as indigenous rights, environmentalism, and activist anthropology have converged in Amazonia in the late 20th century. Lévi-Strauss's seminal *Tristes Tropiques* (1961) departs from the conventional ethnographic format, and subsequent work with Amazonian myth (1970, 1973, 1978, 1981) is in a category of its own, but his lasting influence in terms of shaping the research agenda and emphasizing classic utopian and dystopian themes (e.g., Rousseau and 'noble savagery') is undeniable – hence, the volume's inclusion.

The traveller/explorer/biographical literature (e.g., Biocca 1970; Cotlow 1954; MacCreagh 1985 [1926]; Davis 1996, to name but a very few) is highly variable in quality and in terms of relevance to the anthropological project, but in terms of photographic content and agenda setting –e.g., the kidnap story in Biocca (1970) recurs in Boorman's (1985b) *The Emerald Forest* – it has had an undeniable role in projecting stereotypes and clichés.

Significant Exclusions: Steward and Rondon

The most voluminous photographic documentation of indigenous Amazonian peoples is provided in Volumes 1 and 3 (*Marginal Tribes* and *Tropical Forest Indians*) of Steward's (1948a, 1948b) *Handbook of South American Indians* and in Rondon's (1946, 1953a, 1953b) *Indios do Brasil*. The former is a reference work organized along lines meant to allow extensive cross-cultural comparison (e.g., distributions of culture traits and other now largely out-moded protocols), while the latter is more of a photographic expedition journal than a systematic collection. Both are valuable collections that document Indian peoples of a region undergoing a dramatic deceleration of one colonial/imperial process and the commencement of a new phase of assertive national priorities, but the scope and scale of both provide uncertain bases for generalization. The photographs in Steward (1948), interesting though they are to look at individually, are a hodge-podge of a collection. With a highly fragmented set of materials available, there is little consistency in the image documentation of the tribes in question, and images of artefacts feature as prominently as do those of people.

The Rondon volumes are as much commemoration as they are documentation of the expedition experience, and the Indians – while subjects – are also administrative objects. The Rondon expeditions' primary goal was to wire Amazonia for telegraphy,[13] not to seek out and document native peoples. This is not to say that Rondon's duty to approach Indians as national subjects and lay the groundwork for their assimilation was incidental, merely a detail or side issue, but that these incursions into Indian territory be recognized for what they were: military expeditions, steps toward the goal of 'integrating' Amazonia – a project still being enacted in/inflicted on Amazonia.

Rondon had unusually extensive photographic and cinematic resources. The 1,500 photographs in *Indios do Brasil,* organized roughly by tribe and location feature a mix of observational and posed images. As this period of Brazilian Amazonian history falls between two phases of intense external influence (the rubber industry, in decline after ca. 1910, and the post-World War II modernization), it may be characterized as an era of relative tranquility in which Rondon's presence was a deceptively benign precursor of what was to come. The volumes document from the state's perspective the indigenous constituency that was about to confront a new developmentally oriented bureaucratic apparatus.

Steward's volumes were part of a continental project that reflected a division of labour within the field of anthropology according to area studies (or subarea studies) and subfield criteria (e.g., cultural anthropology, archaeology, linguistics, physical anthropology). Thereafter, a 'highlands' (Andeanist) person would be encapsulated as would be a 'lowlands' person, a 'Caribbeanist', etc. In this period, then (immediately following the end of World War II), Amazonian ethnography came to define and command a specialist arena in a manner it had not achieved earlier. Similarly, in the case of Rondon's expeditions this state-executed approach to the 'Indian problem' defined and objectified Amazonia in a new way within the national perspective, and the accompanying invasion of the field by extractivist entrepreneurs, international captains of industry,[14] ranchers, land-seeking colonists, missionaries, and others overshadowed Rondon and the SPI and any benignness implied in the state's cultivation of the image of the 'society for the protection of Indians'.

Focal Literature

The core list of Selected Monographs (see Table 6.1) includes 140 titles drawn from a larger list of several hundred books that includes excised items, examples of which were given above (edited collections, mono-graphs on non-indigenous peoples, etc.) The core titles – meeting the nar-row criteria of 'Amazonian monograph' – are attributed a canonical status (not to be taken too severely) in the sense that they represent primarily the output of professional anthropologists working under the auspices of scholarly institutions (university departments and museums, in the main); many are the standard references for their specialist subfields; many are published by university presses; and many are the direct result of doctoral research (i.e., they represent contributions to scholarship as well as a crucial stage in career formation).

To say that they are canonical in the aggregate, however, is not to sug-gest that there is necessarily a high degree of concurrence among spe-cialists pursuing research among the same set of anthropological subjects. The Yanomami literature, for example, includes authors with significant, fundamental disagreements. While some anthropological subjects have been recurrently studied,[15] occasionally by different principal researchers, many if not most are represented by a single work.

A central concern is with the accuracy and adequacy of representative images of the Amazon and its indigenous peoples, but that begs three questions: Accurate according to what criteria? Adequate for whom? Why should it matter? The brief guiding/provisional answers are:

- The images generally stand as visual confirmation of textual claims based on long-term, immersive fieldwork. To date, and in general, the authority of ethnographic accounts has not been displaced by accounts from other quarters.
- The images are adequate in terms of establishing and maintaining a body of non-trivial knowledge about the history, worldviews, and quo-tidian concerns of Amazonian social actors who are not mere automata wholly governed by algorithms of nature.
- It matters because poor understanding and appreciation of Amazonian realities inhibits appropriate responses to interventions that have im-plications for human rights and social and ecological justice.

The photographs that illustrate[16] the professional literature are variable in terms of content, particular illustrative intent, aesthetic quality, density, and so on. Rather than try to generalize, therefore, it is preferable first to examine in a more prosaic fashion which the actual images of Amazonia are and reserve judgement and ignore received opinions until after having established the dimensions of the phenomenon.

In narrowing the object of analysis in this way, that is to say only considering images that have emerged in the course of official (i.e., in this context, anthropological) portrayals of Amazonians, there is a de-parture from more reflexive approaches that have characterized much recent interesting work in an anthropology of images. Rony (1996), for example, although dealing mainly with moving images, proposes that the cinematic, ethnographic spectacle is something akin to DuBois's notion of 'double-consciousness' (Bright 1998). Poole's (1997) detailed study of the Andean visual economy, pursuing a very different trajectory, considers the complex transformation of Andean photographic subjects as they – in the role of practitioners – take themselves as subject matter. The aim here is to step back from what is assumed to be true collectively about Amazonian imagery and examine the actual artefacts/images upon which this collective representation – the cliché/stereotype – is based.

The Artefacts of Experience

Prescriptive Photography

Figure 5.31 Dull River I. S. Paternoster ca. 1910.

Figure 5.32 Dull River II. S. Paternoster ca. 1910.

Images of 'green hell'[17] are familiar Amazonian artefacts, as are these two images' timeless[18] and uninformative evocations: unnamed stretches of river with little more than water, forest shoreline, and sky. Brought together, the key elements of an anthropological photograph – a human subject and an unambiguous river/forest setting – are prefigured in the work of Frisch, Pearson, Im Thurn, and other documentarists of the late 19th/early 20th centuries.

In terms of official anthropological prescription, *Notes and Queries on Anthropology* (1951), the handbook of the Royal Anthropological Institute of Great Britain and Ireland, is a source of guidance.[19] The appendix on photography and cinematography (pp. 353–61) begins with the claim that '[a] good photographic record is an essential part of every kind of anthropological work', but the reasons behind that strong claim are not revealed. Most of the text is given over to practical and technical matters ('Apparatus', 'Exposure', 'Development', 'Care of Apparatus', 'Storage of Negatives', 'Printing' and 'Indexing of Prints'), and it is only in the final subsection – 'Subjects' – that much attention is granted image content. Acknowledging that the type of subject will vary according to the interests of the fieldworker, *Notes and Queries* recommends that the researcher record as wide a range of photographs as possible and that '[t]ypical local scenery should not be forgotten' (p. 357).[20] Further recommendations include: take portraits as well as group shots; 'representative individuals should be photographed full face and profile, head and shoulders, close enough to show the features in detail'; identifying numbers (on discs) should be included (p. 358). The photography section concludes that 'it is usually sufficient to explain that the pictures will enable your own people, who live a long way off, to see how their people live and what they do' (p. 359).

The cinematography section is a little over two pages long and mainly concerned with the idea that it is the mastering of technical matters 'which make[s] all the difference between an interesting film and a dull one' (p. 359). There follows a list of points regarding length of shots, the virtues of movement, establishing shots, and other such basics. Sensitive, perhaps, to some of the notorious shortcomings of many ethnographic films, the anonymous author notes that

> [n]o shot should be prolonged after the scene has conveyed its point, when the attention of the spectator begins to wander. This applies in particular to such scenes as native dances and ceremonies, which can become extremely monotonous on the screen, as they often consist of simple actions or movements repeated almost indefinitely. (p. 361)[21]

Whether the cinematographic advice in *Notes and Queries* was persuasive or merely reflected widely held sentiments, it is not difficult to identify an observational orientation that regards the camera – moving or still – basically as a device for gathering information. This notion of a benign or neutral or passive technology continues to be a source of discussion, debate, and at times demonization, but the debate with the alternative view – that the camera is not benign, etc. – hasn't really progressed very interestingly; rather, the pairing of these two 'standard' positions appears only ritually antagonistic. The fact that neither of these positions can plausibly remain resolutely unambiguous for long might lead to speculation of a compromise in the form of a spectrum of views lying between these idealized extremes. There is a case there, but not a very strong one. It is a spectrum, but one with few gradients, more akin to a multiple choice test than one allowing of greater nuance. More appealing is the idea that this crude opposition between an 'objectivist' view and a 'subjectivist' one is obligatory precisely because knowledge – whether in textual or image form – is always open to challenge. The fact that the image, however, is fixed, that it has a materiality seemingly lacking in 'mere speech, argument and the mustering of evidence', makes it particularly dangerous and problematic. Despite the various interpretations put on an image's meaning, it can still float through history detached from efforts to pin it in place.

In this presentation and analysis of the photographic material embedded in Amazonian anthropological monographs, I am setting aside for the moment any ambition to attach meaning to these artefacts. Instead, I am merely identifying them in the first instance and trying to organize them by theme, content or other overt markers. There is no taxonomy-like structure implied or sought after, rather the initial goal is simply to note their presence and distribution. Figure 6-6, for example, simply shows the ratio of pages of text to number of photographs. To recapitulate – the preliminary aim is merely to record and characterize what has thus far ended up in this core literature.

Notes

1 Clastres's (1977) *Society Against the State* is one modern restatement.
2 *Bugre manso* or 'tame buggers' is an expression for Indians allegedly borrowed from the French.
3 See Marcoy (1873) and Coudreau (1977) for representative examples.
4 The sharpness of the departure of these photographs is probably enhanced by their association with events in Casement's dramatic subsequent career (involving treason, public scandal, the *Black Diaries*, Irish republicanism, and secret service intrigue).
5 An important parallel message concerns the conservation of occidental control over rubber production in the face of competition from Southeast

Asian plantations. Woodroffe (1914) – whose introductory chapter is entitled 'The Rubber Industry of the Amazon and How Its Supremacy Can Be Maintained' – cites Hardenburg's (1912) *The Putumayo: The Devil's Pardise* in his chapter on 'the labour question', but neglects to mention what the Putumayo scandal was about. Also see Wright (1912).

6 The role of Indians in standard accounts of the Amazon rubber industry is rather muted. Generally they are portrayed as reluctant employees, although in Murphy's (1960) monograph on the Mundururcú, there is more enthusiasm than is usually conveyed. See Weinstein (1983), Dean (1987), and Collier (1968).

7 This 'refuge' status should be qualified. The position of Indians was not positively advanced; rather, the highly dispersed and constant threat posed by the rubber industry was mitigated.

8 A heavily retouched photograph? Listed merely as 'illustration' in Paternoster, as are all the unretouched photographs.

9 In Brazil, for example, there is currently a debate about whether national scholars should aim to publish in English in order to achieve the academic kudos conferred by participation in the 'international' (which is to say English-speaking) arena or publish first in Portuguese in acknowledgement of the cohesion and autonomy of Brazil's own distinctive tradition(s). Additionally, Brazilian anthropology has a distinctive political profile that has no parallel in the Anglo-American anthropological tradition.

10 The 'explorer' caricature is a bit unfair – except perhaps in the case of the Villas Boas brothers – but in all three cases, relations with Indians are unambiguously defined by state interests: how to deal with the 'Indian problem'. The standard answer is through assimilation.

11 This is not to deny significant parallels or analogies, as in the case of U.S. relations with Native American peoples, but these are by no means easy or mirror-like reflections. For one interesting discussion, see Kickingbird and Ducheneaux (1973).

12 It is not often stated as explicitly as this ('salvage'), but an undeniable theme of anthropological industry in Amazonia has been the location, identification, and documentation of 'final exemplars', the 'last peoples', the 'uncontacted tribes'. This theme is more evident in journalistic and exploration accounts – see Cowell's (1973) *The Tribe That Hides from Men*, for example – but is no less important in the arguments, say, of Neel (1970, 1994) and Chagnon (1974) and, from a different wing of anthropology, in the arguments of contemporary proponents of an anthro-environment 'wise forest management' approach (Posey and Balée 1989).

13 Which is to say, cutting trails, erecting telegraph poles, establishing outposts, connecting cable.

14 Henry Ford and Daniel Ludwig are undoubtedly the most important, Anita and Gordon Roddick the most celebrated.

15 The various peoples known collectively as the Kayapó, for example, and those occupying the upper and lower Xingu regions. Elsewhere – in Colombia, for instance – there are further examples of restudies.

16 This may be a premature attribution of function. Perhaps they don't illustrate at all, but are merely vaguely ornamental.

17 The term 'green hell' is closely associated with early 20th century debates about the Brazilian national trajectory and how to integrate vast interior spaces and their peoples. Euclides da Cunha (1944 [1902]) and Alberto Rangel (1927 [1908]) are key contributors. A suitably clichéd 'green hell' emerges again in the context of a concerted national assault on Amazonia during the construction of the Transamazon Highway and related development initiatives in 1970. A D.C. Comics publication commencing in the 1980s features Green Fury (derived from the character Fire aka Beatriz da Costa) who is the offspring of a surveyor working in Amazonia. She is in contact with a Gê-speaking group and their shaman with whom she collaborates.

18 They date from the early 20th century but could be contemporary.

Figure 5.33 Dull River III. S. Nugent 1976.

A similar photograph (from an unnamed, recent monograph) is published as local people's view of the universe: sky, horizon, river. It is unclear whether the Indians are putting the author on.

19 The sixth – most recent – edition of *Notes and Queries* was reprinted in 1954, 1960, 1964, 1967, and 1971. The first edition was published in 1874. It is not clear how influential the advice in *Notes and Queries* was.

20 The equivalent of cutaways?

21 There is some doubt among viewers of ethnographic films that these specific recommendations have been widely implemented.

6

Method and Data: Framing Indians

Figures 6.1 & 6.2 Indian child in native garb, masked, and isolated from kin dressed in missionary clothing. T. Whiffen 1908–09.

The photographs shown thus far to indicate the general features of Amazonian imagery widely accessible from the mid-19th until early 20th centuries have been drawn unsystematically from diverse sources and were themselves originally produced for diverse purposes (scientific, postcard illustration, journalism). The photographs selected to form the subject matter for this chapter are different in that they share a narrow common purpose: photographs by and large taken by anthropologists in the field, they are meant to illustrate ethnographic work.[1] Subsequently, some have been drawn upon for other purposes (for journalism, advertising, rights advocacy, and so on) without explicit acknowledgement of their primary or original purpose, but initially they appeared in service to the comparative and analytic scope of modern anthropological practice.

The fact is that the restricted scope of the original ethnographic purpose does not seem to result in a radically or even substantially different portrayal of Amazonians from that characteristic of non-specialist Amazonian imagery, and the ubiquity of the cliché/stereotype/received views raises questions about the force of the specialist portrayals. At first glance, specialist portrayals (and the criteria invoked to justify them) may be relatively inconsequential in terms of establishing any kind of authority based on systematicity, scholarship, or fitness for purpose claims. In effect, there may be little difference between *carefully* and *casually* advanced imagery, and this has implications for some of the claims of a visual anthropology; that is to say, an analytic and critical departure resting primarily on claims that the medium per se – still photography or moving image technology in this instance – significantly alters the epistemological space of the discipline.[2] While new media no doubt affect the distribution and accessibility of images, does that necessarily imply that the content of the images is transformed? During the past twenty years, for example, there has been a decline in the frequency of appearance of shrunken heads in the scientific literature (or on museum display), attributable to changes in public perception of the appropriateness of such images (or artefacts). It is not a re-evaluation that comes directly out of anthropological preoccupations, or because of media-based changes in the distribution of such images, but because of a more general public devaluation of such imagery. The centrality of shrunken heads as iconic of the anthropological enterprise has never been a significant feature of the anthropological enter-prise (any more than cannibalism has been), but persistent inference of its relevance seems relatively immune to either the critical posture of anthropology itself or hyper-availability incumbent on new media.

Aside from the ways in which particular media may or may not have heightened significance in terms of the promulgation of notions about Amazonia and Amazonians, in the narrow context of anthropology, it is difficult to establish clear boundaries between specialist and non-specialist image worlds, even if there are widely assumed boundaries between expert (e.g., ethnographic) and non-expert (e.g., *National Geographic*) domains. Feature film portrayals of Amazonians, for example (see Chapter 7) in *The Emerald Forest* (Boorman 1985b) and *At Play in the Fields of the Lord* (Babenco 1991), are accorded a degree of respect and admiration denied *Eaten Alive* (Lenzi 1986) and *Emmanuelle and the Last Cannibal* (D'Amato 1984) for reasons that are not necessarily substantiated by reference to ethnographic authority (much less medium-specific effects).

To try to reduce some of the arbitrariness in judgements offered about the quality, accuracy, and authenticity of images of Amazonians, some methodological issues are raised.

The characterization of the ethno-photographic record provided in earlier chapters has been largely a qualitative one, but in this chapter the emphasis is as much on a quantitative characterization in order to try to reduce, or simply shed light on, some of the arbitrariness resulting from the overlap of photographic images produced for explicit ethnographic purpose and those produced for other purposes. Such an attempt to delimit the ethnographic sphere of representation may help to clarify the role of the Amazonian ethno-photographic record. The aim is to generalize about the ethno-photographic record alone without conceding its similarities to the broader, inclusive photographic account (installed by journalism, travel literature, and other genres). In addition to mitigating some of the arbitrariness of interpretation, there are several other reasons for choosing to isolate the record this way – not all of equal importance, but still germane.

The first is to underscore the role that ethnography plays as a documentary practice regardless of the pressures of the politics of representation. The ethnographic monograph form has always had a split character – part literary narrative, part observational compendium. In recent years, however, and reflecting tendencies of the literary turn, the indeterminate and interpretive aspects of the form have had greater prominence. One result of this has been an emphasis on the intersubjectivity of the anthropological project and scepticism toward, if not outright rejection of, more prosaic modes of presentation. It is possible to document (and count) without having a full-blown epistemological affair. Carroll has made a similar point in relation to forms of film criticism that demand that every meaning be 'read'. The denial of a level of documentary certainty (he uses the example of a factory instruction film about how milk is bottled) entails an extreme philosophical scepticism and 'exorbitant premises about the passing of truth and objectivity' (Privett and Kreul 2001).[3]

The second reason for seeking a quantitative characterization of the photographic material is to offer a transparent device for delimiting a finite set of images that could be said to comprise the professional anthropological record – what is, in the context of Euro-American mass culture, a reasonably authoritative limiting case. The images as presented in this chapter might be thought of less as a collection of singular images (e.g., a Mundurucú family at rest; Maué women grating manioc; etc.) that meet the criteria for inclusion in a monograph than as a profile of a particular kind of knowledge (anthropological). Hence, the interest here is in the type and distribution of images over time (the epoch of modern anthropology, roughly one hundred years) presented in the form of tables and charts.

The reductive character of this mode of representation notwithstanding, for present purposes it is preferable to generalizations based on more vaguely grounded impressions. Before assembling these data, and as minor example, the category 'Grooming' had been pencilled in as one of the likely sets of ethnographic photographs typical in accounts of Amazonian tribal life, an intention abandoned as specimens failed to appear. For me, Lévi-Strauss's lone image of Nambiquara nitpicking had been overgeneralized, falsely remembered as a recurrent Amazonian image.[4]

The third reason for this particular mode of quantitative exposition is in the interest of providing a context that forces a literal rather than metaphoric view of the so-called 'anthropological gaze'. These are not all the images that could be conjured up in the course of considering how anthropological knowledge is configured within the photographic record of Amazonia, from Frisch's (1860–65) early images to Salgado's (2005), and in view of the considerable overlap of expert and non-expert, it may be useful to abstract one element or subset from the aggregate. These are the actual images employed by anthropologists in their professional publications, not the derivatives, yet the gaze revealed does not seem to be so isolated from the broader panoramic of the stereotype/cliché. For a discipline not averse to making strong claims as an authoritative mediator between 'the West and the rest', assessing the gaze could hardly be a trivial matter.

Much recent writing on anthropological photography has sought to redress the indexical bias according to which Western image making of non-Westerners has, to put it as crudely as possible, objectified anthropological (and other) subjects. Instead, the broadly post-colonial project aims to show how the photographic record provides a more complex platform, one on which, according to Pinney (2003a:2), '[P]hotography's mimetic doubling becomes a prism through which to consider questions of cultural and self-identity, historical consciousness, and the nature of photographic affirmation and revelation'.

This ambitious project of post-colonial revision addresses, as did Im Thurn's (1893) critique of forensic photography more than a century ago, failures of the anthropological imagination with respect to the diverse possible uses of photographic images. In Im Thurn's case, the force of the critique rested on the argument that anthropological photography favoured the real or metaphoric dead over the living; its subject matter was the image equivalent of a museum specimen. In the post-colonial case, the force of the critique rests on the argument that not only are anthropological subjects coeval with their interlocutors, but are actively engaged in supplying their own meanings to images and the settings within which those images are manipulated and transformed.

While both critiques obviously bear on the specificity of the anthropological gaze, the force of the arguments depends in part on presenting that gaze as temporally and spatially unbounded, a variation on the notion of the ethnographic present – a move that seems predicated on the notion that it is the medium of photography that provides the necessary unity for engaging the concept of anthropological gaze, even if that is not the precise term used. Poole (1997), for example, recognizes the limitations of that notion and offers an important corrective in the notion of visual economy.

In the Amazonian material considered here, the main issue is neither inter-subjectivity (placed high on the post-colonial agenda) nor the analytic utility of the image-as-material-object (raised by Im Thurn), but rather tracking the subject matter of the focal stereotype/cliché that has come to represent in the 21st century – and after five centuries of cultivation – the archetypal Amazonian forest Indian.

The timelines below (Figure 6.3) illustrate why attention to the particular issues of the representation of time are so crucial to a consideration of how photographs have been used to depict Amazonian Indians. That diagram, as is the case for many of the charts to follow, stands back from the intersubjectivity entailed in interpreting photographic images and draws attention instead to the aggregate product: the corpus of images as a measure of intent.

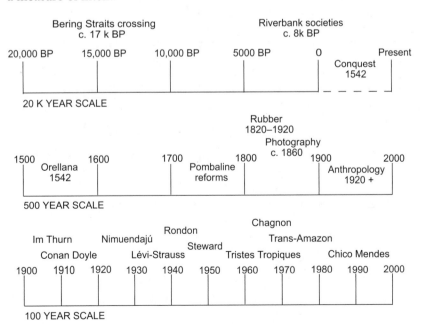

Figure 6.3 Timelines of Brazilian Amazonian Indian prehistory, history, ethnography.

This diagram depicts three different, nested time frames. The first represents roughly the period between human penetration of the New World and the present. The second line covers the colonial-to-present period of approximately five hundred years. The third line represents the life span of anthropological research in the area.

Certain key dates are still subject to re-evaluation. Although there is little dispute about the provenance of early peoples of South America, and massive revision on this front seems unlikely at this point, an adequate characterization of pre-colonial social formations is still under construction. Once well into the historical period, there is less uncertainty about sequence and precise dates;[5] the period of anthropological scrutiny – however far back its putative explanatory reach – constitutes a very small period of time and, crucially, has as its object of analysis what is acknowledged to be a highly fragmentary set of *ethnies* whose unity under the heading 'indigenous Amazonians' is as much sketchily descriptive as it is analytic. Despite the (relative) empirical poverty of the prehistoric and historical records, and however well the dangers of retrospective projection are recognized, such ethnographic knowledge as exists is ineluctably engaged in representing the deep or distant past.

The images we possess are on one hand tied to five hundred years of myth telling and myth making,[6] and on the other are the source material for the critical disassembly of those active myths of representation.

Earnest discussion of method may induce a vegetable-like state among the normally alert and invocation of numbers in the course of cultural interpretation of images may be seen as a needlessly transgressive gesture, typically a kind of pathetic recourse to debased scientism.[7] Here, modest use of tabular/chart presentation of data concerning a mainstream 'interpretivist' topic in sociocultural anthropology – visual anthropology and the analysis of visual representation of ethnographic fieldwork – has been driven by several considerations. One of these is a straightforward legal/property issue: the difficulty (i.e., expense) of gaining publishers' permission to reproduce the ethnographic images contained in Table 6.1. Another is simply the convenience of being able to generalize over a finite body of data without having to address each image individually.

Those two are tied to another issue, and that concerns the claims made for the incompatibility of interpretivist and non-interpretivist forms of explanation said to lie at the core of sociocultural anthropology (see Segal and Yanagisako 2005 for some indicative discussion). The level of hostility/antipathy/incommensurability adduced[8] is symptomatic rather than revelatory. While the polemic continues to find sharp expression, the urgency of the struggle is deflated somewhat by historical precedent. The 'unwrapping of the sacred bundle', as Segal and Yanagisako refer to the decline of 'four-field' holism in anthropology, must include – call it collateral damage – a number of uncontroversial anthropological and sociological platitudes, including the most basic 'theorizing' of Durkheim, Marx, and Lévi-Strauss (just to name a few), such as the notion that one uses comparative, empirical material to get at patterns and (by definition, unseen) structures that would otherwise remain beyond grasp. A basic explanatory gambit in anthropology, model building as a speculative enterprise meant to show that one explanatory account is better than another, is 'unwrapped' as a consequence of this caricature of the anthropological enterprise that insists on the centrality of the 'interpretivist' versus 'positivist' split.[9]

Counting the Figures: Some General Comments on Tables and Charts

Figure 6.4 Postcard, Salesian mission.

In Im Thurn's (1893) early discussion of the modes of portrayal of Amazonian subjects, the posed photograph is compared unfavourably with the observational. In practice, it is often difficult to distinguish between the two, but in many cases the distinction may not carry much weight: the differences between an observational and a posed photograph of someone napping in a hammock are likely not worth much attention.

While moving images provide a narrative structure – even if only registered as the passing of time – a still photograph often demands contextual information.[10] Most images from the Selected Monographs (Table 6.1) are captioned, but rarely in such detail that they stand free from the text. They are, in short, contingent.

Table 6.1

Author	Title	Date of Publication	Place of Pub/ Publisher	Number of images	Number of pages	Labour	Leisure	Portrait	Domestic	Ritual	Historical	Nature
Balée, W. L.	Footprints of the forest: Ka'apor ethnobotany: the historical ecology of plant utilization by an Amazonian people	1994	New York: Columbia University Press	18	396	8	1	0	5	3	0	1
Basso, E.	The last cannibals: a South American oral history	1995	Austin: University of Texas Press	7	319	1	0	0	0	3	0	3
Basso, E.	Kalapalo Indians of Brazil	1973	New York: Holt, Rinehart and Winston	20	157	4	6	0	0	7	0	3
Basso, E.	A musical view of the universe	1985	Philadelphia: University of Pennsylvania Press	18	343	4	3	0	0	11	0	0
Basso, E.	In favour of deceit: a study of tricksters in an Amazonian society	1987	Tucson: University of Arizona Press	11	376	2	1	6	0	2	0	0
Brown, M. & Fernandez, E.	War of Shadows: the struggle for utopia in the Peruvian Amazon	1992	Berkeley: University of California Press	16	280	1	0	2	0	0	13	0

Brown, M.	Tsewa's gift, magic and meaning in an amazonian society	1985	Washington DC: Smithsonian Institution Press	8	220	2	1	2	0	1	0	2
Campbell, A. L.	Getting to know Waiwai:an amazonian ethnography.	1995	London: Routledge	6	253	1	0	3	1	0	0	1
Campbell, A. L.	To square with genesis	1985	Cambridge: Cambridge University Press	6	198	0	0	1	5	0	0	0
Candre, H.	Cool tobacco, sweet coca: teachings of an indian sage from the Colombian Amazon	1996	Tulsa: Themis Books	22	293	17	0	3	0	1	0	1
Chagnon, N.	Yanomamo: the last days of Eden	1992	San Diego: Harcourt Brace Jovanovich	45	309	15	7	8	7	7	0	1
Chagnon, N.	Studying the Yanomamo	1974	New York: Holt, Rinehart and Winston	197	270	5	6	177	3	3	0	3
Chagnon, N.	Yanomamo: The Fierce People, 1st ed.	1968	New York: Holt, Rinehart and Winston	29	224	7	10	4	3	5	0	0
Chernela, J.	The Wanano indians of the Brazilian Amazon: a sense of space	1993	Austin: University of Texas Press	0	185	0	0	0	0	0	0	0

Continued

Continued

Author	Title	Date of Publication	Place of Pub/ Publisher	Number of images	Number of pages	Labour	Leisure	Portrait	Domestic	Ritual	Historical	Nature
Chibnik, M.	Risky rivers: the economics and politics of floodplain farming in Amazonia	1994	Tucson: University of Arizona Press	0	268	0	0	0	0	0	0	0
Clastres, H.	The land-without-evil: Tupi-Guarani prophetism	1995	Urbana: University of Illinois Press	0	129	0	0	0	0	0	0	0
Clastres, P.	Society against the State	1977	Oxford: Blackwell	0	186	0	0	0	0	0	0	0
Clastres, P.	Chronicle of the Guayaki Indians	1998	New York: Zone Books	26	240	1	2	14	0	5	0	4
Coimbra, C.E.A. et al	The Xavante in transition: health, ecology, and bioanthropology in central Brazil	2004	Ann Arbor: University of Michigan Press	19	344	6	5	0	0	2	1	5
Conklin, B.	Consuming grief: compassionate cannibalism in an Amazonian society	2001	Austin: University of Texas Press	11	285	2	4	3	0	1	0	1
Crocker, J. C.	Vital souls: Bororo cosmology, natural symbolism, and shamanism	1985	Tucson: University of Arizona Press	13	380	1	2	6	2	1	0	1
Crocker, W.H. & J.	The Canela (Eastern Timbira), I: an ethnographic introduction.	1990	Washington DC: Smithsonian Institution Press	273	487	45	59	94	0	67	0	8

Author	Title	Year	Place: Publisher								
Crocker, W.H. & J.	The Canela: bonding through kinship, ritual, and sex	1994	Forth Worth: Harcourt Brace College Publishers	31	202	7	4	4	0	14	0	2
Da Matta, R.	A divided world	1982	Cambridge: Harvard University Press	0	186	0	0	0	0	0	0	0
Davis, S.	Victims of the miracle	1977	Cambridge: Cambridge University Press	0	205	0	0	0	0	0	0	0
Descola, P.	The spears of twilight: life and death in the Amazon jungle	1997	London: Flamingo	31	459	10	2	16	0	0	0	3
Descola, P.	In the society of nature: a native ecology in Amazonia	1994	Cambridge: Cambridge University Press	3	372	2	0	0	0	0	0	1
Dumont, J-P.	Under the rainbow: nature and supernature among the Panare Indians	1976	Austin: University of Texas Press	0	178	0	0	0	0	0	0	0
Dumont, J-P.	The Headman and I: ambiguity and ambivalence in the fieldworking experience	1978	Austin: University of Texas Press	19	211	4	2	8	0	2	0	3

Continued

Continued

Author	Title	Date of Publication	Place of Pub/ Publisher	Number of images	Number of pages	Labour	Leisure	Portrait	Domestic	Ritual	Historical	Nature
Early, J. D. & Peters, J. F.	The Xilixana Yanomami of the Amazon: history, social structure, and population dynamics	2000	Gainesville: University Press of Florida	0	324	0	0	0	0	0	0	0
Early, J. D. & Peters, J. F.	The population dynamics of the Mucajai Yanomama	1990	San Diego: Academic Press	10	152	2	1	4	2	0	0	1
Fabian, S. M.	Space-time of the Bororo of Brazil	1992	Gainesville: University Press of Florida	9	253	0	0	2	0	6	0	1
Farabee, W.	The Central Arawaks	1918	Philadelphia: University of Pennsylvania Museum	50	288	10	2	38	0	0	0	0
Farabee, W.	The Central Caribs, Vol. 9	1924	Philadelphia: University of Pennsylvania Museum	72	339	9	1	59	0	0	0	3
Farabee, W.	Indian tribes of Eastern Peru	1922	Cambridge: Peabody Museum, Harvard University	19	194	4	0	14	0	0	0	1

Fejos, P.	Ethnography of the Yagua	1943	New York: Viking Fund Publications in Anthropology, Vol. 3	76	219	30	5	26	0	3	0	12
Fock, N.	Waiwai religion and society of an Amazonian tribe	1963	Copenhagen: Danish National Museum	25	316	4	4	6	0	4	0	7
Goldman, I.	The Cubeo: Indians of the Northwest Amazon	1963	Urbana: University of Illinois Press	10	315	3	0	3	0	4	0	0
Goldman, I.	Cubeo Hehenewas: religious thought	2004	New York: Columbia University Press	0	438	0	0	0	0	0	0	0
Gomes, M. P.	The Indians and Brazil	1992	Gainesville: University Press of Florida	0	300	0	0	0	0	0	0	0
Gow, P.	Of mixed blood: kinship and history in Peruvian Amazonia	1991	Oxford: Clarendon Press	0	331	0	0	0	0	0	0	0
Gow, P.	An Amazonian myth and its history	2001	Oxford: Oxford University Press	4	338	1	0	0	0	4	0	0
Graham, L.	Performing dreams: discourses of immortality among the Xavante of Central Brazil.	1995	Austin: University of Texas Press	16	290	1	7	3	0	4	1	0

Continued

Continued

Author	Title	Date of Publication	Place of Pub/ Publisher	Number of images	Number of pages	Labour	Leisure	Portrait	Domestic	Ritual	Historical	Nature
Gray, A.	The last shaman: change in an Amazonian community	1996	Oxford: Berghahn	0	294	0	0	0	0	0	0	0
Gray, A.	Indigenous rights and development	1997	Oxford: Berghahn	0	354	0	0	0	0	0	0	0
Gray, A.	The Arakmbut: mythology, spirituality and history	1996	Oxford: Berghahn	0	324	0	0	0	0	0	0	0
Gregor, T.	Mehinaku: the drama of daily life in a Brazilian indian village.	1977	Chicago: University of Chicago Press	9	382	1	3	1	1	3	0	0
Gregor, T.	Anxious pleasures: the sexual lives of an Amazonian people.	1985	Chicago: University of Chicago Press	22	223	2	7	1	3	8	0	1
Harner, M. J.	The Jivaro: people of the sacred waterfalls	1973	Garden City, NY: Doubleday	19	234	4	2	8	2	0	0	3
Heckenberger, M.	The Ecology of power: culture, place and personhood in the Southern Amazon, AD 1000-2000	2005	London: Routledge	16	404	8	1	1	0	4	2	0
Hendricks, J. W.	To drink of death: the narrative of a shuar warrior	1993	Tucson: University of Arizona Press	0	316	0	0	0	0	0	0	0

Author	Title	Year	Publisher								
Henley, P	The Panare: tradition and change on the Amazonian frontier	1982	New Haven: Yale University Press	21	263	4	2	3	3	0	5
Henry, J.	Jungle people: a Kaingang tribe of the highlands of Brazil.	1964	New York: Vintage Books	0	215	0	0	0	0	0	0
Hill, J.	Keepers of the sacred chants: the poetics of ritual and power in an Amazonian society	1993	Tucson: University of Arizona Press	0	245	0	0	0	0	0	0
Holmberg, A.	Nomads of the long bow	1969	New York: Natural History Press	13	294	2	6	0	0	0	3
Hugh-Jones, C.	From the milk river: spatial and temporal processes in Northwest Amazonia	1979	Cambridge: Cambridge University Press	0	332	0	0	0	0	0	0
Hugh-Jones, S.	The palm and the pleiades: initiation and cosmology in Northwest Amazonia	1979	Cambridge: Cambridge University Press	0	302	0	0	0	0	0	0
Huxley, F.	Affable savages: an anthropologist among the Urubu indians of Brazil	1957	New York: Viking Press	0	287	0	0	0	0	0	0
Im Thurn, E.	Among the Indians of Guiana	1883	London: Kegan Paul, Trench and Co.	0	445	0	0	0	0	0	0

Continued

Continued

Author	Title	Date of Publication	Place of Pub/ Publisher	Number of images	Number of pages	Labour	Leisure	Portrait	Domestic	Ritual	Historical	Nature
Jackson, J.	The fish people: linguistic exogamy and Tukanoan identity in NW Amazonia	1983	Cambridge: Cambridge University Press	0	287	0	0	0	0	0	0	0
Kaplan, J. O.	The Piaroa, a people of the Orinoco basin: a study in kinship and marriage	1975	Oxford: Clarendon Press	1	236	0	0	1	0	0	0	0
Karsten, R.	Blood revenge, war, and victory feasts among the Jivaro Indians of Eastern Ecuador	1923	Washington DC: Smithsonian Institution, Bureau of American Ethnology, Bull. 79	14	94	0	1	7	0	5	0	1
Karsten, R.	The headhunters of the Western Amazonas: the life and culture of the Jibaro Indians of Eastern Ecuador and Peru	1935	Halsingfors, Finland: Societas Scientiarum Fennica, Commentationes Humanarum Litterarum, Vol. 7, No. 1	37	598	2	4	19	0	9	0	3
Karsten, R.	The civilizations of the South American Indians: with specific reference to religion	1926	New York: Knopf	0	540	0	0	0	0	0	0	0

Author	Title	Year	Publisher	55	305	11	4	30	0	6	0	4
Kensinger, K. W.	How real people ought to live: the Cashinahua of Eastern Peru.	1995	Prospect Heights, IL: Waveland Press	55	305	11	4	30	0	6	0	4
Kloos, P.	The Maroni River Caribs of Surinam	1971	Assen: Van Goram	10	304	2	1	2	0	2	0	3
Koch-Grünberg, T.& Huebner, G.	Die Xingu-Expedition (1898–1900)	2004	Köln: Böhlau	8	503	0	0	8	0	0	0	0
Kracke, W. H.	Force and persuasion: leadership in an Amazonian society	1978	Chicago: University of Chicago Press	10	322	6	2	1	0	0	0	1
Lamb, F. B. & Cordova-Rios, M.	Wizard of the Upper Amazon	1974	Boston: Houghton Mifflin	0	206	0	0	0	0	0	0	0
Lévi-Strauss, C.	Tristes tropiques	1961	London: Hutchinson	22	404	1	1	6	11	2	0	1
Lizot, J.	Tales of the Yanomami: daily life in the Venezuelan forest.	1985	Cambridge: Cambridge University Press	36	197	4	7	12	0	10	0	3
Lukesch, A.	Bearded Indians of the tropical forest	1976	Graz: Akademische Druck	47	143	11	14	12	7	0	0	3
Maybury-Lewis, D.	Akwe-Shavante society	1967	Oxford: Clarendon Press	11	356	3	2	1	0	4	0	1
Maybury-Lewis, D.	The savage and the innocent	1965	London: Evans Bros	34	270	6	9	4	8	4	0	3

Continued

Continued

Author	Title	Date of Publication	Place of Pub/Publisher	Number of images	Number of pages	Labour	Leisure	Portrait	Domestic	Ritual	Historical	Nature
McCallum, C.	Gender and sociality in Amazonia: how real people are made	2001	Oxford: Berg	10	208	3	3	2	0	0	0	1
Meggers, B. J.	Amazonia: man and culture in a counterfeit paradise	1971	Chicago: Aldine	10	182	7	1	0	0	1	0	1
Mentore, G.	Of passionate curves and desirable cadences	2005	Lincoln: University of Nebraska Press	2	375	0	0	1	0	1	0	0
Metraux, A.	The native tribes of Eastern Bolivia and Western Mato Grosso	1942	Washington, DC: Government Print Office	0	182	0	0	0	0	0	0	0
Meunier, J and Savarin, A.	The amazonian chronicles	1994	San Francisco: Mercury House	0	169	0	0	0	0	0	0	0
Mindlin, B.	Unwritten stories of the Surui Indians of Rondonia	1995	Austin: ILAS, University of Texas	40	151	12	4	8	0	12	0	4
Moran, E.	Through Amazonian eyes	1993	Iowa City: University of Iowa Press	3	230	0	0	0	0	0	0	3
Murphy, R.	Headhunter's heritage: social and economic change among the Mundurucú Indians	1960	Berkeley: University of California Press	0	202	0	0	0	0	0	0	0

Author	Title	Year	Publisher									
Murphy, R. F. and Quain, B.	The Trumai Indians of Central Brazil	1955	Seattle: University of Washington Press	7	108	1	0	3	0	0	0	3
Murphy, Y. and R.	Women of the forest	1985	New York: Columbia University Press	0	236	0	0	0	0	0	0	0
Nimuendajú, C.	The Serente	1942	Los Angeles: Southwest Museum.	4	106	4	0	0	0	0	0	0
Nimuendajú, C.	The Apinaye	1939	Washington DC: Catholic University of America Press	14	189	0	2	5	0	6	0	1
Nimuendajú, C.	The Eastern Timbira	1946	Berkeley: University of California Press	54	357	8	2	27	0	17	0	0
Nimuendajú, K.	The Tukuna	1952	Berkeley: Publications in American Archaeology and Ethnology, vol. 45. University of California.	0	209	0	0	0	0	0	0	0

Continued

Continued

Author	Title	Date of Publication	Place of Pub/Publisher	Number of images	Number of pages	Labour	Leisure	Portrait	Domestic	Ritual	Historical	Nature
Novaes, S. C.	The play of mirror: the representation of self as mirrored in the other	1997	Austin: University of Texas Press	18	177	2	0	0	0	5	11	0
Oakdale, S.	I foresee my life	2005	Lincoln: University of Nebraska Press	2	206	0	0	2	0	0	0	0
Oberg, K.	Indians tribes of northern Mato Grosso, Brazil	1953	Washington DC: Smithsonian Institution Institute of Social Anthropology, Pub. No. 15.	39	144	9	3	23	1	1	0	2
Peters, J. F.	Life among the Yanomami	1998	Peterborough: Broadview Press	19	292	5	6	6	0	0	0	2
Picchi, D. S.	The Bakairi Indians of Brazil: politics, ecology, and change	2000	Prospect Heights: Waveland Press	13	217	3	1	6	0	3	0	0
Posey, D	Kayapó ethnoecology and culture	2002	London: Routledge	0	285	0	0	0	0	0	0	0
Price, D.	Before the bulldozer: the Nambikwara Indians and the World Bank	1989	Washington DC: Seven Locks Press	8	212	1	2	3	0	0	0	2

Author	Title	Year	Publisher									
Rabben, L.	Brazil's Indians and the onslaught of civilization	2004	Seattle: University of Washington Press	6	214	1	0	4	0	0	0	1
Ramos, A.	Sanuma memories	1995	Madison: University of Wisconsin Press	10	346	4	3	1	2	0	0	0
Reichel-Dolmatoff, G.	The shaman and the jaguar: a study of narcotic drugs among the Indians of Colombia	1975	Philadelphia: Temple University Press	21	280	3	3	2	0	8	0	5
Reichel-Dolmatoff, G.	The sacred mountain of Colombia's Kogi Indians	1990	Leiden: E. J. Brill	36	86	7	2	16	2	9	0	0
Reichel-Dolmatoff, G.	The forest within: the world-view of the Tukano Amazonian Indians	1996	Totnes, Devon: Themis Books	46	229	10	5	16	0	5	0	10
Reichel-Dolmatoff, G.	Rainforest Shamans: Essays on the Tukano Indians of the Northwestern Amazon	1997	Totnes, Devon: Themis	17	344	2	3	5	0	6	0	1
Reichel-Dolmatoff, G.	Yurupari: studies of an Amazonian foundation myth	1995	Cambridge, MA: Harvard University Press	10	300	0	1	2	0	7	0	0
Reichel-Dolmatoff, G.	Amazonian cosmos: the sexual and religious symbolism of the Tukano Indians	1971	Chicago: University of Chicago Press	12	290	1	0	4	1	3	0	3

Continued

Continued

Author	Title	Date of Publication	Place of Pub/ Publisher	Number of images	Number of pages	Labour	Leisure	Portrait	Domestic	Ritual	Historical	Nature
Reichel-Dolmatoff, G. & A.	People of Aritama	1961	London: Routledge & Kegan Paul	0	483	0	0	0	0	0	0	0
Rival, L.	Trekking through history: the Huaorani of Amazonian Ecuador	2002	New York: Columbia University Press	14	246	1	2	8	0	0	0	3
Riviere, P.	Individual and society in Guyana	1984	Cambridge: Cambridge University Press	0	127	0	0	0	0	0	0	0
Riviere, P.	Marriage among the Trio: a principle of social organization.	1969	Oxford: Clarendon Press	15	353	9	4	0	0	0	0	2
Roe, P. G.	The cosmic zygote: cosmology in the Amazon basin	1982	New Brunswick: Rutgers University Press	1	384	0	0	1	0	0	0	0
Rosengren, D.	In the eyes of the beholder: leadership and the social construction of power and dominance among the Matsigenka of the Peruvian Amazon	1987	Goteborg: Ethnographic Museum	0	231	0	0	0	0	0	0	0

Author	Title	Year	Publisher									
Rubenstein, S.	Alejandro Tsakimp: a shuar healer in the margins of history	2002	Lincoln: University of Nebraska Press	0	322	0	0	0	0	0	0	0
Ryden, S.	A study of the Siriono Indians	1941	Goteborg: Humanistic Foundation of Sweden	18	167	3	5	6	0	0	0	4
Salomone, F.	The Yanomami and their interpreters: fierce peoples or fierce academics?	1997	Lanham: University Press of America	0	140	0	0	0	0	0	0	0
Santos-Granero, F.	The power of love: the moral use of knowledge among the Amuesha of central Peru	1991	London: Athlone	0	338	0	0	0	0	0	0	0
Santos-Granero, F.	Tamed frontiers: economy, society and civil rights in upper Amazonia	2000	Boulder: Westview Press	6	386	1	0	0	0	0	5	0
Seeger, A.	Why Suya sing: a musical anthropology of an Amazonian people	1987	Cambridge: Harvard University Press	5	147	0	0	1	0	4	0	0
Seeger, A.	Nature and society in Central Brazil: the Suya indians of Mato Grosso	1981	Cambridge: Harvard University Press	0	278	0	0	0	0	0	0	0
Siskind, J.	To hunt in the morning	1973	Oxford: Oxford University Press	19	214	6	5	4	0	0	0	4

Continued

Continued

Author	Title	Date of Publication	Place of Pub/Publisher	Number of images	Number of pages	Labour	Leisure	Portrait	Domestic	Ritual	Historical	Nature
Smole, W.	The Yanoama Indians: a cultural geography	1976	Austin: University of Texas Press	23	272	9	1	8	0	0	0	5
Stearman, A. M.	Yuqui: forest nomads in a changing world	1989	New York: Holt, Rinehart and Winston	27	164	8	2	4	0	0	3	10
Stearman, A.M.	No longer nomads: the Siriono revisited	1987	Lanham: Hamilton Press	17	166	7	1	5	0	1	1	2
Stirling, M. W.	Historical and ethnographical material on the Jivaro Indians	1938	Washington, DC: Smithsonian Institution, Bureaus of American Ethnology, Bull. 117	89	186	15	0	73	0	0	0	1
Sullivan, L. E.	Incanchu's drum: an orientation to meaning in South American Religions	1988	New York: Macmillan	0	1003	0	0	0	0	0	0	0
Taussig, M.	Shamanism, colonialism, and the wildman	1987	Chicago: University of Chicago Press	58	517	15	4	4	1	8	26	0
Taussig, M.	The magic of the state	1996	New York: Routledge	8	206	2	0	0	0	6	0	0
Taylor, K.	Sanuma fauna: prohibitions and classification	1974	Caracas: Fundacion La Salle de Ciencias Naturales	13	138	0	4	2	0	2	0	5

Thomas, D. J.	Order without Government: the society of the Pemon Indians of Venezuela	1982	Urbana: University of Illinois Press	0	265	0	0	0	0	0	0	0
Urban, G.	Metaphysical community: the interplay of the senses and the intellect	1996	Austin: University of Texas Press	7	288	1	1	1	0	0	4	0
Verswijver, G.	The club-fighters of the Amazon: warfare among the Kaiapó Indians of central Brazil	1992	Gent: Rijksuniversiteit	45	378	1	9	16	0	6	9	4
Villas Boas, O.	Xingu: the Indians, their myths	1974	London: Souvenir	0	270	0	0	0	0	0	0	0
Viveiros de Castro, E.	From the enemy's point of view: humanity and divinity in an Amazonian society	1992	Chicago: University of Chicago Press	23	407	3	5	4	3	3	0	5
Von Graeve, B.	The Pacaa Nova: clash of cultures on the Brazilian frontier	1989	Peterborough: Broadview Press	22	160	5	9	5	0	0	0	3
Wagley, C.	Welcome of tears	1977	New York: Oxford University Press	50	328	4	7	20	0	15	0	4
Wagley, C. and Galvao, E.	The Tenetehara Indians of Brazil: a culture in transition	1949	New York: Columbia University Press	25	200	1	2	10	0	8	0	4

Continued

Continued

Author	Title	Date of Publication	Place of Pub/ Publisher	Number of images	Number of pages	Labour	Leisure	Portrait	Domestic	Ritual	Historical	Nature
Whitehead, N.	Dark shamans: Kanaima and the poetics of violent death	2002	Durham: Duke University Press	7	310	1	0	3	0	1	1	1
Whitten, N. E.	Sacha Runa: ethnicity and adaptation of Ecuadorian jungle Quichua	1976	Urbana, Ill: University of Illinois Press	28	348	12	4	2	0	6	0	4
Wilbert, J.	Mystic Endowment: religious ethnography of Warao Indians	1993	Cambridge: Harvard University Press	6	308	0	2	3	0	1	0	0
Wilbert, J.	Tobacco and shamanism in South America	1987	New Haven: Yale University Press	13	294	0	1	3	0	8	1	0
Wilbert, J.	Survivors of Eldorado	1972	New York: Praeger	25	212	13	2	0	4	4	0	2
Wright, R.	Cosmos, self and history in Baniwa religion: for those unborn	1998	Austin: University of Texas Press	1	314	0	0	1	0	0	0	0
Yde, J.	Material culture of the Waiwai	1965	Copenhagen: National Museum	38	319	17	1	11	0	1	0	8
Totals				2509	39126	492	311	959	77	379	78	213

Figure 6.5 Posed/observational. M. Schmidt 1926.

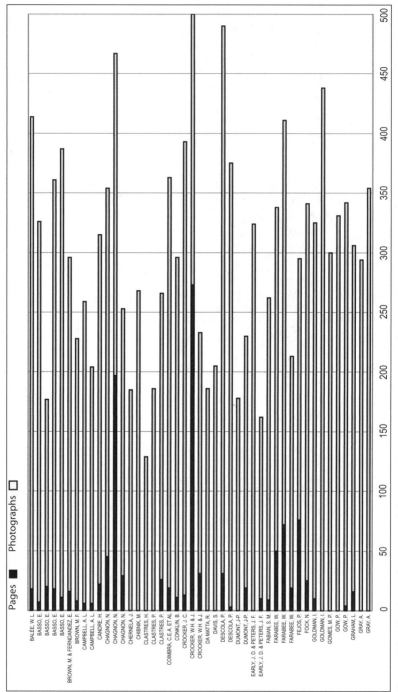

Figure 6.6a Numbers of pages and photographs.

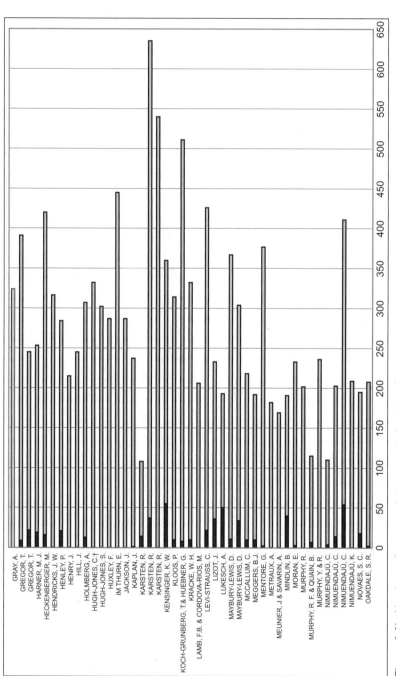

Figure 6.6b Numbers of pages and photographs (continued).

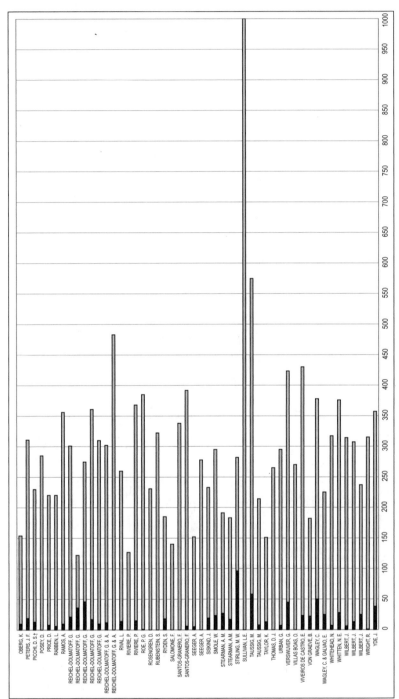

Figure 6.6c Numbers of pages and photographs (continued).

Figure 6.6, Selected Monographs, shows the number of ethnographic images (E) and pages of text (F) in each of the monographs. The images are then sorted into seven categories: Labour (G), Leisure (H), Portrait (I), Domestic (J), Ritual (K), Historical (L), and Nature (M).[11]

These categories are indicative and approximate, some more exact than others, but all somewhat imprecise and/or ambiguous. Are a shaman's ministrations to be taken as Labour or Ritual? Is a dance welcoming visitors to be taken as Leisure or Ritual? Is a posed photograph Leisure or Portrait? And so on. It may be objected that this ambiguity is the product of poorly designated categories, but while this may be true, the prior ambiguity – that concerning being able to discern an observational-ethnographic image from a posed photograph – could be said to introduce this uncertainty.[12] In cases such as the Rondon group presenting clothing to peoples in the Xingu region (Rondon 1946:150–53), the equivocal status of the images, as posed and/or observational, is very much to the fore. They are posed photos, assembled on behalf of the visiting photographer, and the observational content is not provided by (or just by) the Indians but is in fact the encounter itself between Indian and white.

In this sense, the posed/observed contrast that exercised Im Thurn and continues to bedevil writing preoccupied with the demarcation of a visual anthropology clearly driven by field research seems somewhat misdirected. Typically, in the works under consideration, the content of the 'observational' is precisely the anthropological intervention. The 'posed' is a matter, in camera terms, of point of view (POV). By this reckoning, all ethnographic photographs are both posed and observational, yet the weight of the image seems ultimately to rest on the subjects more than the relationship between the subjects and their viewers/documenters.[13] Key to this relationship for the material under consideration here is the embedding or situating of the images within voluminous ethnographic texts.

The high ratio of number of pages of text to number of images is a characteristic not commented on in the professional literature.

While it seems clear that an ethnographic account that depends primarily on photographic images becomes a different kind of (anthropology?) book – a coffee-table book, a book too easy to consume to be taken seriously by professionals, a book with little or no theoretical or ethnological content, a topical book – aside from considerations of cost, it is unclear exactly why it is that in general the use of images in monographs is usually modest, and it is unclear what kinds of usage of or dependence on images leads to 'coffee-table' pollution. Arhem (1998) and Verswijver (1996) are authoritative, image-dominated monographs whose scholarly authority is in no doubt, yet they are virtually alone in attempting to reverse the usual print-to-image ratios. It is likely that the historically high cost of photo reproduction has been a factor that has conventionalized the underuse of images,[14] but that aversion persists even in an era in which the costs of black-and-white image reproduction is relatively trivial. Neither the emergence of offset printing in the 1950s (on a mass scale) nor digital photo-origination has had a dramatic impact on the number of ethnographic images per year. The typical number of photographs per monograph has been quite modest.

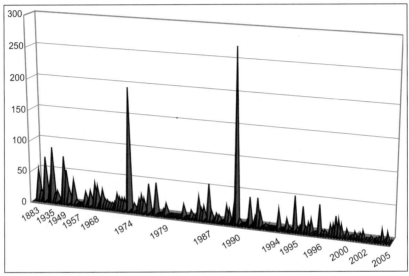

Figure 6.7 Number of photographs by year.

Those monographs with a high number of images tend to be museum publications[15] in which subsidy presumably plays a substantial role. In the Selected Monographs set (Table 6.1),[16] these include Crocker (1985), Crocker and Crocker (1990), Farabee (1918, 1924), Karsten (1935), Lukesch (1976), Nimuendajú (1946), Oberg (1953), Stirling (1938), and Yde (1965).[17] Among other books containing higher-than-average numbers of images are several that ostensibly seek to share both professional and public audiences. These include, for instance, Chagnon (1992), Maybury-Lewis (1965), Mindlin (1995), Reichel-Dolmatoff (1990, 1996), and Descola (1997). Of the remaining books containing high(ish) numbers (the cutoff point is thirty images or more), Wagley (1977), Taussig (1987), and Kensinger (1995) contain disproportionately large numbers of Historical images and/or Portraits.[18]

The largest number and highest proportion (images per text page) of photographs in a 'standard' monograph, however, occurs in Chagnon (1974), a book that is neither a museum publication nor an artefact that falls off the shelf and lands on the coffee table. In fact, *Studying the Yanomamo*

(1974) – the majority of whose photographs are mug shots reminiscent of early, anthropometrically driven anthropology (the object of Im Thurn's ire) – is a very self-consciously 'scientific' work; and although Chagnon collaborated extensively with the imaginative filmmaker Timothy Asch, there is little in Chagon (1968 or 1974) that suggests visual ambitions beyond those motivated by rigorous data gathering and documentary.[19]

At first glance, there is in the corpus of standard ethnographic accounts of Amazonia a visual record that is generally subordinate to the textual record, yet over time (1883–2005) and viewed by decade, there is an upward trend in the number of images appearing (adjusted to smooth atypical spikes).

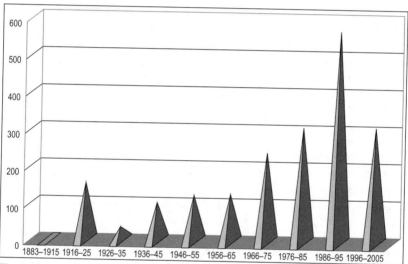

Figure 6.8 Number of photographs by decade.

Despite these trends, though, if the spikes represented by Chagnon (1974) and Crocker and Crocker (1990) – along with a handful of early museum publications – are removed (see Figure 6.7), there are only a handful of monographs throughout the period that have more than a few dozen images. The average number of pages of the monographs in the set is 280; the average ratio of pages/images is 16/1. The disproportionate weight of textual exposition – disregarding the possible truth of the cliché that calculates the value of one image as equivalent to that of one thousand words – seems to assign images to a secondary role. Volumes for which the expositional and representational weight is borne by images are to be found only in the marginal monograph literature – the aforementioned works by Arhem (1998) and Verswijver (1996), for instance – and in those such as Ricciardi (1991), which, although presented with requisite anthropology authority,[20] have explicit aesthetic-cum-documentary goals (that is, they are basically coffee-table books). Even among some of the more recent monographs in which the relative ease of digital capture might be expected to lead to more extensive and measured ethno-photographic documentation, one is just as likely to encounter low-resolution images-as-smudges. In such examples, it seems unlikely that the quality – in several senses – of such images is a coded repudiation of the place of photography in ethnographic rendition (though this may be a fair inference), but it is hard to account for the casualness of gesture. As with the Dull River photographs (see Chapter 5), it may be that too much confidence is placed in an image's capacity to stir a response commensurate with the photographer's own memory.

Tristes Tropiques (Lévi-Strauss 1961) is arguably the only listed work with a significant and lasting impact as both an important anthropological contribution and public/literary artefact;[21] and its influence has been underscored years after publication by the reflective, melancholy *Saudades do Brasil* (1994), which represents a major change of view. Although disdainful in *Tristes Tropiques* of the anthropological use of photographs, in *Saudades* Lévi-Strauss seems to give his photographs (which date from the *Tristes Tropiques* period, 1935–39)[22] licence to provide a photo-narrative alternative to text.

The relative marginality of ethno-photograph content in the monograph set is consistent throughout the ca. 120-year period under consideration, but viewed in terms of decades, a different picture emerges – namely a decade-on-decade increase in output of monographs with images from the 1950s until the present, tracked by similar increase in photo-free monographs. Although the literature is growing, the average number of images per monograph tends to decline as the number of monographs published per year rises.

This sketch of Amazonian images indicates, at a minimum, some of the dynamic and problematic features of what seems at casual glance to be a fairly straightforward 'collection of images'. Even as constrained a set of sources as that contained in Table 6.1 (images of Amazonian Indians published within the professional monograph literature) shows conflicting tendencies. There is, for example, a marked and consistent tendency toward portraiture even though this runs counter to a generically functionalist disavowal of the forensic/anthropometric leanings of 'pre-scientific' anthropology. By contrast, there is a very inconsistent use of historical images. The photographic record, in other words, is embedded in other kinds of records. The photographic medium per se, while allowing the representation of other, new, different dimensions of anthropological inquiry, seems to fall short of delimiting the kind of new space implied by the notion of a visual culture/visual anthropology.

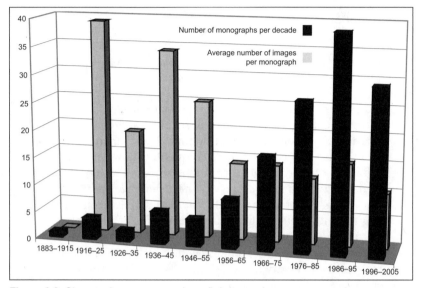

Figure 6.9 Changes in average number of photographs per monograph.

Who/What Is on Show?

Of the 140 monographs considered here, one hundred include ethnographic images. Of those, a third (32) have only 1–10 images. Forty monographs include no ethnographic images.

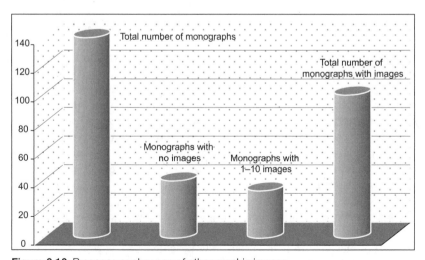

Figure 6.10 Presence or absence of ethnographic images.

The images tend to be illustrations bolstered by captions rather than stand-alone artefacts. In this, they share in one of the quandaries of ethnographic writing: bald description of the by-definition exotic requires artifice (of a rhetorical rather than sleight-of-hand sort), which means that most ethnographic writing is complex translation – never able to rely on a naked, expressive realism, but supported by hedging, approximation, metaphor, and a range of other devices. Images as illustrative/documentary enhancements of the text typically require captions, at a minimum, and occasionally extended textual comment and analysis in order to situate their imputed contribution. Frequently, however, the captions merely underscore the marginal contribution that such photographs are presumed to offer; *that is a man with a knife standing over a dead tapir* hardly raises the game. Whereas most field data are simultaneously presented and analyzed/interpreted, the photographs in this literature are generally not accorded the same level of treatment. They are not often analyzed on their own, but are used and perhaps cited, typically with a minimum of instruction or commentary).

In crucial respects, this unadorned, illustrative function of images in service to Amazonianist text has unhappily ironic implications. Whereas the ethnographic/textual record displays an absence of an overarching, generic, unifying structure (bemoaned in Jackson 1975, Overing 1981, Viveiros de Castro 1996, and Hill n.d.), the photographs in the aggregate show just the opposite: the unifying cliché. Not only do similarities within the image set contradict an assemblage of case studies that defies a pan-Amazonian gloss,[23] but additionally the images tend to reinforce the destructive stereotypes of Amazonian savagery, nomadism, technological backwardness, etc.[24] that subtle anthropological analysis has taken pains to dispute.

In the literature, with some noteworthy exceptions, the cod-observational photograph takes precedence over the portrait or very self-consciously posed photograph,[25] even though many photographs end up being classified as 'portraits' by default. The attempt to portray banal quotidian experience (there are many images of manioc processing) as well as more esoteric activities (trance, ingestion of psychotropics) manages to convey two forms of exoticism, that of material want and that of spiritual complexity, both accurate – that is, based on real examples, albeit unevenly distributed – yet both reinforcing the stereotype of the mythology-laden, Rousseauean, hunter-gatherer agent.

This stereotype in the photo-ethnography, however, falls far short of the rampant caricatures available through cinema, television, and other public sources. There is little that may be construed as representing the cannibalism, depravity, amoralism, gluttony, greed, and other exoto-

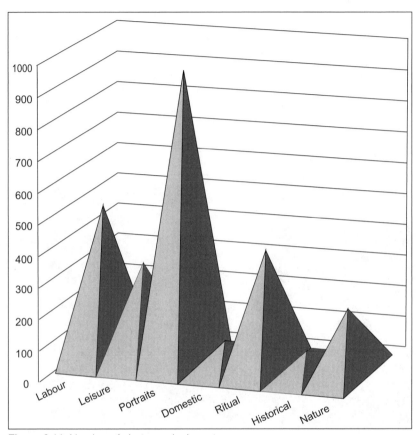

Figure 6.11 Number of photographs by category.

negative attributes frequently featured in exploration/travel writing. Many of the standard green hell accoutrements – venomous or carnivorous snakes, *candirú*,[26] electric eel, fevers, piranha, *curupira*, *mapinguari* – do not feature often if at all (sometimes for the obvious reason of their non-existence) in ethnographic images. The most frequent animal subjects are tapir and peccary, other large species being rare (jaguar) or *yeti*-related fantasies (e.g., *cobra grande*, -a river snake with one headlight-like eye; *mapinguari*, the giant sloth; or the terrestrial dolphin).

A number of different perspectives are represented within the images published as complements to the core, textual representations. These include:

- Some Indians' reality.
- Some anthropologists' expectations.

- Some output generated by explanatory models/theory machines.
- Ideological/political fiction.
- Encapsulated folk narrative.

With respect to the first, for example, the diversity of portrayals of 'typical' Amazonian Indians does not entirely succumb to the expectations of the stereotype/cliché and does reflect to some degree genuine differences among peoples and among the formal studies of such peoples.

Figure 6.12 Iconic beast I. R. Centeno and P. Fernández O. 1998.

Figure 6.13 Postcard, Iconic beast II.

Figure 6.14 On the road to assimilation. R. Centeno and P. Fernández O. 1998.

Figure 6.15 On the way home. C. M. Rondon 1953a.

With respect to the second and third, the choice of anthropological subjects is often motivated by a desire to explain/account for a particular cultural practice or feature. The long-standing – though by no means universally respectable – obsession with protein capture, for example, provides the focus for an important research trend, and through its association with such concepts as 'carrying capacity' is still a significant element in shaping field research.

In terms of theory machines, the photographic portrayal of Amazonian lifeways has for the most part proceeded under the assumption that present-day Indians are significantly representative of their predecessors, as though they were relic populations of Neolithic peoples, members of a world not so much *lost* in spatial terms, isolated on the Mount Roraima mesa (à la Conan Doyle), as *temporally* lost, in suspended animation over several thousand years. Within the cultural evolutionary framework[27] associated with Steward (1955), this kind of suspension made some sense. The argument was that peoples of the humid neo-tropics were materially constrained from advancing culturally and sociopolitically because of the limitations of a biome ('green hell') that tolerated only societies of a low level of complexity, density, and overall size. In view of these 'natural constraints', social agents of the present could be presumed to be broadly similar to their ancient ancestors.

This has not been the only macro-framework for anthropological research in Amazonia (see Viveiros de Castro 1996), but it embodies many underlying assumptions shared across a broad spectrum of researchers. Meggers (1971) expresses most clearly this dominant, but increasingly challenged, view.

The photo-ethnographic renditions of this nature-controlled lifeway do little to contradict the orthodoxy (although historic works such as Im Thurn (1883) often include plates of 'puzzling' petroglyphs that disturb the hunter-gatherer cliché), but the mounting evidence that contemporary Indian societies are little or poorly representative of prehistoric Amazonian societies also calls into question the adequacy of the photographic record that is driven to some considerable degree by the prejudice identified by Blaut (1993) as 'the doctrine of tropical nastiness'.

Regardless of the merits of either side in the debates over the 'representativeness' of present-day Amazonian societies, the fact is that one side of the debate is available for photographic representation and one is not. Present-day Amazonian sociality may be but a faint sliver of what the past held, but however fragmentary and attenuated a version it is, there is little of the revisionist model of typical prehistoric Amazonia that can be so portrayed. Lathrap's (1970) persuasive but largely textual arguments, Palmatary's (1960) images of ceramics, Roosevelt's (1991) hearths and house posts, Heckenberger's (2005) maps, the contributions to McEwan,

Barreto, and Neves (2001), and C. Erickson's (2000) aerial photographs of mounds contribute to a major re-evaluation of Amazonian prehistory and raise awkward questions about the relationships among ethnography and history and prehistory, but the difficulty in realizing this challenge in a cohesive photographic form is not a trivial impediment. Novel forms of satellite imaging in Heckenberger (2005) and C. Erickson (2000), for example, considerably elevate the perceived credibility of revisionist arguments about Amazonian prehistory in a way denied Lathrap's work.

In terms of the political defence of Indians, cultural distinctiveness as displayed – partially, but significantly – through images has had an important role, not least because of the confirmation it provides of the precariousness of the Indians' position. On the other hand, the way in which Indians present or express themselves stylistically (for example, wearing 'Western' clothes and forsaking traditional customs) often deviates from the conditions imposed by cliché. From another quarter, the fact that Indians might present themselves stylistically in ways that deviate from the cliché is often used by the state as evidence of the active disavowal of Indian distinctiveness – as revealed, for instance, but by no means unusually, during the widely reported legal proceedings against Paulo Payakan.[28]

Finally, photographs from the ethnographic record document with great consistency a generic image of the Indian that is resilient against the odds. Declining fortunes (in most respects), legal reconfiguration via the New Constitution (1988), alliances with First Nations Peoples of the north, and

Figure 6.16 Teenage girls. T. Whiffen 1915.

Figure 6.17 Teenage girls. © Stephen Baines 2003.

re-evaluation in the face of new evidence about prehistoric antecedents hardly alter the stable imagery of received public views about the nature of Amazonia and its peoples. The cliché, while mutating rapidly, both maintains an atavistic rooting while simultaneously validating new forms of Indian cultural capital. Ramos has discussed this complex of Indian and non-Indian recognition of the cultural capital available as a particular kind of co-dependency. In *Pulp Fictions of Indigenism* (2001) she says that

> [Altamira] highlighted the phenomenon of an international market of exoticism as manifested in the interplay between non-indigenous consumers and indigenous producers of cultural resources as commodities. It profusely displayed both sides of the same coin: on the one hand, avid white audiences whose close proximity with 'real' Indians served either as inspiration for mystical pursuits or simply as cheap thrills; on the other, equally avid 'real' Indians turning their cultural capital into political muscle against undesirable state policies. Both sides reinforced each other's cravings by parading their affected selves under the enthralled lenses of the media.[29]

The Inductive Indian

A guiding notion of the collection of images drawn from the ethnographic corpus seems to be 'the Inductive Indian' – that is, if it walks like, talks like, and looks like an Indian, it must be so. The historical record displays less sympathy for this notion than might be expected, for the Indian is (perhaps partially as a result of years of practice) commonly out of view. Well-known predictions of the complete removal of the Brazilian Indian,

Figure 6.18 Carajá woman and child. C. M. Rondon 1953a.

most notoriously by Ribeiro (1967), have proved wrong. Brazil's Indian population has risen from a reported 50,000 in 1972 (Brooks et al. 1973), to more than 350,000 in 2005, but such increase does not necessarily translate into greater visibility. Even if there is confusion and serious disagreement about what criteria should be used to identify Indians (and who should have the power to engage them), the photographic record tends to favour the notion of an idealized 'pre-modern' Indian even while there is open acknowledgement that a strict boundary between Indian and Indian *manqué* (defined in many different ways)[30] is not always evident.

In this context, shaped by uncertainty about how to ascertain precisely what 'Indianness' means, the images contained in ethnographic monographs may be realistic depictions: in the face of the complexities of Indian existence in Amazonia and Brazil – in forest, village, or city – how could any image possibly contain or express any more than a fleeting insight? Instead, such an argument might go, an image that is in effect retrospective, harking back to an assumed idealist configuration, encapsulates enough contextual memory to ring true. Such images are projective and adequate in the sense that the figure (the forest Indian, say) does not vary when viewed from different angles – the Indian on the magazine cover, sleeping on a park bench, appearing before a tribunal, and so on. By this reckoning, a minimalist or reductive image is more secure, less risky, because it makes fewer assumptions. It accepts the burden of cliché.

Of the 140 monographs in the set, forty contain no ethnographic photographs at all and a further 32 include only 1–10 images. The fact that such a large proportion of monographs contains few or no images may support the argument that ethno-photography is not centrally concerned with anthropological knowledge but is a casual appendage, essentially ornamental even if attributed a documentary/non-aesthetic function. The inclusion of images is obviously not obligatory in monograph publications, but neither do there seem to be clear conventions governing their imputed contribution.[31] The cliché/stereotype shows great resilience in the face of the trends toward assimilation of Indians into national society – which is to say, remove Indians. Thus, the stereotype/cliché may represent a stylized, rough approximation of 'Indian' yet at the same time be an effective refuge for a notion of Indian who continues to resist domestication, assimilation, obliteration.

Calculating Images

The ways in which specialist knowledge about Amazonia – anthropological knowledge, for instance – is articulated with broader public understanding of the region and its peoples[32] has been both enhanced and complicated by the intense attention paid to Amazonia over recent decades. Not only has the research literature grown dramatically, but disparate and combined effects of journalistic/media coverage and the activities of innumerable interest groups – from campaigning NGOs to world music entrepreneurs[33] and DIY superstores -generate a lot of white noise. In a context in which the volume of information exceeds the capacity of conventional categories to provide organization and frames of reference, it becomes more difficult to distinguish between the accurate/adequate and the trivial/distracting. Estimates of the rate of forest clearance, for instance, a phenomenon linked to global climate change, biodiversity, desertification, and carbon sink capacity (to mention but a few), are not only calculated – with requisite claims of authority – on different bases by different interest groups (and in different time frames, with varying fineness of resolution, etc.), but are also implicated in diverse supervening and by no means mutually intelligible analyses with respect to global changes in resource stocks of primarily materials, rates of speciation, flows of investment, and so on. By comparison with the highly fragmented nature of this more expanded sphere of public knowledge about Amazonia, the image of the 'Indian-in-the-forest' seems relatively stable and reliable however much its adequacy may be found wanting in other respects. If that pseudo-fixity is acknowledged, it makes it even more important to ascertain the reliability of the images in the narrow context that provides them with academic authority.

The graphic depiction of image data does not carry with it any implication of high scientistic purpose, as though it is possible simply to cut through the undergrowth of interpretive confusions by resorting to numerical rendition; but it is done in the spirit of trying to maintain a consistent referential baseline and minimize ambiguity when it comes to generalizing about the images of Amazonia that – shaped by diverse forces and interests – have come to be assembled as 'natural', the clichés and stereotypes of 'green hell', 'Indians of the forest', 'the last frontier' and the like.

In addition to the focus on a narrow literature and an attempt to provide some useful quantitative generalizations, there is also an interest in another kind of de-exoticization. The developmental workout/punishment to which Amazonia has been subjected over the past three decades, what Bourne (1978) accurately labels 'the assault on the Amazon', is in many respects not nearly as exotic as its locale and associate imagery may suggest. Many of the pathologies afflicting the region and its peoples are simply the result of the grotesque ambitions of interests for which Amazonia is little more than a cheap source of quite ordinary, but increasingly scarce, resources. Widely regarded as an enclave whose biodiverse offerings may be dramatically beneficial (cancer cures and the like), the reality is that the region – terrestrial and riverine – is plundered for far less exotic products such as wood, fish, shrimp, soya, and mineral ores. These are not (in the main) uniquely Amazonian resources but are sought there because they are cheap, because there is a notable lack of environmental and fiscal regulation, and because access is sustained in part by the myths of the frontier and 'Indian land'.[34]

The stability of number of images per monograph is a striking feature of the overview for the period (1883–2005), with major spikes attributable to museum publications for which, in many cases, the ethnographic images form only part of the image contents.[35] This (mainly earlier) emphasis on wide documentation is assumed to reflect aspects of museum collecting perhaps more prominent earlier in the century than later; these are, first, the focus on salvage – the acquisition of objects and images of peoples on the verge of extinction, a final record – and second the role of object collections in teaching. This pedagogic role of objects has declined dramatically, and in the contemporary period such collecting is almost unrecognizable as a central aim of anthropological fieldwork.

That tendency toward over-documentation – of material culture, of portraits – is rare and instrumental. In general, it is hard to detect an overall pattern. The high number of portrait numbers for Chagnon (1974) noted in Table 6.1 significantly distorts upward the total number of ethnographic images, but it doesn't reflect the prominence in that work of the Indian visage, however, as much as it reflects the methodological demands of a research strategy in which the identity of and close tracking of individuals forbidden from speaking the names of the dead is crucial to an argument about genetic relatedness. Taussig's (1987) relatively large number of images similarly represents a methodological demand – namely detailing an historical context that has had a persistent effect on contemporary 'traditional', supernatural preoccupations. Reichel-Dolmatoff (1996), though authoritative, tends toward a non-specialist audience but has been included/counted because it is in line with a higher-than-average photograph/page ratio revealed in the largest number of monographs by a single author on the list (Table 6.1). Kensinger (1995), as noted above, contains a large number of photographs of individuals dating from two long-separated periods of fieldwork, again a product of a particular methodological emphasis.

With few – and non-mysterious – exceptions, the photo-ethnographic looks very much like an ethnographic accessory rather than a vital, basic element. Yet the photo-ethnographic cliché/stereotype can hardly be attributed too minor a role in shaping views about what is typical, what is normal, what is natural.

Types of Ethnographic Image

The anthropometric/mug-shot approach apparent in some early field photography and criticized by Im Thurn (1893) was in large part driven

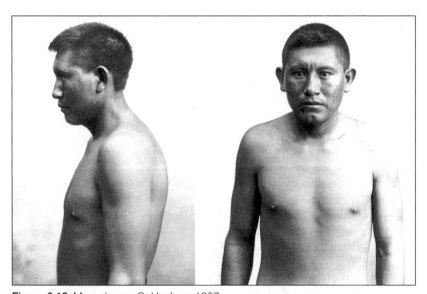

Figure 6.19 Macuxi man. G. Huebner 1907.

by the conviction (stated or not) that phenotypical differences contained, reflected, or were isomorphic with significant, different competencies among human beings – a sentiment still widely expressed today if in more nuanced and devious ways. A successor approach, that represented in the monograph literature considered here, was equally committed to the notion that something of anthropological interest could be revealed in photographs – not necessarily in 'forensic' photos, and not necessarily in photos of Indians per se, but of 'cultures' as embodied in human types. In other words, photographic images were represented as a different kind of data gathering, not necessarily a different kind of data.[36]

Portraits comprise the largest of the seven categories of images drawn from the monograph collection, 37 per cent of the total, nearly twice the size of the next largest category (Labour at 19 per cent). Some of these images seem quite uncomplicated examples of portraits – studies of individuals' faces, for instance –but others are less straightforward. The mug shots above, for example, combine the interactive gaze of the subject and

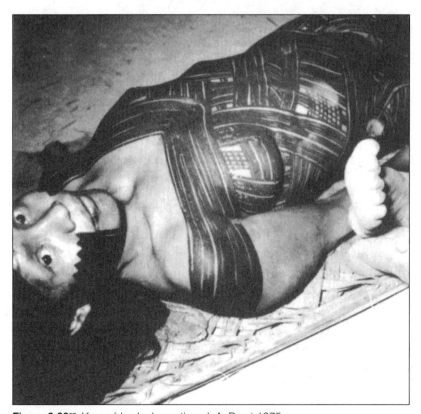

Figure 6.20[37] Kayapó body decoration. J. A. Peret 1975.

Figure 6.21 Tapayuna man. J. A. Peret 1975.

a side view that is more forensic. Many portraits are more than studies of faces but include full bodies (and, not infrequently, shot from the back) or, quite expectedly, feature the adornments for which some Amazonian forest peoples are particularly known (lip plugs; tattooing; forms of hair dressing). Many are clearly posed with subjects staring straight into the camera. In the image below, for example, of a Kayapó woman whose body is decorated with *genipapa* (a non-permanent vegetable dye), the subject is scrutinizing the gaze of the camera as though to say *you look at my body while I look at your face.*

Taking the group of images as a whole, the contrast with Curtis's (2003) *Portfolio* is striking. Not only does the Amazonian material seem to avoid iconicity, but it also shows a disinterest in matters of composition that might lend the images more singularity. This is in keeping with the ethos according to which what is being studied is a system, a culture, a society, not just an assembly of individuals; but this avoidance of being drawn into portraying exemplars – 'the typical X-ian' – as well as a more overtly 'aesthetic' approach often extends even to portraits of named individuals such as key informants. This contrast with Curtis (who usually does provide the names of his subjects, although some do appear just with labels – e.g., 'A Hopi Mother') in the avoidance of personalizing Amazonian subjects reflects a general contrast between the catalogues of images of North and South American Indians: few of the latter are known by name in the way Sitting Bull or Geronimo are. More often, Amazonian Indians are captioned by their tribal names ('a Guarani chief').[38]

Figure 6.22 Macuxi couple. © Stephen Baines 2001.

Curtis's purpose in compiling the twenty volumes of *The North American Indian: The Complete Portfolios* (2003) was explicitly to document peoples who were on the verge of extinction.[39] This salvage aspect is not missing from the Amazonian record – and is most pronounced as part of the museum ethnography project – but there also appears in the Amazonian context a quite different aim, a preoccupation with the future as well as the past. This is revealed in the still-current interest in discovering lost tribes. This is not a wholly unrespectable preoccupation, on par with *yeti* and Bigfoot obsessions, for example, although it is far more pronounced among explorer-adventurers than among ethnographers.[40] The crucial point is that among Amazonian Indians, extinction is the pressing reality, yet this is overlaid with the mysterious possibility of future encounters. This combination of past and present enhances the mythological and mystifying aspects of the stereotype/cliché, the *last* tribe combined with the *lost* tribe.

There are several ambiguities in the ways in which portraits function in this literature. One noted earlier (which affects most of the categories of ethnographic image) is the uncertainty in distinguishing between posed and observational subjects. Perhaps the contrast is not as sharp as it appears. What Im Thurn claims to be observational photographs of his own are not terribly convincing, yet what he is challenging in his claim is the kind of anthropometric, human-subject-as-specimen pose that unsubtly presents people as objects.

Another ambiguity is generated by the discrepancy that lies in an image that is on one hand a unique individual and on the other displays significant typicality. This is often further compounded by the uncertainty of 'typicality' itself given the many tribal[41] identity overlaps characteristic of the region's peoples as well as the indifference this 'dilemma' elicits among 'tribalists'.[42]

These uncertainties about how to position ethnographic subjects is closely related to two methodological issues that, if not unique to anthropological fieldwork, are consistently more pronounced in that discipline. The first of these concerns the length of time that ethnographers typically spend doing fieldwork and the second concerns the mildly oxymoronic notion of participant-observation. With long-term, often intimate insider's knowledge, fieldworkers find themselves in the same sort of gray space as that defined by the posed/observational contrast, and to some degree a fieldworker has the sensibility of a subject without losing the incomer's status (and obligations).

The ethnographic portrait, then, is far from being a simple or straightforward format. On the one hand, its systematic deployment is too closely associated with a clinical census taking or typecasting to be altogether comfortable; but on the other hand, the stories told in people's faces can add dimensions that the text is incapable of addressing. A general tendency that is expressed in some of the ambiguities noted above is that portraits may represent individuals of particular groups as well as representing generic examples, and this confusion of the general and the specific – which is found in other (all?) ethnographic domains as well – carries over into the labelling of Amazonian Indians outside an anthropological context.[43] The controversy surrounding Body Shop International's use of the image of the Indian Pykati-re (who also appears in an Anita Roddick American Express advertisement) was not so much focused on his rights per se as those of the group (Mebengokre) for which he stood. In what amounts to a textual analogy of changing the depth of field, within a single monograph, subjects of portraits may shift from being labelled (a) 'With his daughter on his knee, [named Indian] demonstrates his prowess as a singer' to (b) 'Fathers can be thoughtful parents, but most childcare responsibility is left to women'.

The convergence and mutual reinforcement of archetype and stereotype serves to maintain a clear boundary between 'Indianness' and 'non-Indianness', and the challenges posed by the prehistoric record on one hand, and the not-quite-Indian *mestiço/caboclo* on the other, are subdued. There are compelling reasons for this kind of boundary maintenance, not least of which is the mitigation of threat toward indigenous peoples that can be achieved through stylized images, but one of the costs is to accept that the currency of debate remains closely tied to a highly racialized codification as well as a confidence about continuities between prehistoric and historical Indians that is contentious. It is understandable that in the absence of a single contemporary (or, virtually, historical) example of the kind of Amazonian society whose existence many researchers think is revealed in the archaeological record,[44] there has been no significant displacement or breaching of that boundary in terms of consensual re-assessment of normal-standard-average Amazonian Indianness, but the absence of a visual record is not evidence of anything.

Labour, Leisure, and Ritual

Figure 6.23 Tukano drum. M. Schmidt 1926.

After Portraits, Labour, Leisure, and Ritual are the categories with most entries. As noted earlier, the criteria for inclusion in each category are not always clear, but even if those in Domestic were shifted to Labour or Leisure or Ritual, the impact on the relative ranking of those categories would not be overly disturbed.

In Labour have gone agricultural/horticultural and gathering activities as well as food preparation, tool making, and craft manufacture (weaving, ceramics; see Figure 6.11). Leisure's[45] entries are less certain. They include a certain amount of hammock time, children at play, adults playing with children, non-ritual dancing, and entertaining visitors. As with Leisure, some Ritual entries could be differently allocated, but the effects in terms of relative distribution among categories would not be significant.

In view of the historic emphasis – exaggerated in recent years with growing attention to indigenous knowledge and native science – on the complexities lying behind superficially rude practices such as swidden agriculture, it is surprising how few images move beyond the documenting of forest clearing, garden weeding, tuber harvesting and manioc processing. The centrality of manioc production in many lowland societies is thoroughly documented in the literature, but so are a great many other production forms,[46] yet the range of imagistic portrayal is not extensive.

Figure 6.24 Farinha. C. M. Rondon 1953a.

There are motifs embedded in manioc images that illuminate other aspects of forest Indian life. The most prominent of these is surely the gender division of labour according to which men focus on forest clearing and garden preparation while women are responsible for much weeding and harvesting and have complete control over/responsibility for the many stages of processing between harvest and consumption. This concentration on farming, or that for which we have familiar parallels, may overshadow dependence on production forms that are basically, in a non-pejorative sense, opportunistic – gathering. It is not that examples of the latter are undocumented, but that the relative importance of what seem to be less formal production forms is not clearly conveyed, with the consequence that the complexity of Indians' engagement with nature – the multiple forms of appropriation – is subsumed under a too-simplifying hunting and gathering rubric. In view of the intense and unresolved controversies surrounding the degree to which forests long occupied by indigenous peoples have been significantly modified – so-called 'anthropogenicism' – it is difficult to know how the absence of photographic documentation[47] of what all would agree is a major element in forest dwellers' livelihoods has affected the character of the focal stereotype/cliché, but the discrepancy between textual documentation of extractive complexity and the limited extent of the visual record is marked.[48]

The under-representation of images of extractivist activities also appears in a different light if one considers some of the implications of the opportunism of extractivism. The fact that a cardinal feature of the resource base upon which Indians have depended is the high species diversity/low species density relationship of plants and animals underlies the rationality of this perceived opportunism. The importance of dispersion + extractivism as a central production dimension also highlights the discrepancy between different notions of 'land value'. The value of 'land' from a national perspective of land-as-property does not reflect the capacity to live off it, but its abstract real estate value – hence, the widely voiced claims that Indians want more land than they actually need or, as is frequently made explicit, deserve.[49] The regular dispersal of group members over large areas; political fission at the village level; micro-regional migration; religious order control of Indians through confining women, children and the aged while sending men on extended gathering expeditions: all are structured features linked both to effective exploitation (which is to say, domination over nature) and mystification (which is to say, the appearance that nature is driving the car), and this is what much docu-ethnographic imagery seems to confirm.

This susceptibility of extractivism to being perceived as only a quasi-social kind of productive activity – scavenging as a primary act – also lends it an asystemic character and reinforces the notion of the lazy peasant/native who after catching a couple of fish is happy to tie up his canoe and spend the rest of the day in a hammock – a caricature challenged, for example, by Sahlins (1972) under the rubric 'the original affluent society'. Once immediate consumption needs are met, other valued activities are pursued – lying around, story telling and so on. Although this alternative socio-logic is often depicted as quite exotic, *cold thinking* (following Lévi-Strauss) and fundamentally and qualitatively distinguished from *scientific thinking*, that logic is hardly so esoteric. So-called 'just in time' (JIT) or 'Toyota production design' (TPD) for industrial manufacture, for example, has strong similarities with *forest thinking*.

From the perspective of photographic representation, however, the system does not reveal itself (except in diagrammatic form, which makes an image redundant). An extractive act per se is certainly representable as an image and there are diverse examples of these in the literature. Among the most common are fishing with the use of poison (*timbó, barbasco*), rubber tapping (represented in the current context in the Historical photographs category), and gathering dye plants, but these are iconic and reductive versions of extractivism[50] that tend not to reveal opportunistic extraction as everyday production as ordinary (or extraordinary) as 'going to the office'.

Figure 6.25 Extracting *caucho*. H. C. Pearson 1911.

Many of the ambiguities relating to distinctions between leisure and ritual (and labour, at times) as appropriate labels for the content of images in pre-capitalist/non-valourized/non-market/tribal[51] settings are widely understood to derive from the imposition of historically inappropriate criteria – e.g., 'factory time' in Thompson's (1967) celebrated essay.

In view of the received wisdom that Amazonian Indian societies as a whole display elaborate ritual, mythical, and symbolic structures while being technologically rudimentary and sociopolitically undeveloped, it is not surprising that images of ritual life should feature as prominently as they do. It is surprising, however, that they aren't more prominent – not only because of the relatively greater time often available, but also because of the volume of documentation of material culture artefacts that attests to the high cultural profile of such activities. Much is no doubt excluded from photographic consideration because of the kind of embeddedness characteristic of such pre-modernity (e.g., many forms of customary, symbolic/ritualistic activity associated with – and hence hidden within – mundane horticultural, gathering, and hunting activities), but much is also no doubt necessarily excluded because it is part of interior life expressible only verbally or in ways that do not lend themselves to vivid, imagistic portrayal. Basso's (1973, 1985, 1987, 1995, but especially 1985 and 1995) extensive documentation and analysis of Kalapalo oral and musical traditions does have an imagistic complement, but it is evident that much of the material simply can't be meaningfully expressed or illustrated by photographs.[52] Similarly, Lévi-Strauss's (1970, 1973, 1978, 1981) vast *Mythologiques* – four volumes running to 2,196 pages of text with a mere four photographic/ ethnographic images – offers a panoramic view of a continental, mythic universe with no great potential for photographic representation.[53]

Generally speaking, in light of the performative aspects of the village-level rituals represented photographically in the monograph set, it is not unexpected that the images offer, at best, only fleeting insight,[54] in contrast with journalistic and coffee-table accounts.

What may be significant is how irrelevant the presence or absence of ethnographic photographs is when it comes to complementing or detracting from a monograph's central thesis. That certain kinds of social acts do not lend themselves to photographic representation explains much of the absence, but the question of what is revealed in illustrated monographs remains moot.

The ethno-photographic record for Amazonia does not lend itself to direct critique for it has not explicitly been a major part of the research project. What is available is an almost inadvertent record unsystematically attached to the extensive textual accounts. Abstracted from texts within

Figure 6.26 Bates at wedding. H. Bates 1892.

Figure 6.27 Huitoto dance II. S. Paternoster 1913.

which the images are embedded, the collection provides an uneven glimpse at various aspects of anthropological research over the past hundred years or so.

The dominant images that emerge – the focal images – indicate little of the subtleties of analysis that characterize the texts that they illustrate. Rather, they function in an iconic way as snapshots that capture the rough, general sense, and in this respect they sometimes enhance the texts in an illustrative sense, but equally often seem like crude, reductionist renderings. This reductionist rendering, however, is not necessarily distorting; rather, it may show very accurately the precarious (and often appalling) state in which Indians carry on. The reductionist rendering does have a distorting effect, though, in its portrayal of Indian typicality. Because these Indian subjects are anthropological subjects, their portrayal carries with it the connotation that this is Indianness in its pure, relatively untampered-with form (non-native dress and the like aside), yet the degree to which modern Indians accurately represent their forebears is by no means certain.

While questions about how accurately we can read from the ethnographic record onto the historical and prehistoric record are subjects of intense dispute, scepticism about such a relationship hardly challenges the integrity of those Indians who have managed to persist into the 21st century. What is called into question, however, is the way in which uncertain anthropological knowledge functions outside the professional arena, particularly with respect to the validation inadvertently provided to pernicious beliefs about native peoples. While there may be debate within anthropology about caricature, stereotype, and the fictions entailed in the notion of the 'ethnographic present', outside the field there is much less tolerance or interest. In feature film portrayals – the subject of the next chapter – one encounters a very highly polished form of the stereotype/cliché of the Amazonian Indian, one arguably far more influential than any rigorous anthropological rendering.

Notes

1 Although an important subset comprises those historical images deemed relevant to the 'ethnographic present'.
2 See Carroll's (2003) criticism of 'film theory' for similar reservations.
3 Although Carroll is talking about moving images, the observations with respect to the 'theorizing' approaches within film criticism are consistent with respect to photography in view of his compelling argument that claims for 'medium-specificity' do not hold up. For a discussion, see Carroll (2003), especially Chapters 8 and 14.
4 In fact, of the 140 monographs considered here, only four include grooming photographs (a total of five images out of 2,509).
5 While there is general agreement that the total population of indigenous peoples prior to conquest was much higher than earlier (until ca. 1970) thought, and that the demographic collapse was precipitous, little detail is known.
6 For an instructive example from North America, see Philbrick (2006).
7 Lederman (2005) gently and perceptively frames the conflict in terms of the recurrent 'two cultures' debate of C. P. Snow. While the contrast between 'interpretivists' and 'positivists' is acknowledged as a crude rendition of factionalism within anthropology, it is also acknowledged as a frequently adequate evocation of the tenor and tone of debate.
8 This volume is not being singled out; it is simply a recent and articulate expression of what is, as the volume itself repeatedly reveals, a long-standing discussion/dispute.
9 Outside anthropology, Edward Tufte (1990, 1992, 1997) and Franco Moretti (1998, 2005) provide, in different ways, compelling visual examples that counter the unnecessarily rigid 'two cultures' views that pervade much current anthropological discussion. Tufte's elegant books and arguments impress even the numerophobic of the superiority of thoughtful and provocative displays of quantitative information, and Moretti models literary phenomena in ways that force attention to sociohistorical phenomena whose seemingly defiant anti-literary implications in fact enhance literary analysis and appreciation.
10 A large number of the images in Rondon (1953a) are actually frame grabs from the cinematic footage of Reis, which probably accounts for the relatively large number of 'observational' images in the collection.
11 Material culture photographs have not been counted; nor have landscapes, aerial photographs, or river scenes without people. Further comments on selection criteria follow in each section.
12 These questions pertain more to the photographer than the subjects. From the latter's point of view, the whole 'imaging' exercise may be nonsensical and elicit nothing more than a black hole in terms of anthropological 'reflexivity'.

13 This is presumably part of Faris's (2003) objection to some (all?) of Curtis's images. What is captured is a performance measured for the occasion, although it is hard to see what a 'true' representation would be.

14 In much the same way that the three-minute length of a radio pop song is a legacy of early limits on how much information could be contained on a ten-inch shellac record.

15 And given an implicit or explicit 'collecting' brief, they also contain a larger number of material culture images.

16 While this set is not exhaustive, it is representative. The works cited are drawn from public collections in various London libraries including those of the constituent colleges of the University of London, University of London Senate House Library, the MA collection of the Institute for the Study of the Americas, the Wellcome Library, the British Library, and the British Museum Anthropology Reading Room (Museum of Mankind).

17 Although it may be objected that some of these museum publications do not neatly match a 'single author, bound ethnographic monograph' label, they are counted as such on the grounds that they represent early examples of scientific ethnography, had an undoubted influence, and formally matched the subsequent free-standing monographs.

18 In both Wagley (1977) and Kensinger (1995), the monographs are based on return visits and include photographic documentation from widely spaced fieldwork. Taussig (1987) uses a large number of others' historic photographs. Lizot (1985) has a relatively large number of photographs, but the total number is not distorted by a high frequency in any particular category.

19 There is duplication of photographs in several of Chagnon's publications, but even discounting that, his use of photographs tends toward the higher end. Chagnon (1974) is second only to Crocker and Crocker (1990) – 197 and 273 photographs, respectively.

20 The text is by Marcus Colchester, a regional expert.

21 Chagnon (1983 [1968]) is said to be the most widely read anthropological monograph and its public impact can hardly be doubted (precisely how is unknown), but it functions in the public sphere as an example of anthropological investigation. *Tristes Tropiques*, by contrast, far from being a straightforward monograph, is a text claimed by both academic anthropology and – in the public sphere – as a literary icon. Although the text in different editions remains the same, the number of photographs varies considerably – the first English-language edition including 22, the first French edition including 58.

22 See also the photographs of one of Lévi-Strauss's companions on his field trips, Faria de Castro (2001).

23 There are widely recognized super-ordinate groupings – linguistic families being one of the longest established – but rapid and early demographic collapse and the fragmentary effects of subsequent centuries of persecution lend support to the view that the search for meaningful conceptions of 'pan-Amazonia' lie in prehistory. Against this are claims for an embracing, native notion of conviviality (Overing 2000). Also see Gregor and Tuzin (1998).

24 See Ramos (1998) for a discussion of negative images of Brazilian Indians.

25 The exceptions being Chagnon (1974), as well as the Rondon volumes, which contain a great number of portraits. In terms of portraiture of Native American peoples, however, there is nothing that approaches Curtis (2003).

26 The *candirú* is the ne plus ultra/de facto phallocentrist icon of Amazonian travel writers.

27 Of which 'carrying capacity' is an associated concept.

28 Payakan, a celebrated representative of Kayapó interests, was prosecuted and persecuted in the early 1990s for the alleged rape of a 'white virgin'. Vilified in the national press (Véja 1992), Payakan's political power was greatly reduced. See Ramos (2001) for a broad analysis.

29 Altamira is an Amazonian town (in the state of Pará) that was the site, in 1989, of an Indian protest against the proposed construction of a hydroelectric complex that would have flooded indigenous territory. The event provided much international media coverage. A version of the project has been revived under the name Belo Monte (Beautiful Mountain) without as yet attracting the earlier notoriety (but see Turner 2006).

30 *Mestiço* – or some variant – is the usual depiction. It results, in the case of Indians and anyone else, in being defined negatively as something other than some putative, idealized, 'pure' racial and cultural type – which is to say, like no human yet encountered.

31 The photograph-free *From the Milk River* (C. Hugh-Jones 1979) is unique in employing extensive, effective, and integral hand-drawn diagrams that achieve a level of informative visual representation exceeding that of many photographic image-illustrated volumes.

32 In its most crass form an implausible combination of sun, sea, sand, sex, piranha, Indian, Sugar Loaf, jaguar, and *caipirinha.*

33 The best known, Putumayo, is oddly named in celebration of cultural difference.

34 The degree to which better informed commentary on Amazonia – which includes, of course, extensive use of images – has had any significant effect on mitigating, much less preventing, plunder is taken up later. There is little basis for optimism.

35 These have not been counted, in museum publications or any others.

36 This seems to be the recommendation of *Notes and Queries* (1951), for instance.

37 Note intruding foot, right centre of picture.

38 There are exceptions – Davi Yanomami, Raoni, Mario Juruna, Payakan, Krenak – but they are more analogous to Russell Means and Dennis Banks than Hiawatha.

39 By the time he began, of course, the number of Indians and the number of Indian groups had already been vastly reduced, at least by 50 per cent of the pre-conquest numbers. His patrons included Theodore Roosevelt who, thirty years before becoming involved with Curtis, had written that the Indian was a 'lazy, dirty drunken beggar, whom the . . . frontiersman despised and yet whom they feared; for the squalid contemptible creature might at any moment be transformed into a foe whose like was not to be found in all the wide world for ferocity, cunning, and bloodthirsty cruelty' (quoted in Adam 2003:15).

40 See Bellos (2000) on Sidney Possuelo, FUNAI agent and foremost Brazilian Indian contacter. Hemming (2003) includes a photograph of members of the Zo'e group, contacted ca. 1989 (plate 61), but as in all such cases there is dispute about who first contacted them and when (Hemming 2003:404–6).

41 'Tribe' is widely recognized as a highly problematic category. Often, from a tribe member's point of view, there are 'the people' (us) and the disparaged rest.

42 Of which there is an increasing number. A new form of 'the Indian problem' in Brazil is the emergence of previously unrecognized Indians, in the Northeast for instance (see Warren 2001).

43 In *World Music* terms, for example, 'Malian', 'West African', and 'African' may effectively be synonyms.

44 This is an open and continuing area of discussion. Even those sceptics (in whose ranks Meggers continues to figure prominently) would have difficulty in confidently dismissing as irrelevant the material uncovered to date. Minimally, they would reasonably concede that the typicality of contemporary hunter/gatherer level societies – whose intrinsic sociocultural impoverishment is attributed to an unforgiving humid neo-tropical environment – is challenged. Many would go further than this now (merely challenging typicality) but the archaeological record is still slight. The more that is revealed, however, the less plausible becomes the received hunter-gatherer wisdom.

45 There are well-known problems with applying the Labour/Leisure distinction in pre-capitalist settings, and these are compounded – or further revealed – when Ritual is introduced.

46 Ethnobotanical literature is much better illustrated, Schultes's (1988) being a prime example.

47 The question of validity of ethnographic documentation is a tense issue. From the perspective of other nominally cognate fields (psychology, for instance), the validation of ethnographic evidence is often simply unachievable and much of what is presented as evidence may be dismissed by others as untestable opinion. Controversies in which questions over ethnographic evidence have garnered wider audiences include Casteneda (1968); see also Silverman (1975), Freeman (1983) on Mead, Nance (1975) on the 'Tasady', and Donner (1982).

48 An Amazonian example in which such questions of evidence come to the fore is provided in the dispute between Parker (1992) and Posey (1992) over the extent to which *apêtes* (Kayapó forest islands) are anthropogenic. The contrast between their two positions may not be as great as the sharp tone of their disagreements suggests, but much of the evidence upon which their respective claims are based is simply not available – the botanical specimens having been lost in one case, sterile in the other.

49 Typically more than a suburban federal employee would regard as appropriate. The current president of FUNAI has endorsed the view that the demarcation of Indian land should be scaled back (COIAB 2006), as has senior politician Helio Jaguaribe on a regular basis.

50 For a sustained analysis of extractivism and its particularly Amazonian manifestations, see Bunker (1985). On the ineluctability of extractivism and its departures from normative economic calculation, see Peters, Gentry, and Mendelsohn (1989).

51 I use all three adjectives simply to indicate a broad distinction between types of societies in which the division of labour is (typically) based only on criteria of gender and age and those with class structures, and because the capitalist/ non-capitalist distinction permits the inference that the moral economy is somehow excluded under capitalism.

52 Especially in the early years of photography (and cinema) in Brazil, popular religions were a key subject (see Monte-Mor and Parente 1994; Souza Martins 2001) in much the same way that *carnaval* now has iconic significance.

53 See Prosser (2005) for a discussion of Lévi-Strauss' re-evaluation of the place of photography between *Tristes Tropiques* and *Saudades*.

54 Secrecy and nighttime occurrence are other relevant factors. It is noteworthy that many (most?) feature films involving portrayals of Amazonian Indians include a scene of hallucinogen taking in order to provide an 'image' of interior, religious life. See, for example, *The Emerald Forest* (Boorman 1985b), *Relic* (Hyams 1996), *At Play in the Fields of the Lord* (Babenco 1991).

7

Amazonia on Screen: Building a Lost World

Figure 7.1

Amazonia has provided the setting for, and crucial elements and themes of, a number of feature films of varying ambition and quality. They draw on the same historical documents as those that form the backdrop for anthropological investigation. These include Henry Hoyt's *The Lost World* (2001 [1925]), based on the Conan Doyle (1912) novel (noteworthy as well for its animated sequences of dinosaurs crossing Tower Bridge), which has undergone geographical displacement (to West Africa, for example; Bond 1992a, 1992b)[1] as well as modernization (genomic technology in *Jurassic Park*, Spielberg 1993). It also has an affiliation with the Cold War era space race (*The Creature from the Black Lagoon*, Arnold 1954). In recent decades, Amazonia has been employed in works of greater literary and historical ambition (*The Emerald Forest*, Boorman 1985b; *Aguirre: Wrath of God*, Herzog 1972).

Building a World in Amazonia

The Lost World (Hoyt 2001 [1925])
The Lost World (Bond 1992a)
Return to the Lost World (Bond 1992b)
The Lost World (Orme 2002)
Aguirre: Wrath of God (Herzog 1972)
The Mission (Joffe 1986)
At Play in the Fields of the Lord (Babenco 1991)
The Emerald Forest (Boorman 1985b)
End of the Spear (Hanon 2006)
Medicine Man (McTiernan 1992)
Fire on the Amazon (Llosa 1991)
The Relic (Hyams 1996)
The Creature from the Black Lagoon (Arnold 1954)
Anaconda (Llosa 1997)
Piranha (Dante 1978)[2]

Excluded from more than mention here are a number of marginal films in which the presence of Amazonian themes provides little beyond an excuse for nudity (mainly female) and the sort of violence that gives proper cannibalism a bad name.[3] Although there may be direct Amazonian reference in these films, location and evil native are often generically tropical. The fact that the value of precise or accurate knowledge about such details as geographical setting may rise and fall arbitrarily is also revealed in this excerpt from a review of a Lenzi film.

> Lenzi directs with a considerable degree of verisimilitude. The Thai location and travelogue footage looks authentic – there is no doubt that the toothless and unadorned natives are the real deal. And Lenzi includes little anthropological snapshots – the bleeding of snake venom and dipping of arrowheads in it to make poison arrows – that have a considerable degree of credibility. One has no idea to what extent the film is anthropologically correct or not, but it has the definite ring of authenticity about it. (Scheib 2002)

Deep River Savages/Man from Deep River is one of the earliest examples of the tropical/cannibalism/gore thriller and probably has more in the way of 'anthropological content' than many of its successors. *Cannibal Holocaust* (Deodato 1980) ('four documentary filmmakers disappear in the jungle of South America while shooting a film about cannibalism'),[4] revels in the cannibalism + sex pairing that characterizes many of the Amazonian-tinged films available later. These include Lenzi's (1981) *Cannibal Ferox* and (1986) *Eaten Alive.*

Cannibalism encounters more orthodox branding exercises in films such as *Emmanuelle and the Last Cannibal* (D'Amato 1984) and also veers into candid farce in *Cannibal Girls* (Reitman 1973).

Many of the above-mentioned films belong to genres in which violence, humiliation, and diverse anti-human activities and sentiments are extolled and celebrated, yet they do draw upon a repertoire of Amazonia-related images that overlaps with more mainstream culture products. The main difference between this set of films and those to be looked at more carefully is that the former diffuse the stereotypes/clichés, distracted as they are by content for which the settings and tropical themes appear mere arbitrary dressing. In addition, their purpose – to non-enthusiasts, for example – is persistently contradictory, at loose in the world of faction. The *Amazonia: The Catherine Miles Story* (Gariazzo 1985) image at the head of this chapter, for instance, includes a strapline – 'Based on a shocking true story of inhumanity!' – whose (elemental) facticity is presumably irrelevant to those drawn by the praise blurb printed directly above it: 'This is pure unadulterated exploitation. The blood flows freely and the clothes drop often' (Efilmcritic.com).

While relegation of exploitation fodder to the margins may seem warranted, mainstream films also are subject to similar caveats with respect to the seriousness with which documentary material is employed accurately. Like *Amazonia: The Catherine Miles Story* (aka *Captive Women 7: The White Slave* and *Forest Slave*), Boorman's very respectable (1985b) *The Emerald Forest* is described by its makers as 'based on a true story'.[5] Both stories draw on a legacy of documented 'kidnappings' of which Biocca (1970) is one of the more widely recognized, credible accounts, yet the infrequency of such events – and the erroneous analogy with highly demonized kidnap-for-ransom – means nothing in the face of the propulsive power of the folk tale of white-child-or-nubile-kidnapped-by-Indian.[6] Kidnapping and slave raiding among Indian groups themselves is widely reported, but it is not known to what degree – if at all – Indian recruitment through kidnapping is a response to the parlous demographic circumstances in which Indians have found themselves post-conquest or the degree to which it reflects features of pre-colonial societies as well. From a contemporary perspective, the practice of 'kidnapping' (and other modes of recruitment of new members) suitably reinforces the image of Indian society as a fragile enterprise, dangerously close to absorption back into nature/green hell.

The Lost World

Henry Hoyt's (2001 [1925])[7] cinematic version of Conan Doyle's (1912) novel *The Lost World* adheres closely to the text, itself derived from explorer/naturalist/ethnographer Im Thurn's account of his team's ascent of Venezuela's Mount Roraima (made public in a report read to the British Association meeting in Aberdeen in 1885). It is Conan Doyle's version of the lost world atop Mount Roraima that has endured, whereas Im Thurn's last book in print appears to have been a Dover reprint (1969) of his 1883 *Among the Indians of Guiana: Being Sketches Chiefly Anthropologic from the Interior of British Guiana.* Mount Roraima itself continues mainly to attract the attention of climbers while the fictional *Lost World* has continued to mutate, appearing in updated Darwinian form as a site for genomic mischief (Spielberg's 1993 *Jurassic Park* and 1997 *The Lost World: Jurassic Park II*) and again as historic costume drama updated to reflect (mildly) a new conservationist mentality (Orme 2002).[8]

There have also been a television series based on the novel and cinematic reprises (including shifts of scene to West Africa and Siberia), but most of the fundamentals are unchanged. Following is a summary.

> Professor Challenger has returned from an expedition to South America where he claims to have discovered a lost land where dinosaurs are still to be found. Ridiculed by the scientific establishment (represented by such bodies as the Royal Geographical Society and the Royal Anthropological Institute of England and Wales), Challenger manages to assemble a team to reinvestigate. This includes a journalist – Ed Malone, in whose voice the story is told, a sceptical scientist – Professor Summerlee, and a gentleman explorer – Lord John Roxton. In the course of the investigation of the jungle plateau (following betrayal by a *mestiço* guide with a grudge) the explorers encounter dinosaurs as well as two primate species, hostile 'Ape-men' and sympathetic Indian-like people who ultimately aid in their escape from the mesa. Upon returning to London they have one pre-historic specimen (a boxed pterodactyl) to substantiate their claims (which are accepted). The narrator, Malone, has lost his fiancée to an accountant and Roxton has – unbeknownst to the others – procured a diamond the value of which he shares with his colleagues. (The four explorers are re-assembled for a non-Amazonian adventure in Conan Doyle's [1913] *The Poison Belt.*)

As Hoyt's film version of *The Lost World* is silent, many subtleties of speech are lost in the subtitled text, but it is clear from the outset that the film does not shirk its responsibility to stereotype. A London newspaper, threatened by a suit from Professor Challenger over ridicule of his claim that dinosaurs still exist in South America, characterizes him as 'insane' (the mad scientist). The cub reporter ordered to cover Challenger's press conference at the Zoological Society is ambitious and seeks opportunity for career advancement through a dangerous assignment.[9] Lord Roxton, examining a dinosaur skeleton in the great hall of the Zoological Society, observes to Malone that '[t]he back country of the Amazon contains over fifty thousand miles of unexplored water-ways. Who can say what may be living in that jungle – as vast as all Europe'. The accompanying scientist, coleopterist Sumerlee, is of course 'eminent'. Challenger – bearded and fierce – responds to ridicule ('Bring on your mastdadons, bring on your mammoths') by questioning whether any of the 'spineless worms' in the largely student audience is brave enough to accompany him into 'trackless jungles' replete with 'monsters', and in this setting 'the lost world' is first mentioned. The premise for the expedition is a drawing of a brontosaurus/apatosaurus contained in the diary of the eyewitness daughter of a presumed dead/lost explorer.

A newspaper headline announces that 'Explorers reach last outpost of civilization', a fact confirmed by the screen appearance of a canoe, an Indian on a river bank, a jaguar, a snake, a monkey, a sloth, spectacled bears, ape-men, a chimpanzee, a pterodactyl (with peccary prey), brontosaurus/apatosaurus, allosaurus, tyrannosaurus, triceratops (plus baby), stegosaurus.

Escape from the mesa blocked by a dinosaur's removal of the access bridge, the expedition has to resort to a pet monkey's willingness to ascend the sheer wall bearing a rope ladder, supervised by a blacked-up retainer, suitably accented: 'Jock goin be mighty lonesome down here without Miss Paula – he climb dat big rock dis mo'nin' to git to her – he cain't bear dat girl outen his sight!').[10] A specimen brontosaurus is crated and shipped to London to provide evidence for Challenger's claims, but it escapes while being unloaded from the boat. Tower Bridge is not capable of bearing its weight, and while crossing, the brontosaurus crashes through to the River Thames and is last seen swimming away.

The Lost World has considerable form as a tropical ur-text and the Hoyt movie version projects elemental features that continue to find expression in public sphere representations. Im Thurn himself embodied a number of colonial ambitions: exploration, natural history, ethnography (in Amazonia and elsewhere). That the folklorically, iconic explorer endures as Colonel Fawcett rather than Im Thurn is one indication of the extent to which a mythologized Amazonia seems more apprehendable than a prosaic one.[11] Although there is considerable dramatic content and in some senses a complicated social landscape in *The Lost World*, the emphasis is on examples of an exaggerated natural landscape and its denizens. In terms of the former, for instance, there is the geology and geophysical setting of Mount Roraima itself, the 'fifty thousand miles of unexplored water-ways', and the allegedly threatening humid atmosphere. In terms of the latter, the distortions provided by dinosaurs lie not only in the fantastical idea that megafauna ('Bring on your mastodons' cried the student hecklers at the Zoological Society) still existed, but also in the idea that Amazonia has much in the way of megafauna. The tapir (*t. terrestris*) is not a particularly small animal, but as megafauna go, it is not a compelling specimen. Jaguars, peccary, various species of fish, caiman, harpy eagle, manatee, anaconda, and dolphins pretty much exhaust the large animal menagerie. The search for 'lost' animals, however, continues – as does the search for 'lost' tribes.

Figure 7.2[12] Giant ground sloth (Argentinian postage stamp).

Field researchers still function under the mantle of 'the challenge of the tropics',[13] unwittingly bearing heroic postures while simultaneously allied with diverse ideological and technical dispositions (none of which intrinsically demands intrepid explorer apparatus). 'The challenge', as employed by some nationalist enthusiasts for instance, is little more than a declaration that Brazil – 'the sleeping giant'[14] – will pursue the frontier colonization strategy as eagerly and brutishly as North Americans did. For Brazilian military officers since the time of Rondon, Amazonia has – in the absence of many overseas opportunities – been an important locale for career development.

The anthropological project, while successfully and substantively seeking to distance itself from the explorer idiom, is still obliged to share quite a lot with it as a consequence of the implacability and wide general acceptance of key conceits about the tropics (and particularly the pathologies of the tropics; see Blaut 1993; Garfield 2002; Stepan 2001). This partial acquiescence to the intrepid explorer mode is reinforced by the highly individualized character of most ethnographic research; collaborative or team-oriented efforts such as the Maybury-Lewis-directed Harvard project (Maybury-Lewis 1979) are unusual and most Amazonian ethnography has been single authored. Additionally, the ascendant research programs in Amazonia following the Transamazon assault have had an applied character at odds with traditional ethnographic styles of research. Research programs addressing such notions as biodiversity, short nutrient cycling, atmospheric recycling, and the like function at a scale that exceeds the 'many Amazonias' orientation that persistently casts the ethnographer in sole-operator, heroic mode.

One effect of the coexistence of these miscalibrated Amazonias – the detailed ethnographic, the grand biological, the public sphere mythological, and so on – is an inconsistency of scale of representation that permits and perhaps encourages caricature. It makes possible, for example, the transposition of the 'lost world' tale to West Africa – Bond's (1992a) *The Lost World* and (1992b) *Return to the Lost World* – without much loss of coherence. The main characters are constructed around the familiar stereotypes – loose-cannon scientist, sober scientist, ambitious writer, cynical adventurer, etc. – augmented by variants of 'local peoples'. As in Conan Doyle's novel, in the West African lost world, there is a distinction drawn between authentic natives and others (men on the run from the law, an 'odious collection of gold prospectors'), sentiments not dissimilar from those expressed by Im Thurn's contemporary Enock (1907) when he bemoans the polluting effects of racial mixing in South America; and this West African version of the story re-inserts the original betrayal of Challenger by a half-caste (whose Indian companion, in the novel, remained loyal to Challenger).

A modern twist is revealed in the acknowledgement of a new version of precious native medicine pioneered, among other places, in Amazonia. While there are long traditions – both reputable and less so – acknowledging and venerating folk medicines of various sorts, the fetishization of 'jungle cures' has shifted from the margins to centre stage (see Plotkin 1993), especially with the prospect of patenting newly discovered alkaloids in the wake of widely aired threats to biodiversity.[15] In the Bond/West African version, an adolescent pterodactyl is cured by expedition members using a local plant remedy. 'It's a miracle', says one. 'No, just good science', says his companion. In the same film, jungle pharmacology is also employed when the pulp of a forest fruit is used to repel a carnivorous dinosaur, an act that reinforces the repeated distinctions made between herbivorous (good) and carnivorous (bad) megafauna. And there is a new ideological layer: the scientist who uses plants to cure the dinosaur is pleased at the confirmation of a theory; his companion photographer chides him, 'That's all you think about, your theory, while this poor animal is suffering'. The non-period animal welfare theme recurs in the closing scenes of the film when the evidence brought back from the Lost World – Percy the Pterodactyl – is confined as an exhibit in the London Zoo, only to be surreptitiously released by his captors when he is diagnosed as depressed.

Other ideological/cultural refits are also evident in the new *Lost World* versions, noteworthy among which are the *mise en scène* use of cameras to provide evidence to substantiate contested eyewitness accounts. Although the natives are credited with having moved on from direct cannibalism to cannibalism-at-a-distance (i.e., feeding enemy humans to dinosaurs by way of placating them), they are still foolish enough to be distracted by such 'modern' gimmicks/inventions as hot air balloons. In a move away from the original *Lost World's* association between evil/pre-humanness (through the agency of the so-called 'Ape-men') and virtue/atavistic-humanness (the helpful plateau Indians), the new *Lost World* employs two categories of humans, good and bad Indians – later used to great effect in *The Emerald Forest*.[16] The association between evil and pre- or non-humanness comes to be consigned to fantasy and science fiction (as in *The Creature from the Black Lagoon*, for instance).

Return to the Lost World (Bond 1992b), also set in West Africa, retains little of the lost plateau premise of the Conan Doyle original, yet has a strong Amazonian link in the form of flesh-eating, piranha-like fish. The antagonists in this film are insensitive oil explorers rather than truculent natives, and like the animal rights-aware companion movie (Bond 1992a), includes a topical ideological update in the form of admonitions to save remote peoples who are unique and should be left alone.

The original *Lost World*, cultivated in the image of Im Thurn's pre-professional anthropological investigations, exploits in unsubtle fashion a number of elements of received wisdom about remote, tropical peoples and settings, but there is little occasion for mistaking scientific for entertaining ambitions. In one crucial respect, however, there is a vital similarity between the two genres. The fictional narrative of *The Lost World* requires a familiar kind of suspension of belief: it is storytelling, after all; the ethnographic tale, however much ostensibly pitched within a positivistic, evidence-based framework, typically requires another kind of suspension of belief with respect to the plausibility of the ethnographic present. That is to say that the representation of the social life of the anthropological subjects takes place not in historical time, but in suspended historical time. In the generic 'lost world', the familiar world almost always becomes 'outside', as in 'we've lost touch with the outside world'. In the generic ethnographic world, the ethnographic present achieves a similar effect. The real, nonfictional life is abstracted from its historical dimension and becomes – story-like – timeless.

The anthropology (or, perhaps better, incipient ethnographic sensibility) from which Conan Doyle's *Lost World* was drawn was a transitional form, Victorian anthropology at the edge of scientific or modern anthropology. International – especially European and North American – interest in the region was simultaneously undergoing a shift as the region's long-standing role as near-unique supplier of rubber to foreign industry abruptly disappeared. The subsequent period (roughly from 1915 until 1970), widely characterized as one of economic stagnation and retreat from the global economy, was the era during which modern anthropology laid claim to an important interlocutory role. While a revised anthropological representation and interpretation of Amazonia would, over the next century, result in an authoritative literature in which Amazonian subjects took precedence over an erstatz, mythologized, and folklorical Amazonia, that literature has not fully displaced cardinal features of the prior green hell. These features include caricatures of Amazonian peoples, exotic and/or unusual flora and fauna, cannibalism (or allusions to), and Amazon (women) warriors, as well as geophysical and climatological peculiarities.

While the exploitation of such imagery may not seem surprising in films candidly presented as example of entertainment/exploitation genres, they are no less prominent – whether warranted or not – in serious films. In *The Mission* (Joffe 1986), for example, the presence of a sloth as a pet provides the same measure of tokenistic, exotic-beast cachet as the cutaways to spiders, jaguars, piranhas, etc. that are ubiquitous in manifestly B-type films. If the *Lost World* novel (1912) and film (1925) provided the baseline panoramic setting for subsequent cinematic portrayals, both serious and genre Amazonian films draw upon the same set of image props to establish and reinforce received notions of the exotic peculiarities of the region; and anthropological narrative, far from standing alone or outside such renditions, is also part of the process of reinforcement.

Films in the Setting of Amazonia

The sets of films ('serious' and 'exploitation/B-film') discussed below are not comprehensive, but they are representative. In the first set are feature film productions (primarily U.S. in production/origin) that are historical reconstructions (*Aguirre: Wrath of God,* Herzog 1972; *The Mission,* Joffe 1986; *End of the Spear,* Hanon 2006), literary (*At Play in the Fields of the Lord,* Babenco 1991), or topical/general interest (*The Emerald Forest,* Boorman 1985b; *Medicine Man,* McTiernan 1992; *Fire on the Amazon,* Llosa 1991).

With the exception of *End of the Spear* and partial qualification for *Aguirre*, these serious films are typical, star-driven vehicles.[17]

Aguirre: Wrath of God (Herzog 1972) is acclaimed for its cinematic qualities as well as for the accuracy of its reflection of the historic events upon which it is based.[18] The degree to which the film is perceived as a reasonably faithful or accurate account of events that took place in the 16th century no doubt reflects the relative paucity of primary sources, as well as the sense that the neo-tropical lowlands are intrinsically 'unknowable' in a way that the monumental Andean societies are not. The fact that Lope de Aguirre,[19] the key historical figure, appears to have been more outlandish than Herzog's version (portrayed by Klaus Kinski), or the fact that the careful chronicling of the descent of Amazon by the friar Gaspar de Carvajal actually took place on a prior voyage by Orellana, does not seem to undermine the view that much of the force of the film derives from its jungle/explorer/voyager authenticity.

Following is a synopsis.

> Francicso Pizarro sends a group of explorers Eastward into the jungles of the upper Amazon in search of the rumored El Dorado, the legendary city of gold. Along with practical supplies, a line of Indian slaves move a cannon, a horse, a likeness of the Virgin Mary, and nobleman's chairs containing the wife of the commander, Don Pedro de Ursua (Ruy Guerra) and the daughter of the military captain. He is Don Lope de Aguirre (Klaus Kinski), an intimidating thug who broods and plots mutiny almost from the start. The group intends to claim El Dorado as their own new empire, and has brought along nobility, the clergy, and the women precisely for that purpose. Burdened by their Spanish customs as much as by their unlikely cargo, the group falls prey to the mysteries of the jungle. The river rises without warning and washes away their camp. A third of their soldiers are lost on a raft that becomes caught in a perpetually spinning whirlpool. And unseen Indians are picking off the explorers one by one, with snares and poison darts. When Don Pedro decides to turn back, the possibly insane Aguirre mutinies. Butchering any and all dissenters, the snarling captain continues the expedition further downriver. His megalomaniac plans include breaking away from Spain, and starting a pure dynasty by marrying his own daughter (G. Erickson 2000).

The apparent credibility of the representation of Amazonia available in *Aguirre* confronts many obstacles. During their descent of the eastern slopes of the Andes, the commitment to heavy European dress – including metal helmets and body armour – may be justified (as is the wearing of ponchos and wool hats by Andean slaves), but the maintenance of such taxing costume drama standards once the expedition reaches the less temperate zones in the Amazon valley is not credible. When Canby (1977) writes in his *New York Times* review that the film 'is tactile. One can feel the colors of the jungle and see the heat', this may be the underlying cause of the 'peculiar languor' he identifies in the film. The sedan chairs, the immaculate dress of the female members of the expedition, and the discrepancy between the high degree of threat by Indians and their limited presence all undermine the 'based-on-historic-fact' claims of the film – while at the same time, green hell associations are cultivated (the odd break from arbitrary violence in order to be distracted by and admire a baby sloth; the man traps; the food shortages) and the available historical record is ignored. The actual journey chronicled by Carvajal involved passage through riverbank territories continuously populated – for many kilometres – by Indian settlements (Porro 1996), a rather more striking image than that provided by the few abandoned thatch buildings assaulted by Kinski and crew; yet the authority of the stereotype/cliché prevails: Amazonia at the time of first contact – and presumably, from time immemorial – was inhabited by sparse groups of Indians, technologically and socioculturally rudimentary,[20] armed with potent (if limited) weaponry. *Aguirre*, of course, is a feature film and not a documentary, and its director is obviously under no obligation to adhere to any conventions regarding the reading/translation of history; yet it is the bolstering of the dramatic account with assertions of reliance on the historical record that favours mystification over an account more in line with the facts as known.

Does that mystification have more than trivial consequences? Within the world of film criticism, the merger of fact and mystification appears quite convincing and is sufficient to licence further cultivation of cliché and stereotype. German critic and professor of film studies Petzke (1992) claims that the tale of Aguirre deals with 'possibly the most obsessed group of people in history, the Spanish conquistadors' and that 'a few lines in an old chronicle is all that remains of the historical facts, thus leaving plenty of room for Herzog to employ his imagination and re-arrange the facts.'

The historical facts are more replete than indicated by Petzke but insufficient to dislodge cliché. Herzog's subsequent Amazonian film,[21] *Fitzcarraldo* (1982), provoked in one anonymous critic (Anonymous 6, n.d.) the following compendium of familiar, jungle-related hyperbole: 'the largest drought in history' followed by the 'wildest rainy season in history'; 'a crew member was bitten by a snake with venom so poisonous that cardiac arrest typically followed within seconds [so he] picked up a chain saw and cut off his own foot'; a man paralyzed; another drowned; a cinematographer with a split hand was operated on with no anaesthesia; and 'one of the two camp prostitutes calmed him by pressing his head between her breasts'. And so on.

Herzog, as an independent European filmmaker relatively unaffiliated with/untainted by Hollywood certainties, and an enthusiastic documentary as well as feature film director, carries an authority and argues for a vision that easily overwhelm earnest corrections of the factual record.

From the perspective of both cinema critique and a post-structuralist scepticism about the possibility of ascertaining the denotative meaning of any representations, Herzogian depictions are standard issue, mature examples; yet the very negotiability of 'meaning' in this sense severely under-represents the interests – or meanings – of the depicted subjects and, as is argued here in the case of Amazonians, the dominant images are distorted in ways that seem to grant reproductive rights to the depictions, but not necessarily to the actors/subjects. Green hell is viable, its inhabitants less so.

Recent media depictions of environmental phenomena in Amazonia underscore and enhance this inequality in the weight of received versus approximately accurate images. The widely reported Amazonian drought of 2005 produced dramatic images of stranded canoes and beached fish, yet the impact and significance of 'the drought' was far more complex than what is suggested in such dramatic images, with the many tributaries of the Amazon – such as the Tapajós, for example – producing no such photographable evidence of environmental impact in the region. Following in the grand tradition according to which local particulars fall prey to convenient, externally potent images ('the lungs of the world', for instance) are plausible stand-ins for actuality. The fact that the misspoken 'lungs of the world' expression survives as an iconic reference to 'the dilemmas of Amazonian development' indicates the high level of integration of myth and reality: one could charitably interpret the expression as a shorthand reference to recycling functions of 'the forest', but the analogy hardly survives a glance – unless, of course, you happen to be a rare human who exhales oxygen and takes in CO_2.[22]

Boorman's (1985b) *The Emerald Forest*, although a Hollywood production, shares with *Aguirre* a level of respect and recognition as a serious rather than exploitative Amazonian film.

> Based on a true story, *The Emerald Forest* deals with the mystical power of the Amazon rain forest and the bonds of human love. When the son of an American engineer is kidnapped from a dam site on the edge of the forest, he is taken, spirited away through the layers of civilization, to be raised by the 'invisible people', a tribe of Stone-Age Indians.[23]

This seriousness is enhanced by Boorman's (1985a) publication of a memoir of the making of the film, *Money into Light: The Emerald Forest – A Diary*, the use of Amazonian specialists as production consultants, and an updating of green hell to include the predations of developmentalism.

With the insertion of a modernization subtext into the main story of familial separation, Amazonian forest Indians are cast as organized impediments to the march of civilization, working with the assistance of sympathetic outsiders, key among whom is the father of the kidnapped boy. Father – or *Dadee* as he comes to be known in Indian-speak – directly articulates Indian interests as a result of his son having been integrated into Indian society (roughly fashioned after the Kamaiurá of the upper Xingu). Engineer/*Dadee* seems to speak at least one Indian language well, shows an interest in or affinity with Indians through decorating his Belém home with Indian artefacts, has some knowledge of the untoward environmental effects of the work in which he is involved (hydroelectric dam engineering), and has a wife – *Momee* – who displays similar social consciousness through her work with abandoned/street children in Belém. Additional modernization markers include subplots involving exploitative commercial establishments in the forest (bars, brothels) as well as outside media interest in the fate of the forest Indians (*Dadee* is accompanied on his quest for his son by a cynical European photojournalist).

The tribal matriculation of the kidnapped boy provides a convenient device for illustrating Indian life as lived by *The Invisible People* – as the 'good Indians' of the film are labelled. As the boy matures, he is taken on a trek where he has lessons in forest craft, encounters various jungle/ green hell exemplars (e.g., jaguar, toucan), and comes upon the enemy – *The Fierce People*.[24] *Tomee* undergoes an initiation ceremony in which he becomes a man, ingesting psychotropic snuff, enduring the bites of fire ants (likely drawn from Wayana *tocandira* practice), and finally locating his spirit creature during a vision quest. *The Invisible People* family values are aggressively displayed and *Tomee* subsequently acquires a wife and pays a bride price.

It would be tedious and fruitless to track the ethnographic and factual slips (and hyperbole) committed in the course of Boorman's attempt to establish the authenticity of the depictions, for they are numerous and inevitable and probably irrelevant.[25] As in the case of *Aguirre*, this is not a documentary film, but a feature production in which dramatic force is underwritten by a variant truthfulness to the empirical and historical records. 'Variant truthfulness', though, is highly immune to criticism that suffers the weight of earnestness, pedantry, and nitpicking, yet – as in the case of Herzog's film – the legitimacy/authenticity underpinning the story is propounded by the director, not something only ascribed after the fact by guileless critics. Dramatic overreach of this sort contrasts sharply with Conan Doyle's diffidence with regard to the authenticity of his *Lost World*.

The Emerald Forest's general portrayal of Amazonia in the late 20th century adheres to the stereotype cliché – ensemble and reinforces its credibility as fact-enhanced drama-fiction. It compounds the mystification through its layering of seemingly corroborative material, as in the treatment of the hydroelectric dam. The attention to the construction of this monument implies a heightened sensitivity to 'the realities' of contemporary Amazonia, but actually hinders understanding of the situation on the ground.

The dam depicted in the film exists as Tucuruí, a hydroelectric installation on the Tocantins River, which – as the film suggests – was built despite the very real threats it presented to Indians (and others) whose territory was flooded.[26] The construction project was not a one-time event, but part of a region-wide and long-term strategy of 'national integration' according to which Amazonia is to be exploited for its comparative advantage as site of inexpensive primary resources. The battles with hydroelectric projects in Amazonia (Tucuruí was to have been followed by a project on the Xingu River system) have little addressed social matters as much as gross economic ones – another set of relatively invisible elements in Amazonia – and the depiction of Amazonian conflict as primarily residing at the level of Indians-against-the-state is largely a representation cultivated outside of Brazil – in the minds of moviegoers, say, in New York and London. Although Indian interests have been closely linked with 'environmental' ones during the past two decades, such an equation has barely registered the larger picture; and it transpires that after thirty years of 'careful monitoring' of the effects of the concerted assault on the region and its peoples, much less in the way of environmental or social mitigation has been achieved than might be expected in view of the resources, expertise, and political posturing offered.[27]

The representational adequacy of the situation of the Amazonian Indian in *The Emerald Forest* is not exceptional, but its reinforcement of stereotype defuses whatever insight it claims or is claimed on its behalf. The addition of 'the dilemmas of development' to the repertoire of noble and ignoble savage clichés it invokes merely increases the number and density of grey areas separating the mystified situation from the relatively unadorned situation. What is espoused in *The Emerald Forest* (and this film is hardly alone in that regard) is defense of a fantasy: the Indians depicted are unrealistic; Tucuruí dam still stands and functions; and, in general terms, the assault on Amazonia has been accommodated[28] far more than it has been resisted.

By a generous reading, the claim that the film is 'based on a true story' implies that a dramatic narrative is significantly underpinned by non-fantastical or randomly or deceptively organized elements. Less generously, 'Based on a true story' has no more credibility than a spin doctor's claim that 'the plane returned to earth' is an adequate description of the shooting down of an aircraft. Boorman's (1985a) discussion (in *Money into Light*) of negotiations with his specialist consultants provides insight into the way specialist anthropological knowledge may be transformed into an entertainment resource, then projected into the public domain. While there is a literature on internal anthropological disputes that reach beyond professional audiences, as in the cases of Freeman versus Mead (Freeman 1983) or the Tasady (Nance 1975),[29] Boorman's (1985a) memoir directly reveals not only disputes over evidence and epistemology, but the tunnel vision of an agenda in which credible knowledge about other peoples – conventional anthropological subjects – is so irrelevant as to be as trivial as the colour choice for an iPod case.

Money into Light is not an obvious exploitation/cash-in book. Published by the independent and overtly respectable Faber and Faber in the same year that the film was released, despite its plausible status as a stand-alone memoir-artefact, it still can hardly be separated from the marketing of the film itself. Throughout the text – which among many things is an informative 'behind the scenes' account of modern film financing and production – there is repeated reminder of the importance of ethnographic/factual accuracy, not just in relation to the story ('Based on . . .') but also the back-story. Writing of his visit to the Xingu Indian Park, Boorman says that 'I am embarrassed to know so much about these people. They have been studied in every respect by anthropologists' (1985a:83).

This is a usefully reflective comment by a visitor aware of how strange he is in this context even though he has access to so much documentary, objective (as opposed to experiential) knowledge about these people, yet these 'people' are clearly more his imagined subjects than actual ones. They are the Kamaiurá (or Kamaira in the text; p. 80), but also Mehinaku (p. 84). They are Tupí speakers, but they are also Aruak speakers. They are native to the region, and they are also incomers. It doesn't matter. His professional consultants (an anthropologist and a geographer)

> have been helpful, recommending studies and books, correcting errors and omissions in the script. They are a bit patronizing about my profound experience with the Xingu (sic). They too have witnessed many extraordinary mystic events, but academe would be sceptical of such reports, and they have their reputations as men of science to protect, so these things go unreported for the most part. (1985a:97)

But at least one of them 'feels he must withdraw since he cannot approve of our putting together characteristics of various tribes to make up our own invented one' (1985a:97). The anthropologist declines the credit as 'consultant' (although the geographer does not), but Boorman implies that the reason for severing the association is a reservation about Boorman's vision ('my profound experience') and the meaning he attaches to 'Xingu Indianness', not mere matters of fact and their interpretation.

What survives this encounter between ethnographic knowledge/authority and the demands of cinematic representation, what (in a word) has cultural-ecological fit, is the stereotype/cliché, certainly vividly expressed – and more comprehensively than usual– in *The Emerald Forest*, a kind of Indian and Indian society whose agency and structure are, in Ramos's telling phrase, grounded in hyper-reality rather than reality. While the auteurist protocols (aka 'my profound experience') take the bulk of responsibility, it is likely also the case that the highly collaborative requirements of filmmaking encourage a tendency toward convergence around stereotype/archetype, not least when the starting point for the project is a newspaper clipping (Boorman 1985a:3), an encapsulated story that, to be expanded to feature length, requires bulking up via whatever cultural steroids are at hand.

A different kind of process is evident in the film *At Play in the Fields of the Lord* (Babenco 1991) from the Matthiessen (1965) novel of the same name. In this case, the stereotype/cliché is situated within a more complex narrative, one that does not continuously privilege the Indian-versus-modern-society contrast that prevails in *The Emerald Forest*. In terms of the repertoire of jungle elements, APITFOTL draws on similar cultural resources of ethnographic detail and Western cultural folklore – the shaman who is a jaguar; 'You're in the jungle . . . there is no law'; *ayahuasca* taking; innocent nubiles – but it plays the authenticity claims differently. Instead of being introduced as 'Based on a true story', APITFOTL includes in the closing credits: 'Filmed entirely on location in Amazonia', providing – according to one reviewer (Ebert 1991) – 'those real places, the impenetrable, throbbing jungle on either side of the vast indifferent Amazon'. Although the Indians are not key players as they are in *The Emerald Forest*, and despite the much more realistic depiction of the modern Indians' dilemmas,[30] the possibilities for Indian articulacy are swamped by convention (the stereotype/cliché).[31]

The authenticity quantum available through geographical referent ('filmed entirely on location') is not trivial, but it may be deceptive. APITFOTL was filmed near Belém in estuary outskirts that include a former Pirelli rubber plantation, and workers were recruited locally from scattered settlements. The Belém environs also provided settings for a number of other films including the forgotten *Curucu: Beast of the Amazon* (Siodmak 1956).[32]

Separated by genre, intention, and epoch, *The Emerald Forest* and APITFOTL draw upon familiar Amazonian content and cliché, though marking the shift from untamed land of untamed beasts (and people) to domesticated leisure space, replete with flora and fauna, but largely devoid of local social inscription.

Two films that pursue, in very different ways, the search for the hearts and minds of Amazonians against the jungle backdrop are *The Mission* (Joffe 1986) and *End of the Spear* (Hanon 2006). The former, a costume drama recounting the battle between the Marquess of Pombal and the Jesuits over control of (Guarani) Indians and Indian land in the non-Amazonian south of Brazil, engages a generic jungle background, as though the green hell of the Amazon is the typical landscape of the Brazilian Indian in general. Indians in this film are tokens of paradise (along with sloths, iguanas, birds, waterfalls, marmoset) while the active protagonists are Europeans whose religious hypocrisy is underwritten by power struggle. The role of 'Amazonia/Amazonian Indians' is largely passive.

While *The Mission*'s fictionalized account of the expulsion of the Jesuits from the New World accurately depicts the subordination of religious power to secular, *End of the Spear* (2006) is a more prosaic account of religious labour released by a Christian entertainment company whose evangelical ambitions are hardly disguised.[33] Elisabeth Eliott's (1957) account of the slaying of five midwestern missionaries (one of whom was her husband) in Ecuador is the basis of both *End of the Spear* and the documentary *Through the Gates of Splendor* that preceded it (both directed by Jim Hanon). Wives of the missionaries stayed to live with and convert the Waodani killers of their husbands. Aside from being an evangelical polemic, the film resorts to the same image repertoire as most other Amazonian films mentioned, and this consistency with less religiously laboured accounts underscores the generic character of the repertoire.[34] The Jungian overload of *The Emerald Forest,* the white shoe bohemianism of APITFOTL, the *Upstairs/Downstairs* observationalism of *The Mission,* and the Wal-Mart gospel of *End of the Spear* engage an Amazonia of reliable and predictable qualities.

Amazonia as a B-Film

While a number of the preceding Amazon-related films have received serious critical attention, most films on Amazonian themes fall into various marginal genres that rarely merit evaluation beyond simple acknowledgement or ridicule. Examples of this type range from Hollywood brain candy such as *Anaconda* (Llosa 1997) to cult exploitation thrillers for which the specifically Amazonian content often seems superfluous, such as *Trap Them and Kill Them* (aka *Emmanuelle and the Last Cannibal,* D'Amato 1984) or *Eaten Alive* (Lenzi 1986), yet the recurrent elements are familiar neotropicalist ingredients. Often combined with sex, science, and greed – and frequently hybridized with cannibalism – the Victorian fiction/entertainment of the focal *The Lost World* links in unlikely ways with films such as the graphic *Deep River Savages* (Lenzi 1972), said to be a pioneer of the Italianate cannibal subgenre.[35]

The persistence of a theme of scientific exploration, derived from *The Lost World* (Conan Doyle 1912), reinforces the notion that untapped, unexplored regions such as Amazonia hold great promise for the modern explorer pursuing personal, heroic goals as well as collective, knowledge-advancing ones. Conan Doyle himself was clearly aware of the rising popular, social import of science and science culture, and in Im Thurn's expedition to Mount Roraima found a useful model for fiction-narrative-with-science. Soon after *The Lost World,* in fact, he wrote *The Poison Belt* (1913) in which Professor Challenger and other members of the Lost World expedition progress from a terrestrial to extra-terrestrial context, dealing with an asteroidal threat/drama that prefigures, according to Gibson (1989), 'the peculiarly British form of science fiction, the catastrophe novel'.

In the subtitles of Hoyt's (2001 [1925]) *The Lost World* movie, the word 'science' often appears on the screen[36]: for example, when Challenger asks for 'Volunteers to face death – or worse – for science', and when Malone justifies to his editors the value of the story on 'human interest' grounds as well as 'science'.[37] The heroic posture of the scientist is fully mainstream in the undistinguished *Medicine Man* (McTiernan 1992) and embodied in a more complex division of scientific labour in *Jurassic Park* (Spielberg 1993) and its offspring *The Lost World: Jurassic Park II* (Spielberg 1997) and *Jurassic Park III* (Johnston 2001). The film scientist is highly adaptive. Between the original *The Lost World* and the current, genomically troped[38] derivatives he expresses the prevailing scientific subtexts of different eras. While *Medicine Man* (McTiernan 1992) and *Relic* (Hyams 1996) reflect contemporary developments in the biological sciences, *The Creature from the Black Lagoon* (Arnold 1954) is strongly shaped by Cold War preoccupations with new technologies of space exploration.

Probably best remembered as an innovative stereoscopic film,[39] *The Creature from the Black Lagoon* draws a connection between Amazonian primordialism and unexploited natural secrets that could be revealed through advanced scientific research. A sombre voiceover observes that the record of life is recorded on land through the fossil record, but that the 15-million-year-old record in Amazonia has still not been read. An expedition, prompted by the chance discovery of a fossil hand, enters Amazonia in search of a missing link between life in the water and life on land, and encounters a living human-like amphibian species. Expedition members' interpretations of the significance of this discovery are diverse (commercial possibilities; scientific celebrity; evidence that Amazonia is an evolutionary cul-de-sac, the black lagoon in green hell; basis of an advanced, post-SCUBA[40] breathing system that might be exploited by astronauts), but the film ultimately renders a poor copy of *King Kong's* beauty-and-the-beast message.[41]

Although Amazonia is conceptually represented in a familiar way (an evolutionary lost world), the film lacks much of the normal tropicalist apparatus. No Indians appear, for example,[42] and aside from brief shots of sunning crocodiles and the use of a vegetable stuperificant[43] in an attempt to asphyxiate the unusual amphibian, a visual Amazonia is relatively incidental.

Figure 7.3 U.S. postage stamp.

The Creature from the Black Lagoon prefigures a more secure and technically advanced science than that represented in *The Lost World* through looking glass and test tube, while *Relic* (Hyams 1996) attempts to subsume Amazonian mystery under genetically modified smoke and mirrors.

Relic (Hyams 1996) appeared several years after interest in the fate of Amazonia had found a secure position in terms of general public awareness of neo-tropical environmentalism, the crucial groundbreaking for this having taken place in Rio de Janeiro at the so-called 'Earth Summit' in 1992. The film is not serious in the sense in which that term applies to *Aguirre* and *The Emerald Forest* but is no less obedient to key demands of modern tropicalism, and like the B-class *The Creature from the Black Lagoon*, it features a throwback/primordial/evolutionary mystery.

An anthropologist is seen at night, photographing by firelight. He wears an Indiana Jones hat. Native dancers perform in a stamped earth clearing; leaves are added to a cooking pot; the anthropologist is offered a bowl of the soup to drink and soon becomes agitated, perhaps 'possessed', and experiences a disturbing vision while a costumed Indian crawls menacingly toward him. He whispers 'Kathoga' (eventually revealed as the name of the monster star, the 'Relic') before collapsing in hysterical fear. The Amazon-set opening to the film is just over two minutes in length. Aside from a brief sequence in which crates carrying field materials are loaded onto a boat en route to their Chicago museum destination, the remaining Amazonian content in the film is largely conceptual, though no less adhesive for that.

The beast that has found itself in Chicago depends on a narrow diet, a substance found in the hypothalmous – an esoteric adaptation. This food preference (brains of any species will do) appears related to fungal spores found on Amazonian leaves that have also been conveyed in the packing crates, an error in judgement for which the cultural anthropologist is held responsible by his more 'hard science' colleagues. The details of the putative causal links are unclear, but the message that emerges concerns the mismatch between the dynamics of nature in the jungle and science in the city, and the side plot scheming involved in science funding is repeatedly illustrated, as is disdain for superstition and ill-formed alien beliefs (whose emissaries, anthropologists, are appropriately chastised).

The movie is far too confused for a straightforward 'culture wars' skirmish to emerge, but both cultural interpretation and scientific analysis seem to bear culpability, both being less certain than the human agents imagine. The commentary on Amazonian primitivism is quite clear: there are unfathomable dangers in the forest and they are not easily understood. The evil and danger embodied in the exported Kathoga (the Amazonian monster) make sense within the local jungle context, but set loose abroad, they go out of control.[44] The rationale for urban predation by forest monster is efficiently established within a few minutes, in part because of the historical depth of and familiarity with the prototypical stereotype/cliché (alligator-in-New-York-sewer-system being one of the most familiar).

Anaconda (Llosa 1997) exploits familiar elements,[45] and although the jungle ambience provides a generalized background of exotic fear, the central weight is – in the tradition established by *King Kong* – borne by an animal character. Described by one mainstream reviewer as a 'reptilian version of *Jaws* set in the steaming heart of the Amazon rain forest' (Holden 1997), *Anaconda* distributes its heroism across documentary filmmakers and an anthropologist and demonizes a 'big fierce animal' through exaggeration as well as through an 'evil-genius' exploiter of such beasts. The role of Indians is as fleeting as is the Amazonian setting in *Relic*: the documentarists are in search of a lost tribe, the People of the Mist (the so-called 'Shirishama'), who appear only – and very briefly – at the conclusion of the film. Until that point, they are represented only by word and the unlikely deed of totem manufacture. They – like the Indians in *Relic* and the natives in *Return to the Lost World* – are in the business of forlornly trying to appease natural or supernatural forces that are beyond their control, and their subjugation by these forces is conveniently relieved by the intervention of whites.

If *Anaconda* is a reptilian *Jaws*, *Piranha* (Dante 1978) is a genomic *Jaws*. In a number of the films under consideration, the landscape of green hell provides the backdrop for an appropriately monsterish beast – or, in the case of *The Lost World*, a menagerie – and in these films it is usually science[46] that serves as the beast's antagonist. Although in *Piranha*, science is also relied upon to bring the beast to bay, it also has a more complicated, evil-twin role. The movie opens with the death of two backpackers who have interrupted their walk in the Southern California foothills. Entering a swimming pool in what seems to be an abandoned research facility, they are quickly devoured by piranha. Immediately before their demise, a cinematic/Amazonian reference is provided: just after entering the pool, the boy accuses his companion of biting him on the foot. She turns in the water and replies, 'What? Do I look like the creature from the black lagoon?'

These piranha have not just been transported from Amazonia, but are fish modified by the U.S. Army as an exercise in the war effort in Indochina. Operation Razor Teeth was part of an attempt to destroy the river systems controlled by the North Vietnamese, but the war ended before the modified fish could be deployed and some surviving mutant piranha continued to be experimented upon in the Southern California facility. The piranhas' escape from the pool in the course of the search for the missing backpackers threatens downstream leisure facilities as well as the oceans of the world, and the efforts to block their escape – and world domination – commence with a river descent (by lashed-log raft) reminiscent of Aguirre's voyage.

Of all the films discussed, only in *Relic* is anthropology's role as knowledge guide to the Amazon made explicit. In the rest of the films, including those whose production notes acknowledge anthropological input (such as *The Emerald Forest*), other kinds of white Westerners are the main intermediaries, most often in the capacity of scientist or documentarist. In some recent films, such as *Fire on the Amazon* (1991) and *Medicine Man* (1992), which take environmental politics as the point of entry into the domain of tropical cliché, the central roles occupied by white people represent significant changes in status for both Indians and white interlopers, the former having been upgraded – if only perversely and symbolically – from natural beings (socially relatively unburdened; 'noble savages') to natural resources ('wise forest managers'; holders of 'indigenous knowledge')[47] and the latter shifted across from the scholarly realm (naturalists/explorers) to a more technocratic realm (NGO employees/activists/journalists).

Although these films highlight issues of social justice in a manner not often seen in earlier Amazonian genre films,[48] the new emphasis is hardly subtle and the result is more caricature than added depth. *Fire on the Amazon* (1991), for example, is accurately described in a review as a 'tropical-topical' movie, 'part potboiler, part work of conscience . . . a cheesy but effective drama set against the ecological disaster of South America's disappearing rain forest'.[49] In addition to the expected tropical elements of (in order of appearance) monkeys, snakes, turtles, and parrots, there are also clear-cutting, chainsaws, bulldozers, hardhats, and flamethrowers, as well as the sobering subtitle coda: 'Every day, more than 70,000 acres of rain-forest are destroyed. The loss to humanity and science is incalculable'. The platitudinous foregrounding of 'social awareness' is casually cynical and adds rather than removes layers of mystification.

The Emerald Forest (1985) and *At Play in the Fields of the Lord* (1991), arguably the most serious – and certainly ambitious – of the films under consideration, represent earnest attempts to depict Indians with a degree of ethnographic accuracy.[50] In recent films, however, those whose cumulative access to knowledge of Amazonia and its peoples is greatest, the Indian has been reduced to a largely ornamental/symbolic (and non-speaking, truly spear-carrier) function and screen time has been reduced to a minimum. In *Relic*, the Indian is a crucial part of the authenticating back story (ingestion of *ayahuasca*-like potion by naïve interloper), but after that the native disappears entirely. In *Anaconda*, the Indian appears only in the concluding moments when monstrous nature (the overgrown serpent) has been subdued by outsiders (a mixed ethnos-and-gender A-Team). In the sequence of films commencing with Hoyt's (2001 [1925]) *The Lost World* and concluding (for the moment) with *Anaconda* (1997), the Amazonian Indian moves from being an inhabitant of a 'lost world' to being itself a 'lost world', a representation that in one sense matches the historical record, but which in another sense is an inversion of what has actually happened.

The lost world depicted in the original novel/film of the same name was one that contained living examples of evolutionary precursors – human and non-human - that had somehow evaded the motors of history. As argued by anthropologists claiming allegiance to a variety of otherwise (and to varying degrees) incompatible theoretical dispositions, such human examples occupied self-contained worlds (cultures) that coexisted with and within an historical world. Over time, however, the connotation of the lost world shifts to one of disappearance rather than remoteness or out-of-sightness. The shift in meaning is exemplified in the most celebrated series of ethnographic television productions, Granada Television's *Disappearing World* (1970–93)[51], as well as in a theoretical sea change in the discipline as the anthropological gaze shifted away from its original social scientific/scientific aims and toward a self-conscious, reflexive consideration of its own objects – texts – rather than traditional objects of analysis, the lost/disappearing worlds.

Fire on the Amazon (Llosa 1991) and *Medicine Man* (McTiernan 1992) unsubtly encode this shift. Both are set in a post-exploratory Amazon in which the role of interloper (activist/journalist in one case, scientists in the other) is to domesticate rather than decimate. In the face of crude commercial enterprise, the protagonists of both films aim to conserve aspects of the 'lost world'. The subtext, of course, is that conservation is unfeasible but some sort of mitigation is worth pursuing. What is lost in this 'lost world' is its absolute difference from the conquerors' world. Although there are a few intact elements (the usual cast of animals, including the ubiquitous *candirú*; some Indians; *ayahuasca*; bad weather; and unforgiving geography), what is actually conservable (possibly) has been narrowed down to an object/concept that requires no translation, subtle calibration of different cultural spheres. In *The Medicine Man*, it is the holy grail of green hell: a cure for cancer, the Periwinkle Reprise. In *Fire on the Amazon*, it is soap operatic moral redemption.

Cinematic depictions of Amazonia draw upon a familiar repertoire of themes and elements that, while having undoubted accuracy in various respects, also systematically distort through objectification. This tendency, while neither mysterious nor unique – most of the colonial world is articulated with conqueror cultures in this way – does have effects that are specific and consequential and that cannot be casually elided with those evident elsewhere on the periphery. In the Amazonian case, the specificities of its distortions lie in having been part of a process of global modernization for five hundred years but subject to a particularly haphazard, discontinuous, stop-and-start mode of incorporation – a tropical house destroyed and successively rebuilt by architects with a sense of neither past nor future. One manifestation of this peculiar relationship to the world system to which it has belonged for so long is the habitual reinvention of Amazonia as a frontier, epoch after epoch. In parallel with the disarticulation of the modern world system and modern Amazonia is the oblique relationship that anthropological knowledge has with the public representation of Amazonia and its peoples. Films (and other image artefacts, especially television productions) have a confidence of representational power that is only tangentially related to fact, yet persuasive enough to place specialist critics always on the margins, for the latter command no agenda that challenges the received view.

During the five hundred years that Amazonia has been recognized by non-Amazonians, it has shifted from being one kind of lost world to another. For most of that period, it was lost in the sense that it evaded control and domestication by conquerors – hardly completely, but with enough force to ground the characterization that underpinned the idea of permanent frontier. In the past century, that reading of lost has been joined and challenged by another – namely that in which the region and its peoples pass into memory.

Notes

1 Overall, Africa seems to have been the preferred setting for cinematic jungles as well as those of pulp fiction and comic books.

2 Others, not discussed, include *Green Mansions* (Ferrer 1959); *The Rundown* (Berg 2003); and *Eight Hundred Leagues down the Amazon* (Llosa 1993).

3 These include *Mountain of the Cannibal God* (aka *Slave of the Cannibal God*, Martino 1978); *Emmanuelle and the Last Cannibal* (D'Amato 1984); *Cannibal Apocalypse* (Margheriti 1980); *Jungle Holocaust* (Deodato 1978); *Cannibal Holocaust* (Deodato 1980); *Deep River Savages,* (Lenzi 1972); *Cannibal Ferox* (Lenzi 1981); *Eaten Alive* (Lenzi 1986); and *Cannibal Holocaust II* (Climati 1988).

4 Described by one distributor's reviewer as 'offensive, preposterous garbage. Perfect for fans of rape, animal cruelty, and gratuitous dumpy male frontal nudity' (HK-Flix.com 'Specialty *Is* Our Specialty').

5 Also see the discussion of *End of the Spear* (Hanon 2006) to follow.

6 In the coverage of Paulinho Payakan's 1992 assault case, characteristically great emphasis was placed on the fact that the alleged victim was a white woman (see Turner 2000).

7 In 2001, Lobster Films released a new cut of *The Lost World* based on portions of eight prints (all the original negatives had long been lost). The new cut is substantially longer than the original abridged version. The newly added material does not substantially alter the long-known version but includes a short opening clip of Conan Doyle.

8 In the updated version, Challenger repudiates his discovery of prehistoric life forms in order that the lost world be spared the attention of an hysterical and insensitive public.

9 These broad caricatures are in keeping with the original text. Malone, meeting Lord Roxton for the first time, describes his apartment: 'A dark blue oar crossed with a cherry pink one above his mantelpiece spoke of the old Oxonian and Leander man, while the foils and boxing gloves above and below them were the tools of a man who had won supremacy with each. Like a dado round the room was the jutting line of splendid heavy game heads, the best of their sort from every quarter of the world, with rare white rhinocerous of the Lado Enclave drooping its supercilious lip above them all' (pp. 44–5).

10 There is more than a kernel of *King Kong* in the Paula/monkey relationship. Willis O'Brien was the animator of both *The Lost World* (1925) and *King Kong* (1933).

11 Factual information about Colonel Fawcett's fate is obscure. Im Thurn's activities are well documented and not mysterious.

12 Specimens of the giant sloth – known as *mapinguari* in Brazilian Amazonian folklore – are still being sought, although interest is mainly confined to imaginative cryptozoology enthusiasts.

13 This expression was often invoked during the construction of the Transamazon Highway in the early 1970s, and similar phrases recur in Brazilian political discourse when the question of 'developing the interior' is raised.

14 This dated expression, along with 'awakening giant' – initially referring to the country's post-World War II economic expectations – is frequently revived in business and evangelical circles.

15 In this context, the stereotyped heroic explorer/ethnographer has been overtaken by the explorer/ethnobotanist, modelled after R. E. Schultes; see Davis (1996, 2004). The notion of extinction, once almost exclusively connoting the demise of dinosaurs, shifted to become a key Cold War concept (with humans replacing dinosaurs as the target population), gained a systems reading with Carson's (1962) *Silent Spring*, and – with the maturation of ecological science – was reconfigured as threat to biodiversity.

16 This shift from an evolutionary to structuralist outlook mimics the change in anthropological orientation over the same time period – from Frazer to Lévi-Strauss.

17 *End of the Spear* is a Christian 'independent' film, released though a major studio but without the overt Hollywood associations shared by most of the other films. *Aguirre*, directed by Herzog and starring Klaus Kinski, straddles the 'art film'/feature film line. *Fire on the Amazon* (also known as *Lost Paradise*) is one of the lesser productions linked to the biography of Chico Mendes, but is included here because the better known Mendes film *The Burning Season* (Frankenheimer 1994) emerged from a fraught production battle as, effectively, an exclusively cable/video release.

18 Vincent Canby in the *New York Times* (4 April 1977), for example, refers to the story as 'one of the more bizarre and bloody footnotes to the history of the Spanish conquests'.

19 See Smith (1990) for an account of the career of Lope de Aguirre.

20 When an Indian couple paddles out to meet the expedition raft and is interrogated on board, a short speech given by the male of the couple – and anticipated as a formal response to the expedition leader's 'aims and objectives' delivery – is translated/reported as 'He says he's a jaguar'. This deadpan incommunicability sums up 'culture contact'.

21 In 2004, he released a documentary film on an Amazonian theme, *White Diamond*. Les Blank's (1982) celebrated documentary about the making of *Fitzcarraldo* includes noteworthy interviews with Herzog in which he elaborates vigorously on his personal vision of 'green hell'.

22 Is this also a strong, not to say outstanding, example of the pathetic fallacy?

23 Text from the video packaging.

24 Unlike the Invisible People – who are rather zestful and have a very high proportion of nubiles in their population – the Fierce People are male and tend to grunt and plod as though under the influence. Admittedly, they represent a war party, but the darkened skin, war paint, and consistently aggressive and demented demeanour hardly provides a subtle contrast with the gentle Invisibles. Although the tribal name seems obviously derived from Chagnon's depiction of the Yanomami, the Fierce People are adorned in ersatz, upper-Xingu style and their bloodthirsty/cannibalistic tendencies are strictly dime-

store pulp. The Invisible People are likely based on the Kreen-Akrore/Panará (Boorman 1985a:42), the search for whom is documented in Cowell (1973).

25 A few should be noted, however, by way of documenting the spirited durability of tropicalist myth/mythmaking: the idea that 'big paddle steamers' are typical river craft in 1982 (Boorman 1985a:43) or the comments on the *favelas* of Belém or the 'tumultuous markets' and waterfronts that 'reek of the romance of the Amazon' (1985a:44) add considerable lustre to the ordinary.

26 In *The Emerald Forest*, though, the dam appears to be swept away at the conclusion of the story, destroyed by a combination of human, amphibian, and supernatural intervention.

27 Just to note one indicator: estimates of Amazonian deforestation indicate a pattern of steady increase since the 'development decade' of the 1970s. In 2004, 26,129 square kilometres were cleared (2005 figures indicate a possible decline) to reach a total of 528,000 square kilometres of cleared forest. It must be said that estimates across the various Brazilian and international agencies vary, but there is consensus about trends and rough numbers.

28 Amazonia is widely spoken of in the press as being under threat from diverse enemies, and even the major interests directly and indirectly responsible for the assault speak as though 'the dilemmas' represent an unfortunate – but intractable – situation. The assault on Amazonia is a highly controlled phenomenon the various strands of which are under the command of well-known and allegedly responsible private and public bodies. Crocodile tears have ecological fit.

29 Casteneda's (1968) disputed 'Don Juan', the Yaqui sorcerer, is probably the best known example.

30 The (more candidly) fictitious Indians are riven by compromises and uncertainties comparable to those borne by their religious and secular interlopers.

31 For comparative purposes, *Atanajurat* (Nunuk 2000) discloses a startling multidimensionality in indigenous-inflected cinema.

32 *The End of the River* (Twist 1947), another lost Amazonian film of the same era shot in Belém, has the South Asian actor Sabu playing the role of an 'Akuna' Indian. More recently, this area has been selected as the site for a Disneyland-like Amazonian assault, the *Parque Amazonia,* an eco-tourism development.

33 Their efforts have been somewhat distracted by revelations that the lead actor – playing the role of missionary victim of aboriginal religious intolerance – is a vocal gay.

34 The German film *Lana: Königin der Amazoner* (Cziffra 1964) has an unredemptive missionaries-killed-by-Indians theme combined with the rescue of a blonde kidnap victim.

35 Within Brazilian horror film genres, but without a specific Amazonian connection, the work of Coffin Joe/José Mojica Marins features prominently.

36 As it does in speech in later versions of the movie.

37 In that movie, though, the scientist Summerlee is mildly ridiculed throughout. In subsequent *Lost Worlds* as well as other science-in-Amazonia films, scientists tend to be accorded more respect.

38 Although the political will to protect Amazonia and Amazonians in any serious way remains a remote hope, conserving-society-through-conserving-nature continues to be a widely touted if – on current form, empty – theme. A key premise is that only when commercial value can be demonstrated will abstract values and ideals be recognized and appreciated; thus – the argument goes – an Indian (or, really, any powerless non-cosmopolite) is just a trivial subject of realpolitik and doomed to extinction, but an Indian with knowledge of an uninventoried forest plant alkaloid is a potentially valuable resource (wise forest manager; indigenous knowledge asset; developmentalist stakeholder).

39 Several dozen such films (for which audiences required special spectacles) were produced in the early 1950s, many with exotic settings (e.g., *Bwana Devil* [strapline: 'a lion in your lap, a lover in your arms']; *Drums of Tahiti; Gorilla at Large*) and a number with 'space' themes (e.g., *Cat Women of the Moon; Robot Monster; It Came from Outer Space*).

40 SCUBA (self-contained underwater breathing apparatus) had been co-invented in the previous decade by Jacques Cousteau, later a celebrated Amazonian 'explorer' (see Cousteau and Richards 1984). Cousteau's (1956) *Silent World* film won an Academy Award. *The Creature from the Black Lagoon* did not.

41 The franchise appears to have become exhausted with *Revenge of the Creature* and *The Creature Walks Among Us.*

42 Two *mestiço* workers are killed off early when the creature invades the field camp.

43 Modelled on *timbú/barbasco.*

44 Another interpretation is that the Indians have successfully exported unwanted Kathoga from their midst in the forest to the city, but the non-equivalence of indigenous knowledge and science remains. A similar theme is pursued in a non-Amazonian context in *Q: The Winged Serpent* (Cohen 1982), also a film in which anthropology plays a crucial – albeit cameo – role as bridge between incommensurable belief systems.

45 These include the typical repertoire of animals, including the *candirú* fish and with the addition of a species of poisonous wasp. There are half-hearted acknowledgements of tropical eco-awareness. When the anaconda's companion evil character threatens to use dynamite to stun the monster, one of the expedition members interjects, 'I'm talking about upsetting the ecological balance of this river'.

46 In the case of *Anaconda,* the science is tokenistic: a National Geographic-like expedition.

47 If incidence of *ayahuasca* taking is any indication, a lot of indigenous knowledge is still fairly inaccessible, invested as it is in unfathomable, psychotropic experiences – a characterization that contradictorily acknowledges (a) something akin to science (but as the unqualified/uncredentialed practice it) and (b) an hallucinatory, religion-like body of knowledge (which, being 'native', is out of control and impossible to represent in formal terms). The qualifier 'indigenous' serves to subvert the apparent claim for 'science'.

48 An exception is *At Play in the Fields of the Lord.*

49 From an unattributed Web-posted editorial review. The film is clearly based on Chico Mendes and the Rubber Tappers' Union (also see Frankenheimer 1994). *The Medicine Man* pursues a 'native-science'/genomic-tropics theme that reflects much of the popular science attention closely associated with a revamped version of Amazonia-the-untapped-resource-domain. See Plotkin (1993).

50 In view of the very low quality of the competition, however, this degree of accuracy is highly qualified.

51 See Henley (2004).

8

Conclusion

Ethnographic photography presents itself as a special case of 'the ethnographic present', that 'violation of the normal use of tenses' (Service 1971 [1958]:xv, quoted in D. Nugent 1993:7) according to which the temporal scale of the anthropologist is, in Stocking's (1992:274) phrase 'compressed into a single moment ambiguously situated outside the flow of time'. Stocking continues, 'Although closer perhaps to the real world than "the primal scene" of the archetypal anthropological encounter, it was an imagined space in which that encounter could, after the fashion of Malinowski's mythic charter, be re-enacted again and again' (1992:274).

A photographic image inserted into such an imagined space becomes not just a two-dimensional token of the ethnographic 'total system'. A photograph is already, as Sontag's (1977) celebrated discussion pursues it, both a record of the past – not incompatible with ethnographic ambition – and also a making or representation of the past. This latter notion sits less easily in an ethnographic context in which the continual 'ethnographic present' does not typically concede the involvement of the anthropological investigator in the making of the representation of the subject. Hence, for example, the ethnographic present is often conveyed via a depersonalized narrative, use of passive voice, an air of clinical distance, etc. Just as Malinowski's diary (1967) infamously revealed a parallel ethnographic universe, so do ethnographic photographs threaten to show too much and reveal other perspectives or material with the potential to deflate the pretense of the ethnographic present. Perhaps it is the effort to restrict such uncontrolled expressive qualities of the ethnographic encounter that results in an ethno-photography that so often presents rather flat portrayals of subjects. The actual ethnographic situation that includes subject and researcher – as well as the driver/pilot/bearer/guide who delivered him or her to the field, colonial baggage and all – would challenge the grip of the ethnographic present, which conveniently factors out such complications.

The fully complicit – which is to say *explicit* – ethnographic image – implies more than the 'imagined space of ethnographic encounter'. No ethnographic text can demand more than a charitable suspension of disbelief when it comes to discounting the particular and peculiar effects necessarily incumbent on the author of the ethnographic account, but the artifice of the depersonalized anthropological author is a well-practised and routine part of training. That professional attempt at effacement, however, is harder to achieve with a visual record, but the cost of keeping in check too expressive a visual record is not negligible. A candid visual record of the ethnographic encounter implies something closer to a photo-journalistic approach – that is, one in which the point of view implies a social field in which observed and observer are both contained. The typical ethno-photographic portrayal, on the other hand, is driven by a commitment to the ordinary, the prosaic, the typical, as well as a social field in which there is a strict boundary between observer and observed.

There are positive reasons for that ordinariness, though; one of those is the desire to convey the lives of anthropological subjects in ways that contradict the exoticism and, often, freakishness that is so rigidly associated with ethnography once it leaves the arena of professional interest. While this ambition to defuse stereotyped notions of the anthropological exotic is well illustrated in textual accounts, and is in part achieved through the device of the ethnographic present that aims for an omniscient rather than selective view of 'life in the village/hut/etc., a photograph always contains the potential to disrupt that sober equanimity as it is selective in terms of both time and place. The well-crafted ethnography is meant to give a sense of proportion in that it unpacks and reveals the interdependencies of various aspects of social organization and habitus, while photography – as Sontag points out (Movius 1975) – does exactly the opposite: it annihilates our sense of scale.

The annihilation of scale observed by Sontag refers, in the main, to what happens to an image as it is processed within the same cultural field from which it originates; but as Jenkins (1993) has argued in his discussion of the genealogy of North American Indian photography, the co-emergence of photographic technology and professional anthropology in the late 19th century may have resulted in a kind of fetishized annihilation as those few Indian societies still living at arm's length from white society began the slide into fully administered existence as wards of the state.

> [P]hotographs of Indians entered into new systems of popular and scientific representation [and] they began to take the place of those persons who were represented, render them mute, and speak on their behalf. The legitimacy, the 'great value and interest' in these photographs was thus based in part upon the silence and apparent passivity of those who were represented (Jenkins 1993:10).

He continues, 'As putatively accurate depictions of other peoples, photographs had become semiotic objects that simultaneously functioned as symbols, icons and indices, a mixed form of representation that did not exist prior to the invention of photography' (1993:10). From this perspective, some of the well-known criticism of photographers such as Curtis looks misplaced; for whatever the defects of romanticization of the disappearing world of North American Indians (and such tendencies were severe), the photographs actually capture, indeed embody, an ethnographic reality – that is, Indians in a subject position that epitomizes their waning status as outsiders. Those photographs depict a now missing world whose current analogue is often shocking in the distortions of its 'on-the-ground' form, from trailer camps and prison schools to casino ownership.

In some ways, the establishment of iconic images of Native American peoples in North America is expressed in a parallel process in the Amazon. There is certainly a high recognition factor of the stereotype/cliché and there is a shared sense of the so-called 'Indian problem', but the geographical remoteness and marginality of most Brazilian Indian groups that survived through the 20th century has meant that anthropology as a field has been a key source and reference point for much public understanding of and knowledge about extant Amazonian Indians since the mid-20th century. One of the implications of this special and complex mediating role is that even if the ethno-photographic record presented in the professional monograph literature is uneven or inconsistent, in the sense that the presence or absence of photographs in a scholarly account has little evaluative consequences in terms of scientific standing, there is a generic portrayal – the stereotype/cliché – that still functions as a focal image from the point of view of public consumption. While the relationship between ethno-photography and ethnography can be described as diffident at best, the collective portrait that emerges overlays a long history of photographic representation from diverse public sources. The symbolic authority of the ethno-photographic record allies with the more prosaic authority of postcards, popular encyclopaedias, and the like.

Figure 6.9 shows how recent the actual body of anthropologically informed images – ethno-photography – is. To whatever degree these images complement and solidify the authority of professional accounts of Amazonian Indians, they do so against a broad and historically deep background of popular representation.

The persuasiveness of a recent image record that is taken to represent a broad historical and prehistoric sweep is in keeping with received views about Amazonia. As an ethnographic region and specialist area, Amazonia is not suffused with ambiguity: there is a bold nature/culture contrast; there are numerous examples of strong, almost doctrinaire theoretical

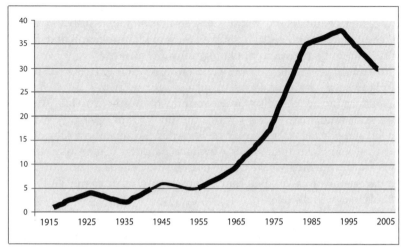

Figure 8.1 Monographs per decade.

tendencies in the traditions of cultural evolutionism and materialism, structuralism, and symbolic systems; there is the recurrent typological contrast between civilized highlands and culturally depauperate lowlands; there are vivid examples of hunter-gatherers, symbolically rich and materially poor societies; and so on. That lack of ambiguity in characterizing 'anthropological Amazonia' – an oversimplification, it has been argued – is complemented by a general depiction of the colonial experience that tends not to be periodized with great subtlety: there was conquest, subjugation, and then marginal survival into the modern period. These simplifying characterizations are enhanced by the tendency for Amazonia to be continuously nested within a recurrent, and often mythologized, notion of the frontier: the colonial frontier, the frontier of green hell, the frontier of Brazilian nation building, the advancing frontier of commercial agriculture, pastoralism, and extraction, conjuring up a pristine remoteness just out of reach that overwhelmed indigenous societies are seen to exemplify. One of the consequences, if theses characterizations have any purchase, is that Amazonian Indian societies seem to evade history and historicization.

Even if there is a kind of 'out-of-history-ness' about a basic conception of Amazonian Indian societies, there is definitely a history of the anthropology of Amazonian Indians, one that recovers the Indian – in the sense of rescuing it from behind the shrouds of tropical naturalism – but which of necessity exaggerates the significance of recent historical examples. In addition to the over-representation of accessible examples of Amazonian Indian society afforded by the ethnographic literature, perhaps there is also an over-sensitivity about the importance of images in displaying crucial knowledge about such peoples. This would seem to be borne out in part by the generally small role allocated to images in presenting ethnographic data, but it may also indicate uncertainties about the control that anthropology as a field has over the meanings attributed to its research results.

While images associated with a particular ethnographic account have a kind of coordinated existence defined by the text – as illustrations, as evidence, as non-textual knowledge, as mementos of experience, as records of relationships – the collectivity of images associated with a broad body of ethnographic material is detached from that logic of exposition. As a compendium, it reveals contradictory tendencies: its capacity to offer generalizations is not shaped by the criteria that determined the initial collection of individual images, but by its meeting other expectations and dispositions. It tells us, for example, as much about anthropology as a culture industry – as a discipline whose particular forms of knowledge production slot into a category already in place – as it does about anthropological subjects. Hence, one of the difficulties posed by the stereotypicality of photographic imagery of Amazonian Indians is that it consolidates and reinforces the historically particular as generic.

While the power of the photographic image may constrict appreciation of the complexity of the notion 'Amazonian Indian', it may also open it up. Evidence that the typicality of 'the Amazonian Indian' as depicted in the modern ethnographic record is suspect has been available for some time, but arguments for its being taken very seriously have not commanded much attention until very recently. There are several reasons that these arguments have been marginal to modern anthropological theory in Amazonia. These include:

- The speed of demographic collapse in the Amazon region, which created a social landscape of dispersed, small-scale, hunter-gatherer/horticulturalists (joining other such groups driven from the desirable riverine habitats by more powerful societies).
- The haphazard, erratic character of the development of colonial society in the region (in view of the absence of the most highly desirable extractive products, the consolidation of colonial rule was a sloppy affair).
- The inaccessibility of much of the interior and inter-fluve terra firma – hence, little direct knowledge by colony/state.
- The economic and intellectual marginality of the region in relation to the development of the modern Brazilian state.

In recent years, there has been a cohering re-evaluation of the degree to which the present state of Indianness (represented iconically as noble hunter-gatherer as well as wise forest manager) is an adequate representation of the past; and although these arguments have been present for decades, the kinds of evidence now being brought forward command an attention previously, strenuously denied – for example, by Meggers, long a champion of the so-called 'counterfeit paradise' argument. In short, archaeological evidence tends to confirm early eyewitness accounts of Amazonian riverine societies at the time of conquest, but – interestingly – moves into the interior as well, as Heckenberger's work on the upper Xingu so strikingly reveals. It is not coincidental, and not a little ironic, that the persuasiveness of the demands to reconsider the Amazonian ethnographic record and its past should be aided by photography as a means of presenting evidence. C. Erickson (2000) and Heckenberger (2005), for example, are able to exploit new imaging technologies in ways that engage the widespread susceptibility to visual representation. Two related areas in which photographic evidence has been part of a significant revision tendency are rock art and the imaging of stratigraphic soils, especially revealing so-called 'black soils' (*terra preta*).[1]

The kind of photographic image offered by archaeological revisionists in Amazonia not only obliges narrowly ethnographic arguments to engage with the past in critical ways, but also highlights a crucial ambiguity in the way ethno-photography has been invoked in the past. Whereas the photography-in-aid-of-archaeological-revisionism clearly relies on the evidential status of the images, this is by no means clear for much of the ethno-photographic record. Within a sociocultural anthropological tradition of ethnographic fieldwork, already burdened with vagaries produced by reliance on the ethnographic present as a time frame, what counts as evidence has tended to be inconsistently appraised. In this context, the truism 'the camera never lies' is subject to a number of disabling qualifiers, which perhaps accounts for the uncertainty of the very notion of visual anthropology, as well as the inconsistency with which photographic images have been engaged as a central feature of the ethnographic project (historical, technical, and economic barriers notwithstanding).

In the absence of programmatic notions of what ethno-photography might do, it is less surprising that what it does do in the case of Amazonian anthropology is orient itself around conventions already available in non-anthropological discourse. In one of the few overviews of the notion of ethno-photography, Sapir (1994) offers an uncontroversial typology of the uses to which the camera is put in anthropology:

- Camera as research tool.
- Camera in service to others.
- Camera providing relaxed, intuitive impressions.

The first is strongly expressed in Collier (1967) and has been central to the ethnographic film genre. The second typically takes the form of political advocacy and reportage, of which Salgado (1997) is a central example; the Kayapó are the Amazonian group best known for seizing upon the use of images for advancing their cause (see Turner 1992). Pierre Verger (1990) is a French-Brazilian example of the third.

Evidentiary use of photographic images in Amazonia has re-emerged in the course of political struggles around indigenous rights and social-ecological justice and is also clear in archaeology's extension of relevance into the study of historical societies, but is rarely straightforward within a modern anthropology, post-anthropometrics. When a lab technician spots

Figure 8.2 *Treponema pallidum*. Center for Disease Control 2006.

under the microscope, the identification (syphilis) is fairly straightforward, yet an ethnography reader presented with two ordinary images of what seem to be Amazonian family groups needs more information: one group may indeed be a man and his wives and children; the other may be survivors of a measles epidemic (the referent images are in Tierney 2000:164-5).

The ambiguity of the ethno-photographic image is neither a matter to be particularly bemoaned nor celebrated, but it does reveal a certain fragility in the oft-repeated assertion that anthropology's distinctiveness and defense against disciplinary erosion lies in an ethnographic method still often cast in a mode of the early 20th century. Fundamental incompatibilities between the ethno-photographic record (although we have yet to see a really developed version of this) that is time based and a suspended tense ethnographic approach put too much strain on what seems at first sight to be a pleasing affinity: an illustrated ethnography. To the degree that the ethno-photography succeeds, it reveals too much that disturbs the still necessary (if partial) fiction of the ethnographic present, and it often reveals – uncomfortably – the fact that within the anthropological endeavour, there are limits to a reflexivism that attempts to mitigate the fact that the ethnographic subject is in fact objectified and historicized. The timeless image of the Amazonian Indian that has come to be firmly encoded in the photographic record risks being mistaken for the other versions of Amazonian Indian pushed out of the frame by selective historical reckoning.

Notes

1   Black soils have been typified in the past simply as (a) rare instances of good soil surrounded by poor soils; (b) then as passively anthropogenic soils, in the sense that they represent long periods of human occupation with resulting build-up of organic material; and (c) most recently as actively anthropogenic, in the sense that they represent intentional human intervention in creation of socially desirable soils.

References

Adam, H. C. 2003. Introduction. In *The North American Indian: The complete portfolios*. E. Curtis, ed. Koln, Germany: Taschen. pp. 6–32.

Agassiz, L. 1896. *A journey in Brazil*. Boston: Houghton, Mifflin.

Akers, C. E. 1912. *The Amazon valley: Its rubber industry and other resources*. London: Waterlow and Sons.

Alden, D. 1987. Late colonial Brazil, 1750–1808. In *Colonial Brazil*. L. Bethell, ed. Cambridge, UK: Cambridge University Press. pp. 284–343.

Anderson, R. L. 1999. *Colonization as exploitation in the Amazon rain forest: 1758–1911*. Gainesville: University Press of Florida.

Anonymous. n.d. Werner Herzog on *Fitzcarraldo*. Humanities Advanced Technology and Information Institute, University of Glasgow. http://www.hatii.arts.glas.ac.uk/multimediastudentprojects/00-0/00

Arhem, K. 1998. *Makuna: Portrait of an Amazonian people*. Washington, DC: Smithsonian Institution Press.

Arnold, J. 1954. *The creature from the black lagoon*. Universal Pictures.

Arnold, L. 1955. *Revenge of the creature*. Universal Pictures.

Asad, T. ed. 1974. *Anthropology and the colonial encounter*. London: Ithaca Press.

Asch, T. 1992. The ethics of ethnographic filmmaking. In *Film as ethnography*. P. Crawford and D. Turton, eds. Manchester, UK: Manchester University Press. pp. 196–204.

Ayler, T. D. 1994. Very loveable human being: The photography of Everard Im Thurn. In *Anthropology and photography*, E. Edwards, ed. New Haven, CT: Yale University Press. pp. 187–92.

Babenco, H. 1991. *At play in the fields of the lord*. Universal Pictures.

Bahn, P. 1991. Dating the first American. *New Scientist* 131:26–8.

Balée, W. L. 1994. *Footprints of the forest: Ka'apor ethnobotany – The historical ecology of plant utilization by an Amazonian people*. New York: Columbia University Press.

Balick, M.J. 1996. *Medicinal resources of the tropical forest: Biodiversity and its importance to human health*. New York: Columbia University Press.

Banks, M. and H. Morphy. eds. 1999. *Rethinking visual anthropology*. New Haven, CT: Yale University Press.

Barthes, R. 1993. *Camera lucida: Reflections on photography*. London: Vintage.

Basso, E. 1973. *Kalapalo Indians of Brazil*. New York: Holt, Rinehart and Winston.

———1985. *A musical view of the universe*. Philadelphia: University of Pennsylvania Press.

——1987. *In favor of deceit: A study of tricksters in an Amazonian society.* Tucson: University of Arizona Press.

——1995. *The last cannibals: A South American oral history.* Austin: University of Texas Press.

Bates, H. W. 1892. *The naturalist on the river Amazons.* New York: D. Appleton.

Bates, M. and the Editors of *Life.* 1964. *The land and wildlife of South America.* New York: TIME-LIFE International.

Beckerman, S. 1979. The abundance of protein in Amazonia: A reply to Gross. *American Anthropologist* 81:533–60.

Bellos, A. 2000. Close encounters. *The Guardian,* 7 January. http://www.guardian. co.uk/g2/story/0,,250266,00.html

Benjamin, W. 1992 [1968]. *Illuminations.* London: Fontana.

Berg, J. 2003. *The rundown.* Universal Pictures.

Bergman, R. 1980. *Amazon economics: The simplicity of Shipibo wealth.* Tucson: University of Arizona Press.

Bethell, L. ed. 1987. *Colonial Brazil.* Cambridge, UK: Cambridge University Press.

——2003. *Brazil by British and Irish authors.* Oxford: Centre for Brazilian Studies.

Biocca, E. 1970. *Yanoama: The narrative of a white girl kidnapped by Amazonia Indians.* Dennis Rhodes, trans. New York: Dutton.

Bisch, J. 1958. *Across the river of death: True adventure in the green hell of the Amazon.* London: Souvenir Press.

Bishop, E. 1962. *Brazil.* London: Sunday Times.

Blank, L. 1982. *Burden of dreams.* Criterion Films.

Blaut, J. M. 1993. *The colonizer's model of the world.* London: Guilford Books.

Bleiler, E. 1996. Lost worlds and lost opportunities: the Pilot Rodin edition of the Lost World. *Science Fiction Studies* #70. http://www.depauw.edu/sfs/reviews_ pages/r70.htm

Bond, T. 1992a. *The lost world.* Medusa Films.

——1992b. *Return to the lost world.* Medusa Films.

Boorman, J. 1985a. *Money into light: The emerald forest – A diary.* London: Faber and Faber.

——1985b. *The emerald forest.* MGM/UA Films.

Borofsky, R. ed. 2005. *Yanomami: The fierce controversy and what we can learn from it.* Berkeley: University of California Press.

Bourne, R. 1978. *Assault on the Amazon.* London: Gollancz.

Bright, B. 1998. Ethnographic film as popular imagination. *American Quarterly* 50:183–91.

Brooks, E., R. Fuerst, R. Hemming, and F. Huxley. 1973. *Tribes of the Amazon basin in Brazil 1972: Report for the Aborigines Protection Society.* London: Charles Knight.

Brown, L. 2005. *Outgrowing the earth: The food security challenge in an age of falling water tables and rising temperatures.* New York: Norton.

Brown, M. 1985. *Tsewa's gift: Magic and meaning in an Amazonian society.* Washington, DC: Smithsonian Institution Press.

Brown, M. and E. Fernandez. 1992. *War of shadows: The struggle for utopia in the Peruvian Amazon.* Berkeley: University of California Press.

Bunker, S. G. 1985. *Underdeveloping the Amazon: Extraction, unequal exchange, and the failure of the modern state.* Urbana: University of Illinois Press.

Campbell, A. L. 1985. *To square with genesis.* Cambridge, UK: Cambridge University Press.

———1995. *Getting to know Waiwai: An Amazonian ethnography.* London: Routledge.

Canby, V. 1977. Review of Herzog's *Aguirre. New York Times,* 4 April.

Candre, H. 1996. *Cool tobacco, sweet coca: Teachings of an Indian sage from the Colombian Amazon.* Tulsa, OK: Themis Books.

Carelli, M. ed. 1995. *Hercules Florence.* Sao Paulo: Marca D'Agua.

Carmichael, E. 1985. *Hidden peoples of the Amazon.* London: British Museum.

Carneiro da Cunha. M. ed. 1992. *Historia dos índios no Brasil.* Sao Paulo: Ed. Schwarcz.

Carneiro, R. L. 1973 [1961]. Slash-and-burn cultivation among the Kuikuru and its implications for cultural development in the Amazon Basin. In *Peoples and cultures of native South America: An anthropological reader.* D. Gross, ed. Garden City, NY: Doubleday/Natural History Press.

Carroll, N. 2003. *Engaging the moving image.* New Haven, CT: Yale University Press.

Carson, R. 1962. *Silent spring.* New York: Houghton Mifflin.

Carvajal, G. de. 1934 [1555]. *Discovery of the Amazon according to the accounts of Friar Gaspar De Carvajal and other documents.* H. C. Heaton, ed. New York: National Geographic Society.

Casteneda, C. 1968. *The teachings of Don Juan: A Yaqui way of knowledge.* Berkeley: University of California Press.

Centeno, R. and P. Fernandez O. 1998. *Imagens del auge de la goma.* La Paz.

Chagnon, N. 1974. *Studying the Yanomamo.* New York: Holt, Rinehart and Winston.

———1983 [1968]. *Yanomamo: The fierce people,* 3rd ed. New York: Holt, Rinehart and Winston.

———1992. *Yanomamo: The last days of Eden.* San Diego: Harcourt Brace Jovanovich.

Chernela, J. 1993. *The Wanano Indians of the Brazilian Amazon: A sense of space.* Austin: University of Texas Press.

Chibnik, M. 1994. *Risky rivers: The economics and politics of floodplain farming in Amazonia.* Tucson: University of Arizona Press.

Churchward, R. 1936. *Wilderness of fools: An account of the adventures in search of Lieut-Colonel P. H. Fawcett.* London: Routledge.

Clastres, P. 1977. *Society against the state.* Oxford: Blackwell.

———1998. *Chronicle of the Guayaki Indians.* New York: Zone Books.

Cleary, D. 1990. *Amazon gold rush.* Iowa City: University of Iowa Press.

Climati, A. 1988. *Cannibal holocaust II.* Vipco.

Cohen, L. 1982. *Q: The winged serpent.* Anchor Bay Films.

COIAB (Coordinating Body of Indigenous Organizations of the Brazilian Amazon). 2006. Brazil: Indians attack FUNAI (press release 17 January). Manaus: COIAB.

Coimbra, C. E. A., N. M. Flowers, F. M. Salzano, and R. V. Santos. 2004. *The Xavante in transition: Health, ecology, and bioanthropology in central Brazil.* Ann Arbor: University of Michigan Press.

Collier, J. 1967. *Visual anthropology: Photography as a research method.* New York: Holt, Rinehart and Winston.

Collier, R. 1968. *The river that god forgot: The struggle of the Amazon rubber boom.* London: Collins.

Committee of the Royal Anthropological Institute of Great Britain and Ireland. 1951. *Notes and queries on anthropology.* London: Routledge and Kegan Paul.

Conan Doyle, A. 1912. *The lost world.* London: Hodder and Stoughton.

—— 1913. *The poison belt.* London: Hodder and Stoughton.

Conklin, B. 2001. *Consuming grief: Compassionate cannibalism in an Amazonian society.* Austin: University of Texas Press.

Corry, S. 1993. The rainforest harvest. *The Ecologist,* July/August. pp. 148–53.

Cotlow, L. 1954. *Amazon head hunters.* London: Viking Press.

Coudreau, H. 1977. *Viagem ao Xingu.* São Paulo: Edusp.

Cousteau, J. 1954. *The silent world.* New York: Pocket Books.

Cousteau, J. and M. Richards. 1984. *Jacques Cousteau's Amazon journey.* New York: Harry Abrams.

Cowell, A. 1960. *The heart of the forest.* London: Gollanz.

Cowell, A. 1973. *The tribe that hides from man.* London: Bodley Head.

Cowell, A. 1990. *Decade of destruction.* London: Hodder and Stoughton.

Crichton, M. 1990. *Jurassic park.* New York: Knopf.

Crocker, J. C. 1985. *Vital souls: Bororo cosmology, natural symbolism, and shamanism.* Tucson: University of Arizona Press.

Crocker, W. H. and J. Crocker. 1990. *The Canela (Eastern Timbira) I: An ethnographic introduction.* Washington, DC: Smithsonian Institution Press.

——1994. *The Canela: Bonding through kinship, ritual, and sex.* Fort Worth, TX: Harcourt Brace College Publishers.

Crosby, A. 1972. *The Columbian exchange: The biological and cultural consequences of 1492.* Westport, CT: Greenwood Press.

——1986. *Ecological imperialism: The biological expansion of Europe, 900–1900.* Cambridge: Cambridge University Press.

Curtis, E. ed. 2003. *The North American Indian: The complete portfolios.* Koln: Taschen.

Cziffra, G. von. 1964. *Lana: Königin der Amazoner.* Arca Studio.

da Cunha, E. 1944 [1902]. *Rebellion in the backlands.* Chicago: University of Chicago Press.

D'Amato, J. 1984. *Emmanuelle and the last cannibal* (aka *Trap them and kill them*). Shriek Show.

Da Matta, R. 1982. *A divided world.* Cambridge, MA: Harvard University Press.

Dalziell, R. 2002. The curious case of Sir Everard im Thurn and Sir Arthur Conan Doyle: Exploration and the imperial adventure novel, *The lost world. English Literature in Transition 1880–1920* 45:131–57.

Dante, J. 1978. *Piranha.* United Artists.

Davis, W. 1996. *One river: Exploration and discoveries in the Amazon rain forest.* New York: Simon and Schuster.

——2004. *The lost Amazon: The photographic journey of Richard Evans Schultes.* San Francisco: Chronicle Books.

Dean, W. 1987. *Brazil and the struggle for rubber: An environmental history.* Cambridge, UK: Cambridge University Press.

Denevan, W. ed. 1976. *The native populations of America 1492.* Madison: University of Wisconsin Press.

Deodato, R. 1978. *Jungle holocaust.* Shriek Show.

———1980. *Cannibal holocaust.* EC Entertainment.

Descola, P. 1994. *In the society of nature: A native ecology in Amazonia.* Cambridge, UK: Cambridge University Press.

———1997. *The spears of twilight: Life and death in the Amazon jungle.* London: Flamingo.

Donner, F. 1982. *Shabono.* New York: Delacorte.

Dumont, J-P. 1976. *Under the rainbow: Nature and supernature among the Panare Indians.* Austin: University of Texas Press.

———1978. *The headman and I: Ambiguity and ambivalence in the fieldworking experience.* Austin: University of Texas Press.

Dwyer, J. P. ed. 1975. *The Cashinahua of Eastern Peru.* Providence, RI: Haffenreffer Museum of Anthropology,Brown University.

Dyott, G. 1930. *Man hunting in the jungle: Being the story of a search for three explorers lost in the Brazilian wilds.* Indianapolis: Bobbs-Merrill.

Early, J. D. and J. F. Peters. 1990. *The population dynamics of the Mucajai Yanomama.* San Diego: Academic Press.

———2000. *The Xilixana Yanomami of the Amazon: History, social structure, and population dynamics.* Gainesville: University Press of Florida.

Ebert, R. 1991. Review of *At play in the fields of the lord. Chicago Sun Times* 6 December. http://rogerebert.suntimes.com/apps/pbcs.dll/article?AID=/19911206/REVIEWS/112060301/1023

———1997. Review of *Anaconda. Chicago Sun Times* 11 April. http://rogerebert.suntimes.com/apps/pbcs.dll/article?AID=/19970411/REVIEWS/704110301/1023

Edwards, E. 2001. *Raw histories.* Oxford: Berg.

Edwards, E. ed. 1994. *Anthropology and photography.* New Haven, CT: Yale University Press.

Edwards, E. and J. Hart, J. eds. 2004. *Photographs objects histories.* London: Routledge.

Elkins, J. 2003. *Visual studies: A skeptical introduction.* London: Routledge.

Elliot, E. 1957. *Through the gates of splendor.* London: Hodder and Stoughton.

Enock, C. R. 1907. *The Andes and the Amazon.* London: T. Unwin Fisher.

Erickson, C. 2000. An artificial landscape-scale fishery in the Bolivian Amazon. *Nature* 408:190–3.

Erickson, G. 2000. Review of *The Herzog/Kinski/Selva trilogy.* http://www.dvdtalk.com/dvdsavant/

Fabian, S. M. 1992. *Space-time of the Bororo of Brazil.* Gainesville: University Press of Florida.

Farabee, W. 1918. *The Central Arawaks.* Philadelphia: University of Pennsylvania Museum.

———1922. *Indian tribes of Eastern Peru.* Papers of the Peabody Museum of American Archaeology and Ethnology, Vol. 10. Cambridge, MA: Peabody Museum, Harvard University.

——1924. *The Central Caribs, Vol. 9.* Philadelphia: University of Pennsylvania Museum.

Faria de Castro, L. 2001. *Um outro olhar: Diaria da expedição a derra do Norte.* Rio de Janeiro: Ed. Ouro Sobre Azul.

Faris, J. 1992. Anthropological transparency: Film, representation and politics. In *Film as ethnography.* P. Crawford and D. Turton, eds. Manchester, UK: Manchester University Press. pp. 171–82.

——2003. Navajo and photography. In *Photography's other histories.* C. Pinney and N. Peterson, eds. London: Duke University Press. pp. 85–99.

Fawcett, B. 1953. *Lost trails, lost cities.* New York: Funk and Wagnalls.

Fawcett, P. H. 1968 [1953]. *Exploration Fawcett.* London: Arrow Books.

Fejos, P. 1943. *Ethnography of the Yagua.* New York: Viking Fund Publications in Anthropology, Vol. 3.

Ferguson, R. B. 1995. *Yanomami warfare: A political history.* Santa Fe, NM: School of American Research Press.

Ferguson, R.B. and N. Whitehead. eds. 1992. *War in the tribal zone: Expanding state and indigenous warfare.* Santa Fe, NM: School of American Research Press.

Ferrer, J. 1959. *Green mansions.* MGM.

Ferrer, G. and W. Naef. 1976. *Pioneer photographers of Brazil, 1840–1920.* New York: Center for Inter-American Relations.

Fisher, W. H. 2000. *Rain forest exchanges: Industry and community on an Amazonian frontier.* Washington, DC: Smithsonian Institution Press.

Flaherty, R. 1922. *Nanook of the north.* Pathépicture.

Fleming, P. 1933. *Brazilian adventure.* London: Jonathan Cape.

Fleming, V. n.d. Fieldwork notes/personal communication.

Florence, H. 1977. *Viagem fluvial doTietê ao Amazonas: de 1825 a 1829.* São Paulo: Cultrix/Edusp.

Fock, N. 1963. *Waiwai religion and society of an Amazonian tribe.* Copenhagen: Danish National Museum.

Fodor, J. 1979. *The language of thought.* Cambridge, MA: Harvard University Press.

Frankenheimer, J. 1994. *The burning season: The Chico Mendes Story.* HBO.

Freeman, D. 1983. *Margaret Mead and Samoa: The making and unmaking of an anthropological myth.* Cambridge, MA: Harvard University Press.

Furneaux, R. 1969. *The Amazon: The story of a great river.* London: Hamish Hamilton.

Furst, P. ed. 1972. *Flesh of the gods: The ritual use of hallucinogens.* London: Allen Unwin.

Garfield, S. 2000. Review: Recent works on Amazonian Indians. *Ethnohistory* 47:755–66.

——2001. *Indigenous struggle at the heart of Brazil: State policy, frontier expansion, and the Xavante Indians, 1937–1988.* Durham, NC: Duke University Press.

——2002. Review of *Race, place, and medicine: The idea of the tropics in nineteenth century Brazilian medicine* (Peard) and *The spectacle of the races: Scientists, institutions, and the race question in Brazil, 1870–1930* (Schwarcz). *Ethnohistory* 49:433–6.

Gariazzo, M. 1985. *Amazonia: The Catherine Miles story.* Shriek Show.

Gell, A. 1998. *Art and agency: An anthropological theory.* Oxford: Clarendon Press/Oxford University Press.

Gibson, W. 1989. Introduction to A. C. Doyle *The lost world* and *the poison belt.* San Francisco: Chronicle Books.

Ginsburg, F. 1995. Indigenous media and the rhetoric of self-determination. In *Rhetorics of self-making.* D. Battglia, ed. Berkeley: University of California Press. pp. 121–38.

Goldman, I. 1963. *The Cubeo: Indians of the Northwest Amazon.* Urbana, IL: University of Illinois Press.

——2004. *Cubeo hehenewas: Religious thought.* New York: Columbia University Press.

Gomes, M. P. 1992 [1988]. *The Indians and Brazil.* Gainesville: University Press of Florida.

Good, K. 1991. *Into the hart: One man's pursuit of love and knowledge among the Yanomama.* New York: Simon and Schuster.

Gow, P. 1991. *Of mixed blood: Kinship and history in Peruvian Amazonia.* Oxford: Clarendon Press.

——2001. *An Amazonian myth and its history.* Oxford: Oxford University Press.

Gow, P. and O. Harris. 1985. The British Museum's representation of Amazonian Indians. *Anthropology Today* 1:1–2.

Graham, L. 1995. *Performing dreams: Discourses of immortality among the Xavante of Central Brazil.* Austin: University of Texas Press.

Gray, A. 1996a. *The Arakmbut: Mythology, spirituality and history.* Oxford: Berghahn.

——1996b. *The last shaman: Change in an Amazonian community.* Oxford: Berghahn.

——1997. *Indigenous rights and development.* Oxford: Berghahn.

Gregor, T. 1977. *Mehinaku: The drama of daily life in a Brazilian Indian village.* Chicago: University of Chicago Press.

——1985. *Anxious pleasures: The sexual lives of an Amazonian people.* Chicago: University of Chicago Press.

Gregor, T. and D. Tuzin. 1998. Amazonia and Melanesia: Gender and anthropological comparison. *Current Anthropology* 39:274–7.

Gross, D. ed. 1973. *Peoples and cultures of native South America: An anthropological reader.* Garden City, NY: Doubleday/Natural History Press.

Gross, D. 1975. Protein capture and cultural development in the Amazon basin. *American Anthropologist* 77:526–49.

Hanon, J. 2005. *Beyond the gates of splendor.* Every Tribe Entertainment.

——2006. *End of the spear.* Fox Faith Films.

Hardenburg, W. E. 1912. *The Putumayo: The devil's paradise – Travels in the Peruvian Amazon region and an account of the atrocities committed upon the Indians therein.* C. R. Enock, ed. London: T. Fisher Unwin.

Harner, M. J. 1973. *The Jivaro: People of the sacred waterfalls.* Garden City, NY: Doubleday/Anchor.

Harner, M. J. ed. 1973. *Hallucinogens and shamanism.* New York: Oxford University Press.

Harris, M. 2000. *Life on the Amazon: The anthropology of a Brazilian peasant village.* Oxford: Oxford University Press.

Harris, M. and M. Sahlins. 1979. Cannibals and kings: An exchange. *New York Review of Books,* 11, 28 June. http://www.nybooks.com/articles/7752

Hastrup, K. 1992. Anthropological visions: Some notes on visual and textual authority. In *Film as ethnography.* P. Crawford and D. Turton, eds. Manchester, UK: Manchester University Press. pp. 8–25.

Hattenstone, S. 2006. The peaceful warriors. *The Guardian,* 11 February. http://arts.guardian.co.uk/salgado/story/0,,1708839,00.html

Hautman, G. 1987. Interview with Malcolm McLeod. *Anthropology Today* 3:4–8.

Hecht, S. and A. Cockburn. 1989. *The fate of the forest: Developers, destroyers and defenders of the Amazon.* London: Verso.

Heckenberger, M. 2005. *The ecology of power: Culture, place and personhood in the Southern Amazon, AD 1000–2000.* London: Routledge.

Heckenberger, M., J. Peterson, and E. Neves. 2001. Of lost civilization and primitive tribes, Amazonia: A reply to Meggers. *Latin American Antiquity* 12:328–33.

Hemming, J. 1978. *Red gold.* Cambridge, MA: Harvard University Press.

———1987a. *Amazon frontier: The defeat of the Brazilian Indians.* London: Macmillan.

———1987b. Indians and the frontier. In *Colonial Brazil.* L. Bethell, ed. Cambridge: Cambridge University Press. pp. 145–89.

———2003. *Die if you must: Brazilian Indians in the twentieth century.* London: Macmillan.

Hendricks, J. W. 1993. *To drink of death: The narrative of a Shuar warrior.* Tucson: University of Arizona Press.

Henfrey, C. 1964. *Through Indian eyes: A journey among the Indian tribes of Guiana.* New York: Holt, Rinehart and Winston.

Henley, P. 1982. *The Panare: Tradition and change on the Amazonian frontier.* New Haven, CT: Yale University Press.

———2004. Anthropologists in television: A disappearing world? Manchester Working Papers. Manchester, UK: Department of Anthropology, Manchester University.

Henry, J. 1964. *Jungle people: A Kaingang tribe of the highlands of Brazil.* New York: Vintage Books.

Herzog, W. 1972. *Aguirre: Wrath of god.* Tartan.

———1982. *Fitzcarraldo.* Filmverlag der Autoren.

———2004. *White diamond.* Werner Herzog Productions.

Hight, E. and G. Sampson. eds. 2002a. *Colonialist photography: Imag(in)ing race and place.* London: Routledge.

Hight, E. and G. Sampson. 2002b. Introduction: Photography, race and postcolonial theory. In *Colonialist photography: Imag(in)ing race and place.* E. Hight and G. Sampson, eds. London: Routledge. pp. 1–19.

Hill, J. 1993. *Keepers of the sacred chants: The poetics of ritual and power in an Amazonian society.* Tucson: University of Arizona Press.

———1996. *History, power, and identity: Ethnogenesis in the Americas, 1492–1992.* Iowa City: University of Iowa Press.

———n.d. South America: Lowlands. *Handbook of Latin American Studies Online,* Vol. 53. http://lcweb2.loc.gov/hlas/

Holden, S. 1997. Review of *Anaconda. New York Times* 11 April. http://movies2.nytimes.com/movie/review?_r=2&res=9802E6DC133CF932A25757C0A96 1958260&oref=slogin

Holmberg, A. 1969. *Nomads of the long bow.* New York: Natural History Press.

Hopper, J. H. ed. 1967. *Indians of Brazil in the twentieth century.* ICR Studies, 2. Washington, DC: Institute for Cross-Cultural Research.

Houtman, G. 1988. Interview with Maurice Bloch. *Anthropology Today* 4:18–21.

Howe, D. 1992. Review of *At play in the fields of the lord*. *Washington Post* 24 January. http://www.washingtonpost.com/wp-srv/style/longterm/movies/videos/atplayinthefieldsofthelordrhowe_a0ae98.htm.

Hoyt, H. 2001 [1925]. *The lost world.* Lobster Films.

Hugh-Jones, C. 1979. *From the Milk River: Spatial and temporal processes in Northwest Amazonia.* Cambridge, UK: Cambridge University Press.

Hugh-Jones, S. 1979. *The palm and the pleiades: Initiation and cosmology in Northwest Amazonia.* Cambridge: Cambridge University Press.

Huxley, F. 1957. *Affable savages: An anthropologist among the Urubu Indians of Brazil.* New York: Viking Press.

Hyams, P. 1996. *Relic.* Columbia Tristar Films.

Im Thurn, E. 1883. *Among the Indians of Guiana: Being sketches chiefly anthropologic from the interior of British Guiana.* London: Kegan Paul, Trench and Co.

———1885. *Roraima.* Paper read at meeting of British Association, Aberdeen, September.

———1893. Anthropological uses of the camera. *Journal of the Anthropological Institute of Great Britain and Wales* xxii:184–203.

———1934. *Thoughts, talks and tramps.* London: Oxford University Press.

Jackson, J. 1975. Recent ethnography of indigenous northern lowland South America. *Annual Review of Anthropology* 4:307–40.

———1983. *The fish people: Linguistic exogamy and Tukanoan identity in Northwest Amazonia.* Cambridge, UK: Cambridge University Press.

Jacoby, R. 1995. Marginal returns. *Lingua Franca,* September/October, pp. 30–37.

Jay, M. 2003. *Downcast eyes: The denigration of vision in twentieth-century French thought.* Berkeley: University of California Press.

Jenkins, D. 1993. The visual domination of the American Indian: Photography, anthropology, and popular culture in the late nineteenth century. *Museum Anthropology* 17:9–21.

Joffe, R. 1986. *The mission.* Warners.

Johnston, J. 2001. *Jurassic park III.* Universal Pictures.

Kaplan, J. 1975. *The Piaroa, a people of the Orinoco basin: A study in kinship and marriage.* Oxford: Clarendon Press/Oxford University Press.

Karsten, R. 1923. *Blood revenge, war, and victory feasts among the Jivaro Indians of Eastern Ecuador.* Bureau of American Ethnology, Bulletin 79. Washington, DC: Smithsonian Institution.

———1926. *The civilizations of the South American Indians: With specific reference to religion.* New York: Knopf.

———1935. *The headhunters of the Western Amazonas: The life and culture of the Jibaro Indians of Eastern Ecuador and Peru.* Societas Scientariarum Fennica, Commentationes Humanarum Litterarum, Vol. 7, No. 1. Halsingfors, Finland.

Kensinger, K. W. 1995. *How real people ought to live: The Cashinahua of Eastern Peru.* Prospect Heights, IL: Waveland Press.

Kickingbird, K. and K. Ducheneaux. 1973. *One hundred million acres.* New York: Macmillan.

Kloos, P. 1971. *The Maroni River Caribs of Surinam.* Assen: Van Goram.

Koch-Grunberg, T. 1995. *Dois anos entre os indígenas: Viagens no noroeste do Brasil, 1903–1905,* 2 vols. Manaus, Brazil: Cedem.

Koch-Grunberg, T. and G. Huebner. 2004. *Die Xingu-Expedition (1898–1900)*. Koln, Germany: Böhlau.

Kracke, W. H. 1978. *Force and persuasion: Leadership in an Amazonian society*. Chicago: University of Chicago Press.

Kricher, J. H. 1989. *A neotropical companion*. Princeton, NJ: Princeton University Press.

Lamb, F. B. and M. Cordova-Rios. 1974. *Wizard of the upper Amazon*. Boston: Houghton Mifflin.

Landau, P. S. 1999. Photography and colonial vision. *H-Africa, Africa forum*. http://www.h-net.org/~africaforum/Landau.html.

Langdon, J. and G. Baer. eds. 1992. *Portals of power: Shamanism in South America*. Albuquerque: University of New Mexico Press.

Lange, A. 1912. *In the Amazon: Adventures in remote parts of the upper Amazon River, including a sojourn among cannibal Indians*. New York: G. P. Putnam's Sons.

——1914. The lower Amazon. New York: G. P. Putnam's Sons.

Lathrap, D. 1968. The hunting economies of the tropical forest zone. In *Man the hunter*. R. B. Lee and I. DeVore, eds. Chicago: Aldine. pp. 23–29.

——1970. *The upper Amazon*. New York: Praeger.

——1977. Our father the cayman, our mother the gourd: Spinden revisited, or a unitary model for the emergence of agriculture in the New World. In *Origins of agriculture*. C. A. Reed, ed. The Hague: Mouton. pp. 713–51.

Lederman, R. 2005. Unchosen grounds: Cultivating cross-subfield accents for public voice. In *Unwrapping the sacred bundle: Reflections on the disciplining of anthropology*. D. Segal and S. Yanagisako, eds. Durham, NC: Duke University Press. pp. 49–77.

Lenzi, U. 1972. *Deep River savages*. ROAS/Medusa.

——1981. *Cannibal ferox*. Image Entertainment.

——1986. *Eaten alive*. Medusa Produzione.

Lerner, L. D. 1956. Cliché and commonplace. *Essays in Criticism*, VI:249–65.

Levine, R. 1989. *Images of history: Nineteenth and early twentieth century Latin American photographs as documents*. Durham, NC: Duke University Press.

Lévi-Strauss, C. 1961. *Tristes tropiques*. London: Hutchinson.

——1970. *The raw and the cooked*. London: Cape.

——1973. *From honey to ashes*. London: Cape.

——1978. *The origin of table manners*. London: Cape.

——1981. *The naked man*. London: Cape.

——1988. *The jealous potter*. Chicago: University of Chicago Press.

——1994. *Saudades do Brasil*. Paris: Plon.

Lisansky, J. 1989. *Migrants to Amazonia: Spontaneous colonization in the Brazilian frontier*. Boulder, CO: Westview Press.

Lizot, J. 1985. *Tales of the Yanomami: Daily life in the Venezuelan forest*. Cambridge, UK: Cambridge University Press.

Llosa, L. 1991. *Fire on the Amazon*. New Concorde Films.

——1993. *Eight hundred leagues down the Amazon*. New Concorde Films.

——1997. *Anaconda*. Paramount Studios.

Loizos, P. 1993. *Innovation in ethnographic film: From innocence to self-consciousness 1955–1985*. Manchester, UK: Manchester University Press.

Lorimer, J. 1989. *English and Irish settlement on the river Amazon 1550–1646*. London: Hakluyt Society.

Lukesch, A. 1976. *Bearded Indians of the tropical forest*. Graz: Akademische Druck.

Lyons, P. ed. 1979. *Native South America: Ethnology of the least known continent*. Boulder, CO: Westview Press.

MacCreagh, G. 1985 [1926]. *White waters and black*. Chicago: University of Chicago Press.

MacDougall, D. 1978. Ethnographic film: Failure and promise. *Annual Review of Anthropology* 7:405–25.

——1999. The visual in anthropology. In *Rethinking visual anthropology*. M. Banks and H. Morphy, eds. New Haven, CT: Yale University Press. pp. 276–95.

Machado, L. O. n.d. Financial flows and drug trafficking in the Amazon basin. UNESCO, Management of Social Transformations, Discussion Paper Series No. 22.

MacMillan, G. 1995. *At the end of the rainbow? Gold, land, and people in the Brazilian Amazon*. New York: Columbia University Press.

Malinowski, B. 1967. *A diary in the strict sense of the term*. London: Routledge and Kegan Paul.

Marcoy, P. 1873. *A journey across South America from the Pacific Ocean to the Atlantic Ocean*, 2 vols. London: Blackie and Sons.

Marghereti, A. 1980. *Cannibal apocalypse*. Image Entertainment.

Markham, C. 1859. *Expeditions into the valley of the Amazons, 1539, 1540, 1639*. London: Hakluyt Society.

Martino, S. 1978. *Slave of the cannibal god*. Diamond Ent Corporation.

Mason, P. 1990. *Deconstructing America: Representations of the other*. London: Routledge.

Matthiessen, P. 1965. *At play in the fields of the lord*. New York: Random House.

Maybury-Lewis, D. 1965. *The savage and the innocent*. London: Evans Bros.

——1967. *Akwe-Shavante society*. Oxford: Clarendon Press/Oxford University Press.

Maybury-Lewis, D. ed. 1979. *Dialectical societies: The Ge and Bororo of Central Brazil*. Cambridge, MA: Harvard University Press.

McCallum, C. 2001. *Gender and sociality in Amazonia: How real people are made*. Oxford: Berg.

McEwan, C., C. Barreto, and E. Neves. eds. 2001. *Unknown Amazon*. London: British Museum.

McTiernan, J. 1992. *Medicine man*. Buena Vista Films.

Meggers, B. J. 1971. *Amazonia: Man and culture in a counterfeit paradise*. Chicago: Aldine.

——1996. Review of A. C. Roosevelt, ed. *Amazonian Indians from Prehistory to the Present: Anthropological perspectives. Journal of the Royal Anthropological Institute* 2:194–6.

——2007. Sustainable intensive exploitation of Amazonia: cultural, environmental, and geopolitical perspectives. In *The world system and the earth system*. A. Hornborg and C. Crumley, eds. Walnut Creek, CA: Left Coast Press. pp. 195–209.

Meggers, B. J. and C. Evans. 1957. *Archeological investigations at the mouth of the Amazon*. Washington DC: U.S. Government Printing Office.

Metraux, A. 1942. *The native tribes of Eastern Bolivia and Western Mato Grosso.* Washington, DC: U.S. Government Printing Office.

Mindlin, B. 1995. *Unwritten stories of the Surui Indians of Rondonia.* Austin: Institute of Latin American Studies, University of Texas.

Monté-Mor, P. and J. I. Parente. 1994. *Cinema e antropologia: Horizontes e caminhyos da antropologia visual.* Rio de Janeiro: Interior Edições.

Moran, E. 1981. *Developing the Amazon.* Bloomington: Indiana University Press.

———1993. *Through Amazonian eyes.* Iowa City: University of Iowa Press.

Moran, E. ed. 1983. *The dilemma of Amazonian development.* Boulder, CO: Westview Press.

Moretti, F. 1998. *Atlas of the European novel, 1800–1900.* London: Verso.

———2005. *Graphs, maps and trees.* London: Verso.

Movius, G. 1975. Interview with Susan Sontag. *Boston Review,* June. http://bostonreview.net/BR01.1/sontag.html

Murphy, R. 1958. *Mundurucú religion.* Berkeley: University of California Press.

———1960. *Headhunter's heritage: Social and economic change among the Mundurucú Indians.* Berkeley: University of California Press.

Murphy, Y. and Murphy, R. 1985. *Women of the forest.* New York: Columbia University Press.

Nance, J. 1975. *The gentle Tasady: A stone age people of the Philippine rain forest.* New York: Harcourt Brace Jovanovich.

Neel, J. 1970. Lessons from a primitive people. *Science* 170:815–22.

———1994. *Physician to the gene pool: Genetic lessons and other stories.* New York: Wiley.

Nimuendajú, C. 1939. *The Apinaye.* Washington, DC: Catholic University of America Press.

———1942. *The Serente.* Los Angeles: Southwest Museum.

———1946. *The Eastern Timbira.* Berkeley: University of California Press.

———1949. Os Tapajo. *Boletim do Museu Goeldi* 10:93–106.

———1952. *The Tukuna.* Publications in American Archaeology and Ethnology, Vol. 45. Berkeley: University of California Press.

———2004. *In pursuit of the past: Amazon archaeological researches in the Brazilian Guyana and in the Amazon region.* Goteborg, Sweden: European Science Foundation.

Novaes da Mota, C. 1997. *Jurema's children in the forest of spirits: Healing and ritual among two Brazilian indigenous groups.* London: Intermediate Technology Publications.

Novaes, S. C. 1997. *The play of mirror: The representation of self as mirrored in the other.* Austin: University of Texas Press.

Nugent, D. 1993. *The spent cartridges of revolution.* Chicago: University of Chicago Press.

Nugent, S. L. 1990. *Big mouth: The Amazon speaks.* London: 4th Estate.

———1993. *Amazonian caboclo society: An essay on invisibility and peasant economy.* Oxford: Berg.

———2004. Introduction. In *Some other Amazonians: Perspectives on modern Amazonia.* S.L. Nugent, S. L. and M. Harris, eds. London: Institute for the Study of the Americas, pp.1–11.

Nugent, S. L. and M. Harris. eds. 2004. *Some other Amazonians: Perspectives on modern Amazonia.* London: Institute for the Study of the Americas.

Nunuk, Z. 2000. *Atanajurat.* Aboriginal Peoples Television Network.

Oakdale, S. R. 2005. *I foresee my life.* Lincoln, NE: University of Nebraska Press.

Oberg, K. 1949. *The Terena and the Caduveo of southern Mato Grosso, Brazil.* Washington, DC: Smithsonian Institution.

———1953. *Indians Tribes of northern Mato Grosso, Brazil.* Institute of Social Anthropology, Publication No. 15. Washington, DC: Smithsonian Institution.

Olsen, D. 1996. *Music of the Warao of Venezuela: Song people of the rain forest.* Gainesville: University Press of Florida.

Ondaatje, M. 2002. *The conversations: Walter Murch and the art of editing film.* New York: Knopf.

Orcutt, L. 2000. The continuing chronicles of Colonel Fawcett: Factual and fabulous. http://www.catchpenny.org/fawcett.html

Orme, S. 2002. *The lost world.* BBC Worldwide.

Overing, J. 1981. Amazonian anthropology. *Journal of Latin American Studies* 13:151–65.

Overing, J. ed. 2000. *The anthropology of love and anger: The aesthetics of conviviality in native Amazonia.* London: Routledge.

Pace, R. 1998. *The struggle for Amazon town: Gurupa revisited.* Boulder CO: Westview Press.

Palmatary, H. 1960. The archaeology of the lower Tapajos valley. *Transactions of the American Philosophical Society* (n.s.) 53:1–243.

Parker, E. 1992. Forest islands and Kayapó resource management in Amazonia: A reappraisal of the *apete. American Anthropologist* 94:2:406–28.

Parker, E. ed. 1985. *The Amazon caboclo: Historical and contemporary perspectives.* Studies in Third World Societies, 32. Williamsburg, VA: Department of Anthropology, College of William and Mary.

Paternoster, S. 1913. *The lords of the devil's paradise.* London: Stanley Paul.

Pearson, H. C. 1904. *What I saw in the tropics: A record of visits to Ceylon, the Federated Malay states, Mexico, Nicaragua, Costa Rica, Republic of Panama, Columbia, Jamaica, Hawaii.* New York: India Rubber Company.

———1911. *The rubber country of the Amazon.* New York: The India Rubber World.

Peret, J. A. 1975. *Populacao indigena do Brasil.* Rio de Janeiro: Civilizacao Brasileira

Perrin, M. 1987. *The way of the dead Indians: Guajiro myths and symbols.* Austin: University of Texas Press.

Peters, C., A. Gentry, and R. Mendelsohn. 1989. Valuation of an Amazonian forest. *Nature* 339:655–6.

Peters, J. F. 1998. *Life among the Yanomami.* Peterborough, Canada: Broadview Press.

Petzke, I. 1992. The films of Werner Herzog. *Senses of Cinema,* Issue 19, March–April. Queensland State Library, Brisbane. http://www.fh.wuerzburg.de/petzke/herzog.html

Philbrick, N. 2006. *Mayflower.* London: Harper Collins.

Picchi, D. S. 2000. *The Bakairi Indians of Brazil: Politics, ecology, and change.* Prospect Heights, IL: Waveland Press.

Pinney, C. 1999. *Camera indica: The social life of Indian photographs.* London: Reaktion.

———2003a. Introduction: How the other half . . . In *Photography's other histories*. C. Pinney and N. Peterson, eds. Durham, NC: Duke University Press. pp. 1–14.

———2003b. Notes from the surface of the image: Photography, postcolonialism, and vernacular modernism. In *Photography's other histories*. C. Pinney and N. Peterson, eds. Durham, NC: Duke University Press. pp. 202–20.

Pinney, C. and N. Peterson. eds. 2003. *Photography's other histories*. Durham, NC: Duke University Press.

Plotkin, M. J. 1993. *Tales of a shaman's apprentice: An ethnobotanist searches for new medicines in the Amazon rain forest*. New York: Viking.

Poignant, R. 2004. *Professional savages: Captive lives and western spectacle*. New Haven: Yale University Press.

Poole, D. 1997. *Vision, race, and modernity: A visual economy of the Andean image world*. Princeton, NJ: Princeton University Press.

Porro, A. 1994. Social organization and political power in the Amazon flood plain: The ethnohistorical sources. In *Amazonian Indians from prehistory to the present: Anthropological perspectives*. A. C. Roosevelt. ed. Tucson: University of Arizona Press. pp. 79–94.

———1996. *O povo das águas: Ensaios de etno-história amazônica*. Petrópolis: Vozes.

Posey, D. 1992. Reply to Parker. *American Anthropologist* 94:441–3.

———2002. *Kayapó ethnoecology and culture*. London: Routledge.

Posey, D. and W. Balee. eds. 1989. *Resource management in Amazonia: Indigenous and folk strategies*. Advances in Economic Botany, Vol. 7. New York: New York Botanical Society.

Price, D. 1989. *Before the bulldozer: The Nambikwara Indians and the World Bank*. Washington, DC: Seven Locks Press.

Privett, R. and Kreul, J. 2001. The strange case of Noel Carroll: A conversation with the controversial film philosopher. www.sensesofcinema.com/contents/01/13/carroll.html

Prosser, J. 2005. *Light in the dark room: Photography and loss*. Minneapolis: University of Minnesota Press.

Putra, S. G. 1978. *Primitif/Savage terror*. Rapi Films.

Raffles, H. 2002. *In Amazonia: A natural history*. Princeton, NJ: Princeton University Press.

Ramos, A. 1987. Reflecting on the Yanomami: Ethnographic images and the pursuit of the exotic. *Cultural Anthropology* 2:284–304.

———1990. Ethnology Brazilian style. *Cultural Anthropology* 5:452–72.

———1992. *The hyperreal Indian*. Serie Antropologia, 135. Brasilia: Deparment of Anthropology, University of Brasilia.

———1995. *Sanuma memories*. Madison: University of Wisconsin Press.

———1998. *Indigenism: Ethnic politics in Brazil*. Madison: University of Wisconsin Press.

———2001. *Pulp fictions of indigenism*. Serie Antropologia, 301. Brasilia: Department of Anthropology, University of Brasilia.

Rangel, A. 1927 [1908]. *Inferno verde (cenas e cenários do Amazonas)*. Tours: Arrault.

Redfern. W. 1989. *Cliches and coinages*. Oxford: Blackwell.

Reed, R. 1995. *Prophets of agroforestry: Guaraní communities and commercial gathering*. Austin: University of Texas Press.

Reichel-Dolmatoff, G. 1971. *Amazonian cosmos: The sexual and religious symbolism of the Tukano Indians.* Chicago: University of Chicago Press.

———1975. *The shaman and the jaguar: A study of narcotic drugs among the Indians of Colombia.* Philadelphia: Temple University Press.

———1990. *The sacred mountain of Colombia's Kogi Indians.* Leiden: E.J. Brill.

———1995. *Yurupari: Studies of an Amazonian foundation myth.* Cambridge, MA: Harvard University Press.

———1996. *The forest within: The world-view of the Tukano Amazonian Indians.* Totnes, Devon, UK: Themis Books.

———1997. *Rainforest shamans: Essays on the Tukano Indians of the Northwestern Amazon.* Totnes, Devon, UK: Themis Books.

Reitman, I. 1973. *Cannibal girls.* AIP.

Ribeiro, D. 1967. Indigenous cultures and languages in Brazil. In *Indians of Brazil in the Twentieth Century.* J. Hopper, ed. ICR Studies, 2. Washington, DC: Institute for Cross-Cultural Research. pp. 77–165.

———1972. *The Americas and Civilization.* New York: Dutton.

Ricciardi, M. 1991. *Vanishing Amazon.* London: Weidenfeld and Nicolson.

Richards, P. 1952. *The tropical rain forest.* Cambridge, UK: Cambridge University Press.

Ritchie, M. 1996. *Spirit of the rain-forest: S Yanomamo shaman's story.* Chicago: Island Lake Press.

Rival, L. 2002. *Trekking through history: The Huaorani of Amazonian Ecuador.* New York: Columbia University Press.

Rival, L. and N. Whitehead, eds. 2001. *Beyond the visible and the material: The amerindianization of society in the work of Peter Riviere.* Oxford: Oxford University Press.

Riviere, P. 1969. *Marriage among the Trio: A principle of social organization.* Oxford: Clarendon Press/Oxford University Press.

———1972. *Forgotten frontiers: Ranchers of north Brazil.* New York: Holt, Rinehart and Winston.

———1984. *Individual and society in Guyana.* Cambridge, UK: Cambridge University Press.

Roe, P. G. 1982. *The cosmic zygote: Cosmology in the Amazon basin.* New Brunswick, NJ: Rutgers University Press.

Rondon, C. M. 1946. *Indios do Brasil, Vol I: Indios do centro, do noroeste e do sul de Mato Grosso.* Rio de Janeiro: Conselho Nacional de ProteSao aos Indios.

———1953a. *Indios do Brasil do centro, Vol II: Cabeceiras do Rio Xingu, Rios Araguia e Oiapoque.* Rio de Janeiro: Conselho Nacional de ProteSao aos Indios.

———1953b. *Indios do Brasil, Vol III: Norte do Rio Amazonas.* Rio de Janeiro: Conselho Nacional de ProteSao aos Indios.

Rony, T. 1996. *The third eye: Race, cinema and ethnographic spectacle.* Durham, NC: Duke University Press.

Roosevelt, A. C. 1980. *Parmana.* New York: Academic Press.

———1989. Resource management in Amazonia before the conquest. In *Resource management in Amazonia: Indigenous and folk strategies.* Advances in Economic Botany, Vol. 7. D. Posey and W. Balee, eds. New York: New York Botanical Society. pp. 30–62.

——1991. *Moundbuilders of the Amazon: Geophysical archaeology on Marajo Island, Brazil.* San Diego: Academic Press.

Roosevelt, A. C. ed. 1994. *Amazonian Indians from prehistory to the present: Anthropological perspectives.* Tucson: University of Arizona Press.

Rosengren, D. 1987. *In the eyes of the beholder: Leadership and the social construction of power and dominance among the Matsigenka of the Peruvian Amazon.* Goteborg, Sweden: Ethnographic Museum.

Rubenstein, S. 2002. *Alejandro Tsakimp: A Shuar healer in the margins of history.* Lincoln, NE: University of Nebraska Press.

Ruby, J. 2000. *Picturing culture.* Chicago: University of Chicago Press.

Ryden, S. 1941. *A study of the Siriono Indians.* Goteborg, Sweden: Humanistic Foundation of Sweden.

Sahlins, M. 1972. *Stone Age economics.* London: Tavistock.

Salgado, S. 1993. *Workers: An archaeology of the industrial age.* New York: Aperture.

Salgado, S. 1997. *Terra: Struggle of the landless.* London: Phaidon.

Santos, R. 1980. *Historia economica da Amazonia (1800–1920).* Sao Paulo: Queiroz.

Santos-Granero, F. 1991. *The power of love: The moral use of knowledge among the Amuesha of central Peru.* London: Athlone.

——2000. *Tamed frontiers: Economy, society, and civil rights in upper Amazonia.* Boulder, CO: Westview Press.

Sapir, D. 1994. On fixing ethnographic shadows. *American Ethnologist* 21:867–85.

Scheib, R. 2002. Review of *Deep river savages.* http://www.moria/co/nz/horror/deepriversavages.htm

Scheper-Hughes, N. 1992. *Death without weeping: The violence of everyday life in Brazil.* Berkeley: University of California Press.

Schmink, M. and C. Wood. 1984. *Frontier expansion in the Amazon.* Gainesville: University Press of Florida.

——1992. *Contested frontiers in Amazonia.* New York: Columbia University Press.

Schoepf, D. 2000. *George Huebner, 1862–1935, un photographe a Manaus.* Geneva: Musée d'ethnographie.

Scholte, B. 1987. The literary turn in contemporary anthropology: A review article. *Critique of Anthropology* VII: 33–47.

Schreider, H. and F. Schreider. 1970. *Exploring the Amazon.* Washington, DC: National Geographic Society.

Schultes, R. E. 1979. The Amazon as a source of new economic plants. *Economic Botany* 33:259–66.

——1988. *Where the gods reign: Plants and peoples of the Colombian Amazon.* Oracle, AZ: Synergetic Press.

Schultes, R. E. and R. R. Raffauf. 2004. *Vine of the soul: Medicine men, their plants and rituals in the Colombian Amazon.* Oracle, AZ: Synergetic Press.

Schwarcz, L. 1999. *The spectacle of the races: Scientists, institutions and the race question in Brazil, 1870–1930.* New York: Hill and Wang.

Schwartz, S. and Salomon, F. 1999. New peoples and new kinds of people: Adaptation, readjustment, and ethnogenesis in South American indigenous societies (Colonial era). In *The Cambridge history of the native peoples of the Americas, Volume III, Part 2.* F. Salomon and S. Schwartz, eds. Cambridge, UK: Cambridge University Press. pp. 443–501.

Seeger, A. 1981. *Nature and society in central Brazil: The Suya Indians of Mato Grosso.* Cambridge, MA: Harvard University Press.

——1987. *Why Suya sing: A musical anthropology of an Amazonian people.* Cambridge, MA: Harvard University Press.

Segal, D. and J. Yanagisako. eds. 2005. *Unwrapping the sacred bundle: Reflections on the disciplining of anthropology.* Durham, NC: Duke University Press.

Service, E. 1971 [1958]. *Profiles in ethnology.* New York: Harper and Row.

Shoumatoff, A. 1982. *Rivers Amazon,* New York: Random House.

——1991. *The world is burning: Murder in the rain forest.* London: Fourth Estate.

Silverman, D. 1975. *Researching Casteneda: A prologue to the social sciences.* London: Routledge.

Siodmak, C. 1956. *Curucu: Beast of the Amazon.* Universal/Rank Pictures.

Siskind, J. 1973. *To hunt in the morning.* Oxford: Oxford University Press.

Skidmore, T. 1993. *Black into white: Race and nationality in Brazilian thought.* Durham, NC: Duke University Press.

Slater, C. 1994. *Dance of the dolphin.* Chicago: University of Chicago Press.

——2001. *Entangled edens.* Berkeley: University of California Press.

Slater, C. ed. 2004. *In search of the rain forest.* Durham, NC: Duke University Press.

Smith, A. 1990. *Explorers of the Amazon.* New York: Viking.

Smith, H. H. 1879. *Brazil: The Amazons and the coast.* New York: Charles Scribner's and Sons.

Smith, N. J. H. 1981. *Man, fishes and the Amazon.* New York: Columbia University Press.

——1982. *Rainforest corridors.* Berkeley: University of California Press.

——1999. *The Amazon river forest: A natural history of plants, animals, and people.* New York: Oxford University Press.

Smole, W. 1976. *The Yanoama Indians: A cultural geography.* Austin: University of Texas Press.

Sontag, S. 1977. *On photography.* London: Penguin.

Souza Martins, J. 2001. The unusual image: Photography and faith in Brazil. Paper delivered at conference 'Popular Religion and Visual Culture in Brazil', Centre for Brazilian Studies, Oxford, November.

Sperber, D. 1980. Cognition and the semiotic function. In M. Piattelli-Palmarini, ed. *Language and learning.* London: Routledge. pp. 244–9.

Spielberg, S. 1993. *Jurassic park.* Universal Pictures.

——1997. *The lost world: Jurassic park II.* Universal Pictures.

Spix, J. B. and C. F. P. Martius. 1976. *Viagem pelo Brasil, 1817–1820.* Sao Paulo: Edicoes Melhoramentos.

Spruce, R. 1908. *Notes of a botanist on the Amazon and Andes,* 2 vols. A. R. Wallace, ed. London: Macmillan.

Stafford, B. 1984. *Voyage into substance: Art, science and the illustrated travel account, 1760–1840.* Cambridge, MA: MIT Press.

Stanfield, M. 1998. *Red rubber, bleeding trees: Violence, slavery, and empire in northwest Amazonia, 1850–1933.* Albuquerque: University of New Mexico Press.

Stearman, A. M. 1989. *Yuqui: Forest nomads in a changing world.* New York: Holt, Rinehart and Winston.

Stearman, A. M. 1987. *No longer nomads: The Siriono revisited.* Lanham, MD: Hamilton Press.

Steichen, E. 1955. *The family of man.* New York: Museum of Modern Art.

Steinen, K. von den. 1942. *O Brasil Central: expedição de 1884 para a exploração do Xingu.* São Paulo: Companhia Ed. Brasiliana.

Stepan, N. 1982. *The idea of race in science: Great Britain 1800–1960.* Hamden, CN: Archon Books.

———2001. *Picturing tropical nature.* London: Reaktion Books.

Steward, J. ed. 1948a. *Handbook of South American Indians, Vol 1: Marginal tribes.* Washington, DC: Bureau of American Ethnology, Smithsonian Institution.

———1948b. *Handbook of South American Indians, Vol 3: Tropical forest Indians.* Washington, DC: Bureau of American Ethnology, Smithsonian Institution.

Steward, J. 1955. *Theory of culture change: The methodology of multilinear evolution.* Urbana: University of Illinois Press.

Steward, J. and L. Faron. 1959. *Native peoples of South America.* New York: McGraw-Hill.

Stewart, I. S. 1994. *After the trees: Living on the Transamazon Highway.* Austin: University of Texas Press.

Stirling, M. W. 1938. *Historical and ethnographical material on the Jivaro Indians.* Bureau of American Ethnology, Bull. 117. Washington, DC: Smithsonian Institution.

Stocking, G. 1983. The ethnographer's magic: Fieldwork in British anthropology. In *Observers observed: Essays on ethnographic fieldwork.* G. Stocking, ed. Madison: University of Wisconsin Press. pp. 70–120.

———1987. *Victorian anthropology.* London: Collier Macmillan.

———1992. *The ethnographer's magic and other essays in the history of anthropology.* Madison: University of Wisconsin Press.

———1993. The camera eye as I witness: Skeptical reflections on the 'hidden messages' of anthropology and photography, 1860–1920. *Visual Anthropology* 6:211–8.

Stoler, A. L. 1995. *Race and the education of desire: Foucault's history of sexuality and the colonial order of things,* Durham, NC: Duke University Press.

Street, B. 1994. British popular anthropology: Exhibiting and photographing the other. In *Anthropology and photography.* E. Edwards, ed. New Haven, CT: Yale University Press. pp.122–31.

Sullivan, L. E. 1988. *Incanchu's drum: An orientation to meaning in South American religions.* New York: Macmillan.

Survival International. 2006. Brazil: Indians attack FUNAI. http://www.survival-international.org/related_material.php?id=371

Taussig, M. 1987. *Shamanism, colonialism, and the wildman.* Chicago: University of Chicago Press.

———1993. *Mimesis and alterity.* New York: Routledge.

———1996. *The magic of the state.* New York: Routledge.

Taylor, A-C. 2003. Les masques de la mémoire. Essai sur la fonction des peintures corporelles jivaro, L'Homme, 165, Image et anthropologie. http://lhomme. revues.org/document204.html

Taylor, K. n.d. *Sanuma Fauna: Prohibitions and Classification.* Monografia No. 18. Caracas: Fundacion La Salle de Ciencias Naturales.

Thomas, D. J. 1982. *Order without government: The society of the Pemon Indians of Venezuela.* Urbana: University of Illinois Press.

Thomas, N. 1994. *Colonialism's culture: Anthropology, travel, and government.* Princeton, NJ: Princeton University Press.

——1999. Collectivity and nationality in the anthropology of art. In M. Banks and H. Morphy eds. *Rethinking visual anthropology.* New Haven, CT: Yale University Press. pp. 256–75.

Thomas, N. and C. Pinney. eds. 2001. *Beyond aesthetics: Art and the technologies of enchantment.* Oxford: Berg.

Thompson, E. P. 1967. Time work-discipline and industrial capitalism. *Past and Present* 28:56–97.

Tierney, P. 2000. *Darkness in El Dorado: How scientists and journalists devastated the Amazon.* New York: Norton.

Tufte, E. 1990. *Envisioning information.* Cheshire, CT: Graphics Press.

——1992. *The visual display of quantitative information.* Cheshire, CT: Graphics Press.

——1997. *Visual explanations: Images and quantities, evidence and narrative.* Cheshire, CT: Graphics Press.

Turner, T. S. 1992. Defiant images: The Kayapó appropriation of video. *Anthropology Today* 8:5–16.

——1995. Neoliberal ecopolitics and indigenous peoples: The Kayapó, the 'rainforest harvest', and the Body Shop. *Yale Forestry and Environmental Studies Bulletin* 98:113–27.

——2000. Indigenous rights, environmental protection, and the struggle over forest resources in the Amazon: The case of the Brazilian Kayapó. In *Earth, air, fire, and water: The humanities and the environment.* J. Conway, K. Keniston, and L. Marx, eds. Amherst: University of Massachusetts Press.

Turner, T. S. ed. 1993. *Cosmology, values, and inter-ethnic contracts in South America.* Indian Studies, Vol. 9. Bennington, VT: Bennington College Press.

Turner, T. and V. Turner-Fajans. 2006. Political innovation and inter-ethnic diplomacy: Kayapó resistance to the developmentalist state. *Anthropology Today* 22:3–10.

Twist, D. N. *The end of the river.* General Film Distributors.

Urban, G. 1996. *Metaphysical community: The interplay of the senses and the intellect.* Austin: University of Texas Press.

Urton, G. ed. 1985. *Animal myths and metaphors in South America.* Salt Lake City: University of Utah Press.

Véja. 1992. The savage: The leading symbol of environmental purity tortures and rapes a white student and then flees to his tribe. 10 June. http://veja.abril.com. br/30anos/p_089.html

Verger, P. 1990. *Retratos da Bahia.* Salvador, BA: Ed. Corrupio.

Verswijver, G. 1992. *The club-fighters of the Amazon: Warfare among the Kaiapó Indians of central Brazil.* Ghent, Belgium: Rijksuniversiteit.

——1996. *Mekranoti: Living among the painted people of the Amazon.* Munich: Prestel-Verlag.

Villas Boas, O. 1974. *Xingu: The Indians, their myths.* London: Souvenir.

Viveiros de Castro, E. 1992. *From the enemy's point of view: Humanity and divinity in an Amazonian society.* Chicago: University of Chicago Press.

——1996. Images of nature and society in Amazonian ethnology. *Annual Review of Anthropology* 25:179–200.

Von Graeve, B. 1989. *The Pacaa Nova: Clash of cultures on the Brazilian frontier.* Peterborough, Canada: Broadview Press.

Wagley, C. 1953. *Amazon town.* New York: Macmillan.

———1977. *Welcome of tears.* New York: Oxford University Press.

Wagley, C. ed. 1974. *Man in the Amazon.* Gainesville: University Press of Florida.

Wagley, C. and E. Galvao. 1949. *The Tenetehara Indians of Brazil: A culture in transition.* New York: Columbia University Press.

Wallace, A. R. 1889. *A narrative of travels on the Amazon and Rio Negro.* London: Ward and Lock.

Warren, J. 2001. *Racial revolutions: Antiracism and Indian resurgence in Brazil.* Durham, NC: Duke University Press.

Watriss, W. and L. P. Zamora, eds. 1998. *Image and memory: Photography from Latin America, 1966–1994.* Austin: University of Texas Press.

Watson, J. F. and J. W. Kaye. 1868–75. *The people of India, 1868–75.* London: Indian Museum.

Wauchope, R. 1962. *Lost tribes and sunken continents.* Chicago: University of Chicago Press.

Weinstein, B. 1983. *The Amazon rubber boom, 1850–1920.* Stanford, CA: Stanford University Press.

Weir, P. 1986. *Mosquito coast.* Jerome Hellman Productions.

Werner, D. W. 1984. *Amazon journey: An anthropologist's year among Brazil's Mekranoti Indians.* New York: Simon and Schuster.

Whale, J. 1940. *Green hell.* Universal Pictures.

Whiffen, T. 1915. *The north-west Amazons: Notes of some months spent among cannibal tribes.* London: Constable and Company.

Whitehead, N. 2002. *Dark shamans: Kanaima and the poetics of violent death.* Durham, NC: Duke University Press.

Whitehead, N. ed. 2002. *Histories and historicities in Amazonia.* Lincoln, NE: University of Nebraska Press.

Whitehead, N. and R. Wright. eds. 2004. *In darkness and secrecy: The anthropology of assault sorcery and witchcraft in Amazonia.* Durham, NC: Duke University Press.

White, C. 2004. The middle mind: Why consumer culture is turning us into the living dead. London: Penguin.

Wilbert, J. 1972. *Survivors of Eldorado.* New York: Praeger.

———1987. *Tobacco and shamanism in South America.* New Haven, CT: Yale University Press.

———1990. *Folk literature of the Yanomami Indians.* Los Angeles: Latin American Center Publications, UCLA.

Wilbert, J. and K. Simoneau. eds. 1983. *Folk literature of the Bororo Indians.* Los Angeles: Latin American Center Publications, UCLA.

Willis, M. 1971. *Jungle rivers and mountain peaks.* London: Readers Digest.

Wilson, R. 1999. *Indigenous South Americans of the past and present.* Boulder, CO: Westview Press.

Wolf, E. 1982. *Europe and the people without history.* Berkeley: University of California Press.

Woodroffe, J. F. 1914. *The upper reaches of the Amazon.* London: Methuen.

Woodroffe, J. F. and H. H. Smith. 1915. *The rubber industry of the Amazon and how its supremacy can be maintained.* London: John Bale, Sons and Danielson.

Wright, H. 1912. *Hevea brasiliensis or Para rubber.* London: Maclaren and Sons.

Wright, R. 1998. *Cosmos, self, and history in Baniwa religion: For those unborn.* Austin: University of Texas Press.

Yde, J. 1965. *Material culture of the Waiwai.* Copenhagen: National Museum.

Index

About the Author

Stephen Nugent teaches anthropology at Goldsmiths, University of London, and is director of the Centre for Visual Anthropology. His long-term interest in Brazilian Amazonia is represented in *Big Mouth* (1990), *Amazonian Caboclo Society* (1993), and *Some Other Amazonians* (2004). He is an editor of the journal *Critique of Anthropology*.